KAIJUMAX

SEASON SIX

FOR ALL
MANKIND

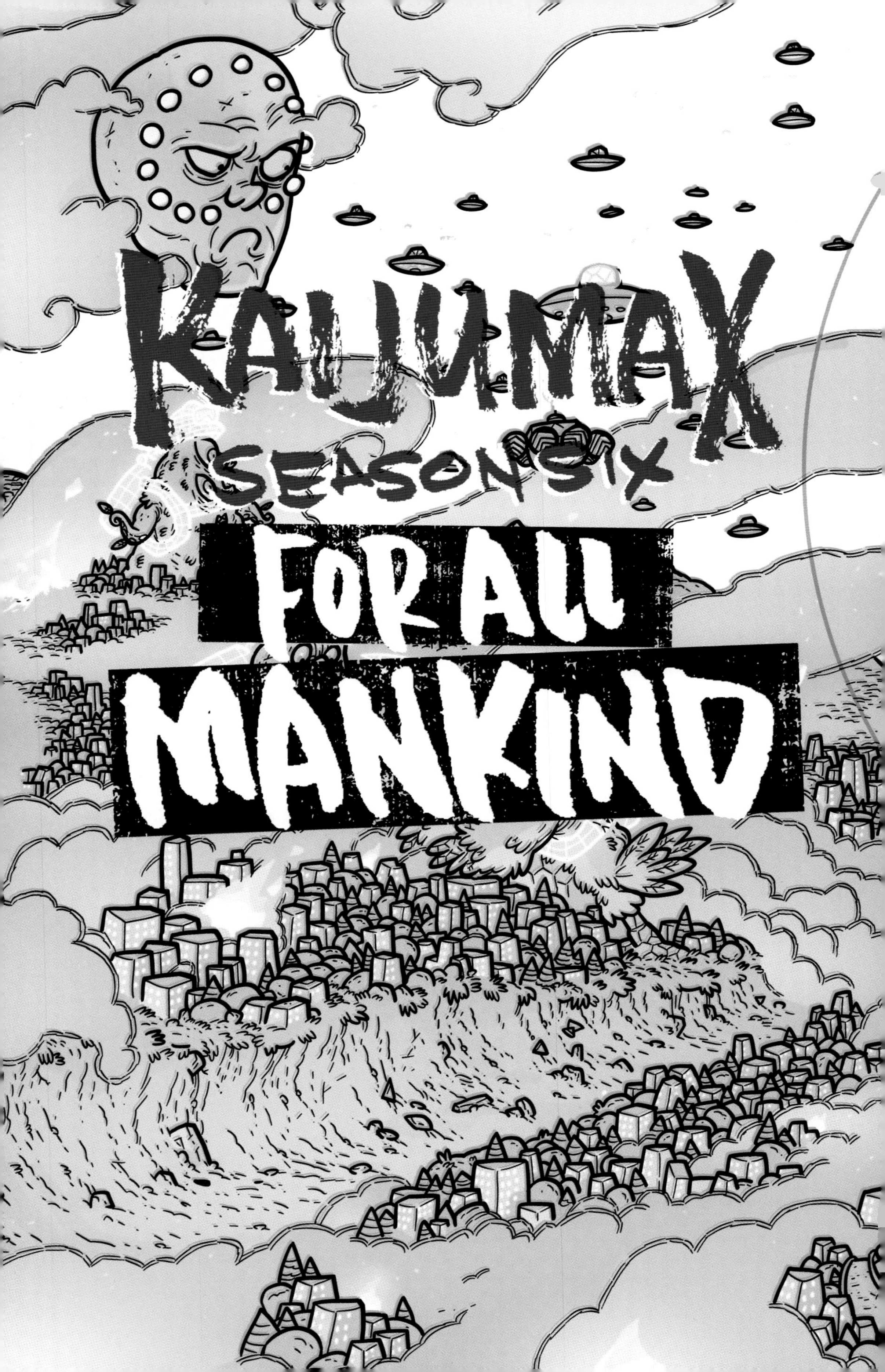
KAIJUMAX
SEASON SIX
FOR ALL
MANKIND

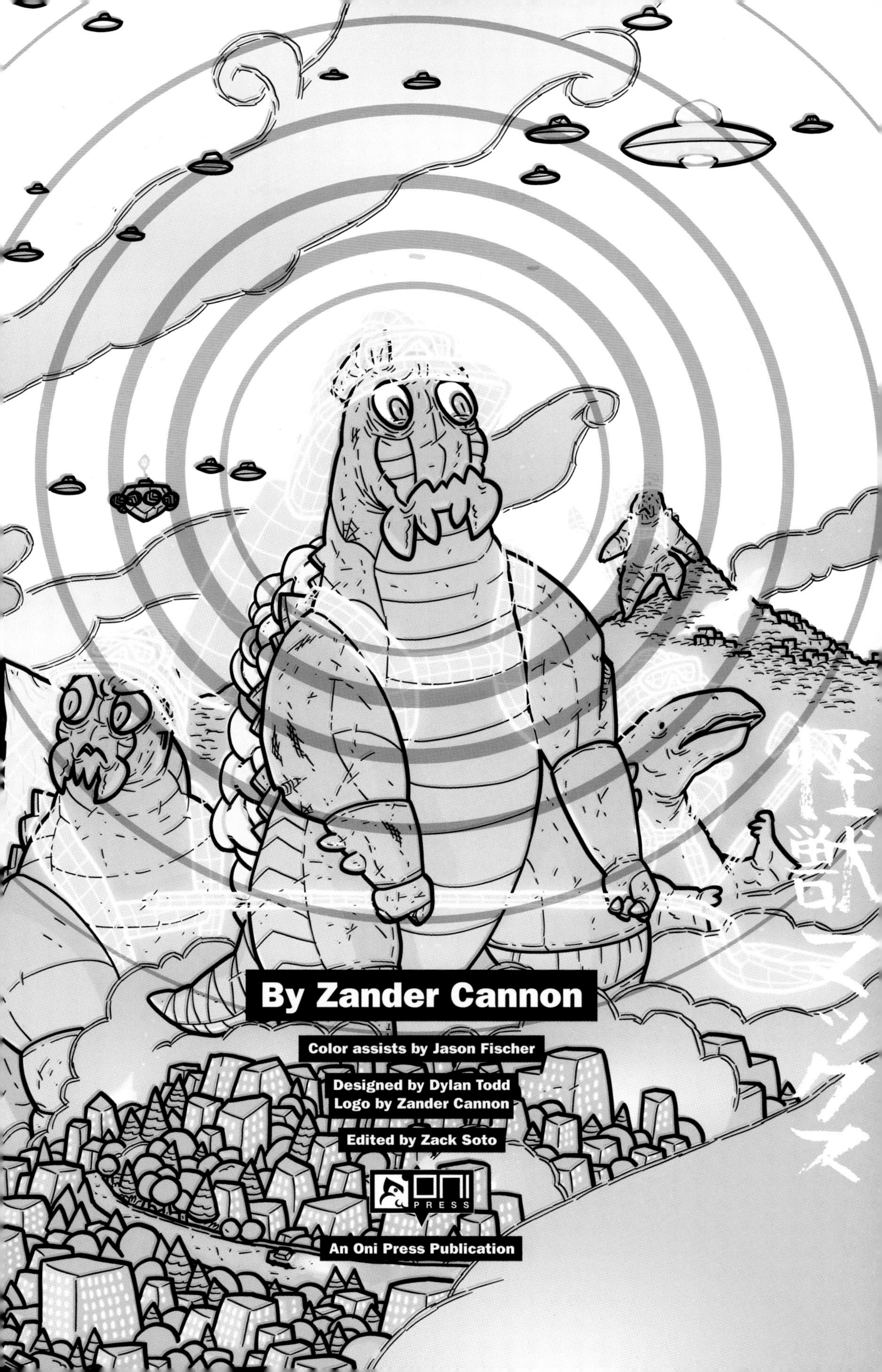
怪獣マックス

By Zander Cannon

Color assists by Jason Fischer

Designed by Dylan Todd
Logo by Zander Cannon

Edited by Zack Soto

ONI PRESS

An Oni Press Publication

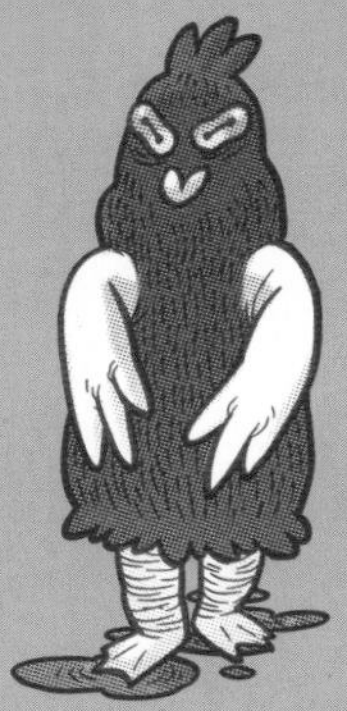

Published by Oni-Lion Forge Publishing Group, LLC.
James Lucas Jones, president & publisher
Charlie Chu, e.v.p. of creative & business development
Steve Ellis, s.v.p. of games & operations
Alex Segura, s.v.p. of marketing & sales
Michelle Nguyen, associate publisher
Brad Rooks, director of operations
Amber O'Neill, special projects manager
Margot Wood, director of marketing & sales
Katie Sainz, marketing manager
Henry Barajas, sales manager
Tara Lehmann, publicist
Holly Aitchison, consumer marketing manager
Troy Look, director of design & production
Angie Knowles, production manager
Kate Z. Stone, senior graphic designer
Carey Hall, graphic designer
Sarah Rockwell, graphic designer
Hilary Thompson, graphic designer
Vincent Kukua, digital prepress technician
Chris Cerasi, managing editor
Jasmine Amiri, senior editor
Shawna Gore, senior editor
Amanda Meadows, senior editor
Robert Meyers, senior editor, licensing
Desiree Rodriguez, editor
Grace Scheipeter, editor
Zack Soto, editor
Ben Eisner, game developer
Sara Harding, entertainment executive assistant
Jung Lee, logistics coordinator
Kuian Kellum, warehouse assistant

Joe Nozemack, publisher emeritus

onipress.com
facebook.com/onipress
twitter.com/onipress
instagram.com/onipress

KAIJUMAX.COM

zandercannon.com / @zander_cannon

studiojfish.com / @studiojfish

@bigredrobot

This volume collects issues #1-6 of Season Six of the Oni Press series *Kaijumax*.

First Edition: August 2022

ISBN 978-1-63715-049-8
eISBN 978-1-63715-066-5

Printed in China

Library of Congress Control Number: 2021950137

1 2 3 4 5 6 7 8 9 10

圣獣マックス

PREVIOUSLY IN KAIJUMAX...

On a secluded island in the south Pacific Ocean
sits **KAIJUMAX**, the infamous prison
for giant monsters. There, inside the
forcefields, power and influence ebb and flow
as easily as radioactive goo, and amid
the gangs, drugs, and intimidation, kaiju serve
their sentences and try to avoid trouble.

But sometimes trouble comes for them...

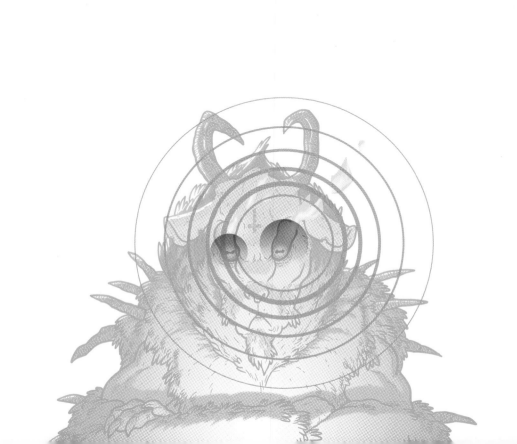

EPISODE 1

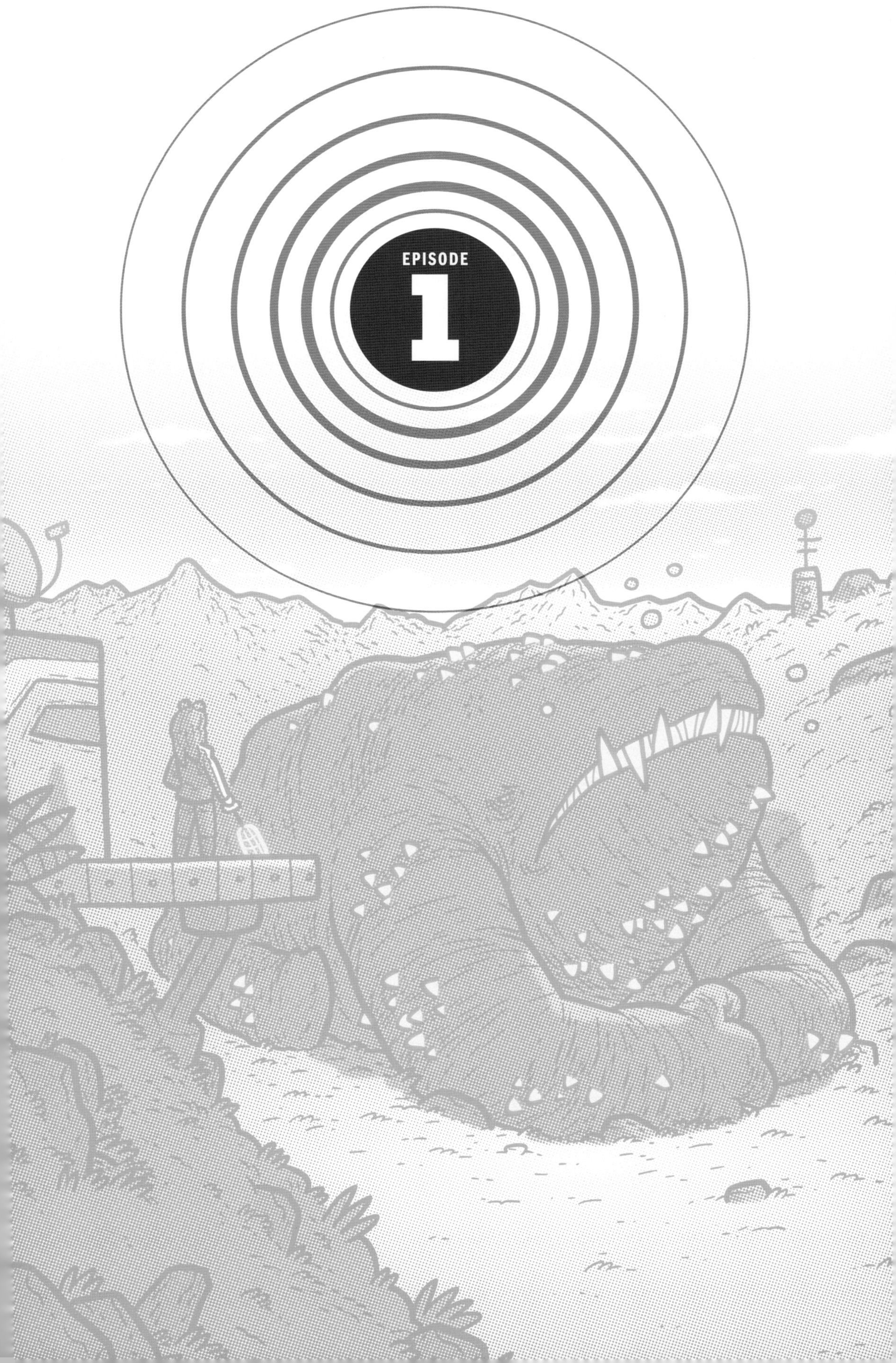

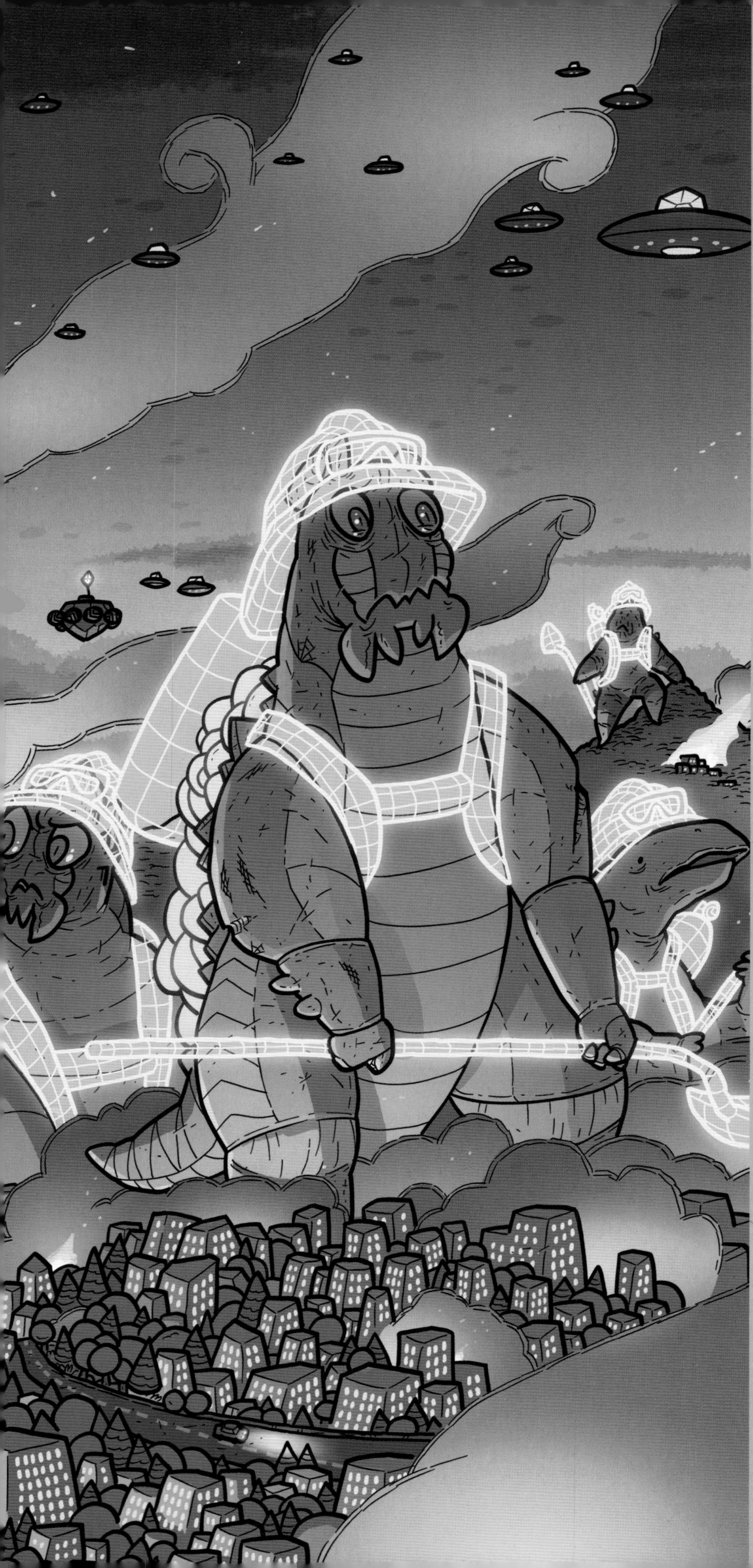

怪獣マックス

ENIGMIRIANS™

MATSUMOTO™

CHARKMON™

SPRINKLES™

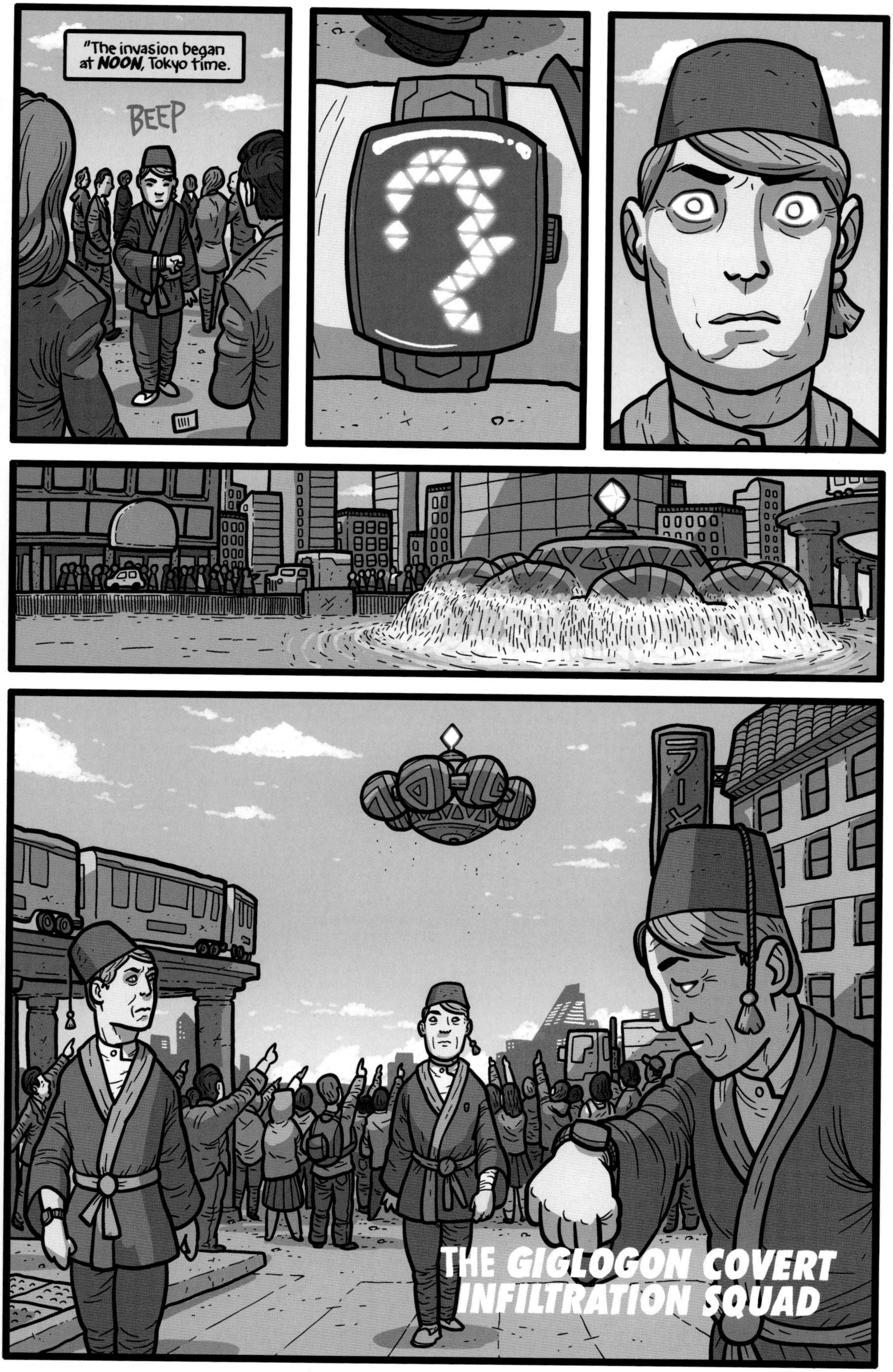
"The invasion began at NOON, Tokyo time.
BEEP
THE GIGLOGON COVERT INFILTRATION SQUAD

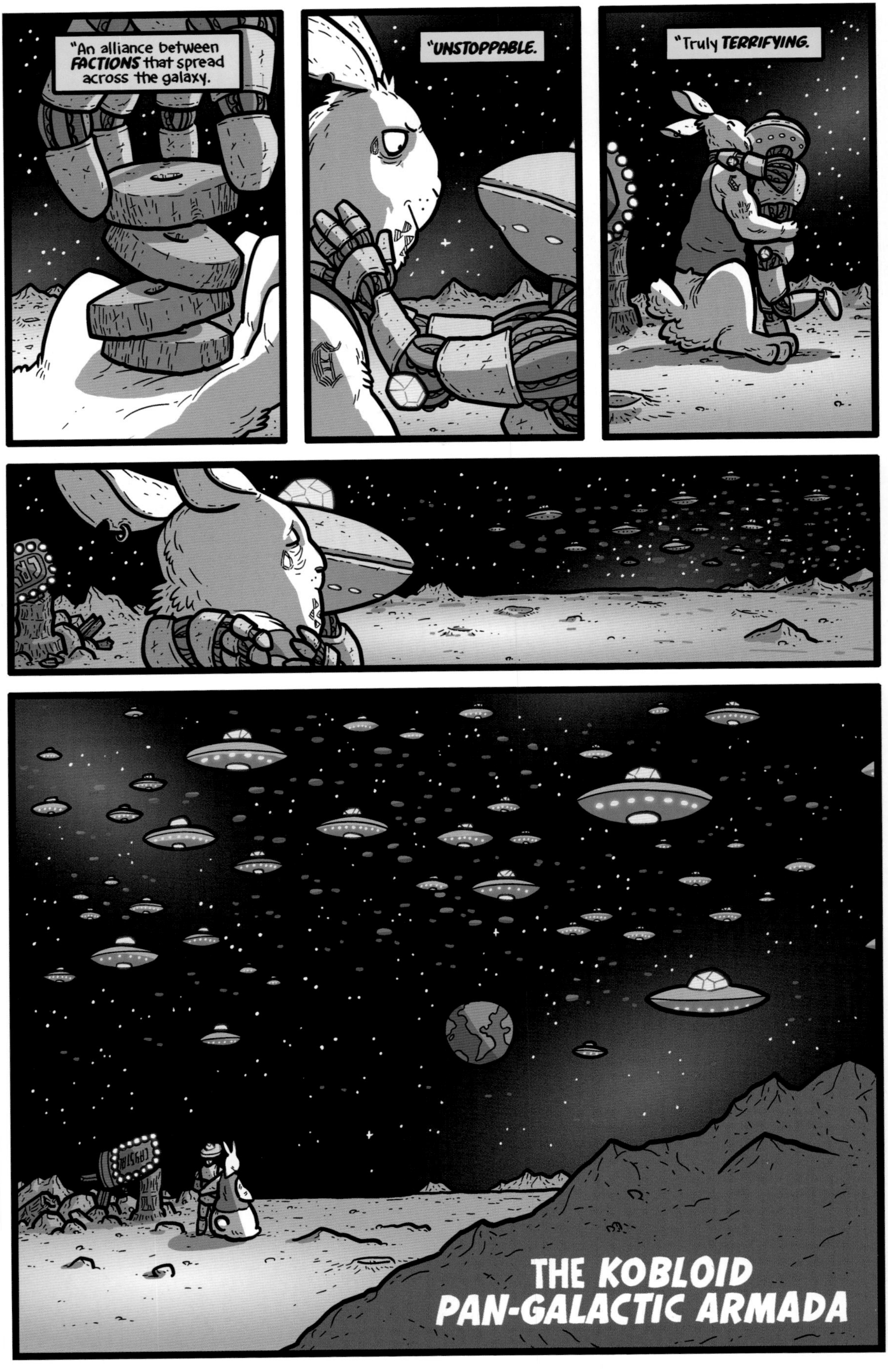
"An alliance between FACTIONS that spread across the galaxy.
"UNSTOPPABLE.
"Truly TERRIFYING.
THE KOBLOID PAN-GALACTIC ARMADA

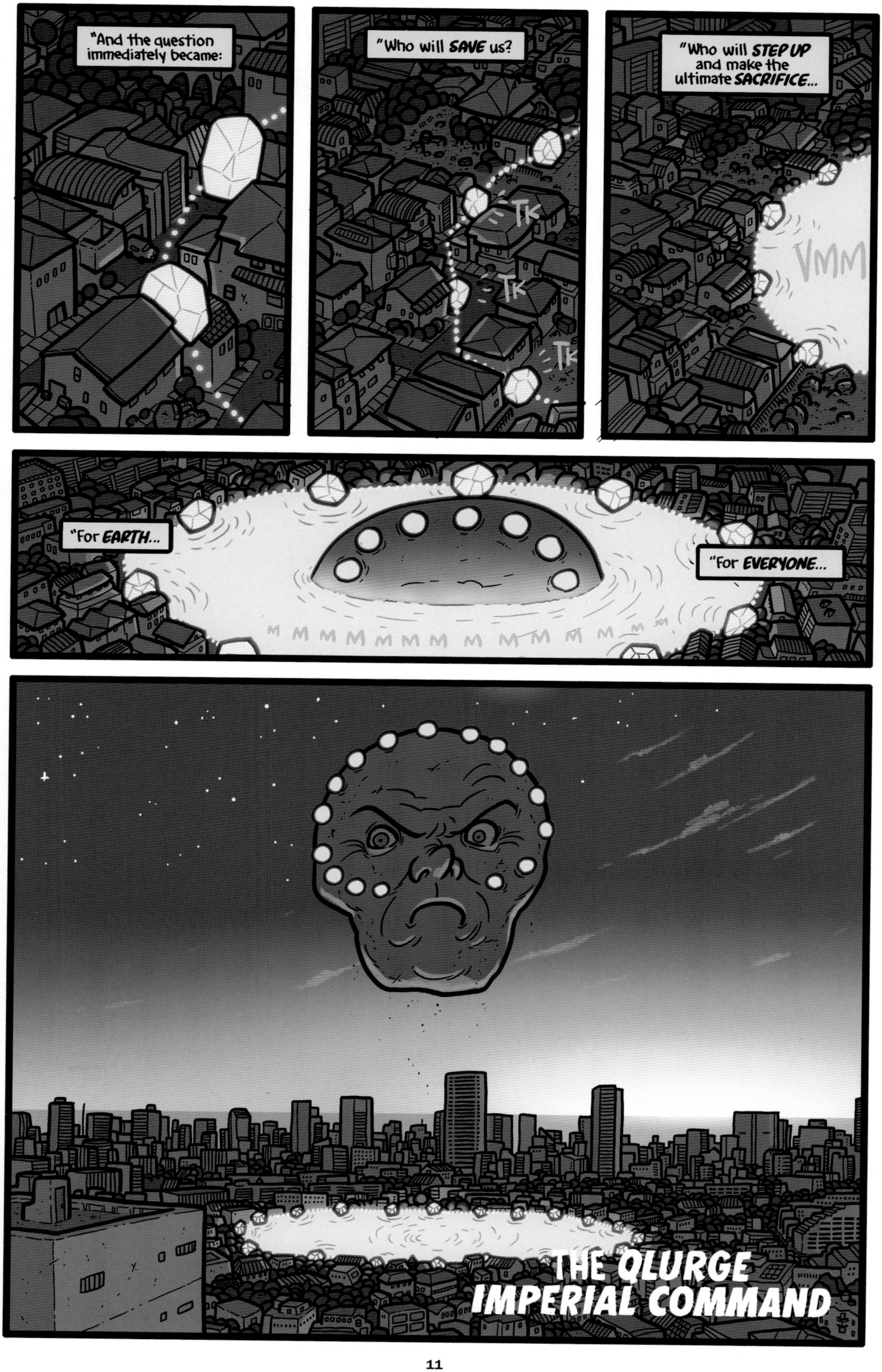
"And the question immediately became:
"Who will SAVE us?
TK
TK
TK
"Who will STEP UP and make the ultimate SACRIFICE...
VMM
"For EARTH...
"For EVERYONE...
MMMMMMMMMMMMMMM
THE QLURGE IMPERIAL COMMAND

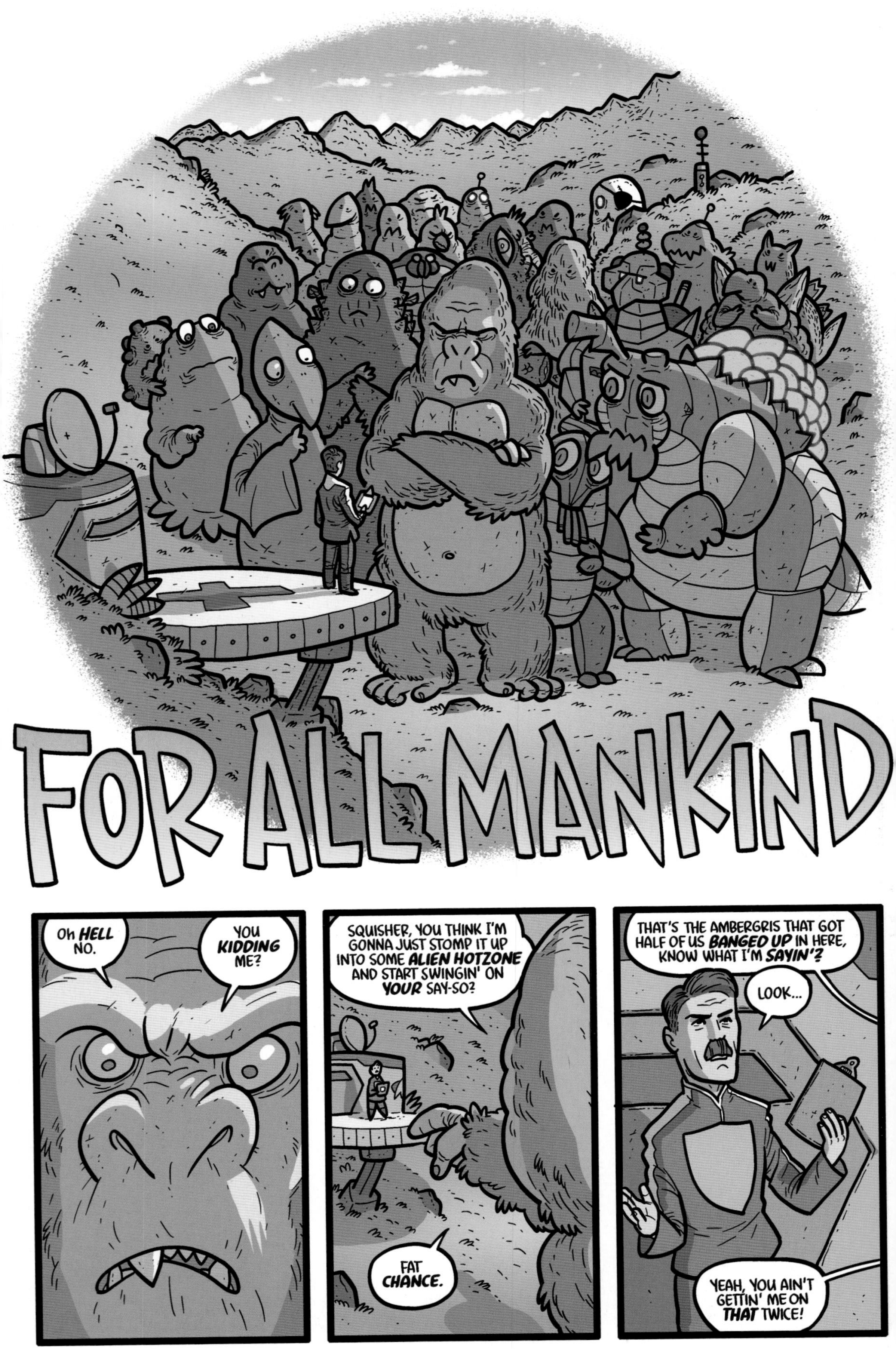
FOR ALL MANKIND
Oh HELL NO.
YOU KIDDING ME?
SQUISHER, YOU THINK I'M GONNA JUST STOMP IT UP INTO SOME ALIEN HOTZONE AND START SWINGIN' ON YOUR SAY-SO?
FAT CHANCE.
THAT'S THE AMBERGRIS THAT GOT HALF OF US BANGED UP IN HERE, KNOW WHAT I'M SAYIN'?
LOOK...
YEAH, YOU AIN'T GETTIN' ME ON THAT TWICE!

AND DON'T GET ME *STARTED* ON THE *OTHER* HALF OF US.

FOR *THEM*...

...THOSE SHUMWAYS UP THERE ARE *FAMILY*.

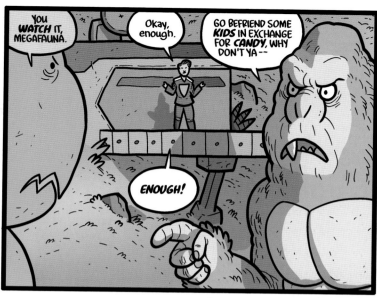

YOU *WATCH IT*, MEGAFAUNA.

Okay, enough.

GO BEFRIEND SOME *KIDS* IN EXCHANGE FOR *CANDY*, WHY DON'T YA --

ENOUGH!

Here's the *DEAL*.

VOLUNTEERS from *BOTH* Kaijumax prisons will receive both *TRAINING* and *EQUIPMENT*, as well as a nominal *PAYMENT*.

But *PRISONERS* will be support *ONLY*.

The *MAJORITY* of the work will be taken on by a *HUMAN BATTALION* of tanks and planes, as well as the professionals in the *EARTH DEFENSE AND ESCAPED KAIJU MURDER SQUAD*.

THE *WHAT* SQUAD?!!

Okay, *RELAX*. It's just an old name from when it was *FOUNDED*.

They're *WORKSHOPPING* new names. They'll get to it.

Fact is, this is an *OPPORTUNITY* for a lot of you.

We've got *WORD*, straight from the *ROTATING LAW-CUBE* at the center of the *UNIVERSE*...

For volunteers, there will be *SENTENCE REDUCTIONS* across the board.

Not to mention *CLEMENCY* for minor crimes.

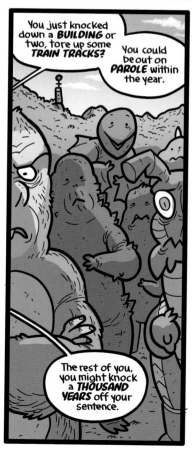

You just knocked down a *BUILDING* or two, tore up some *TRAIN TRACKS*?

You could be out on *PAROLE* within the year.

The rest of you, you might knock a *THOUSAND YEARS* off your sentence.

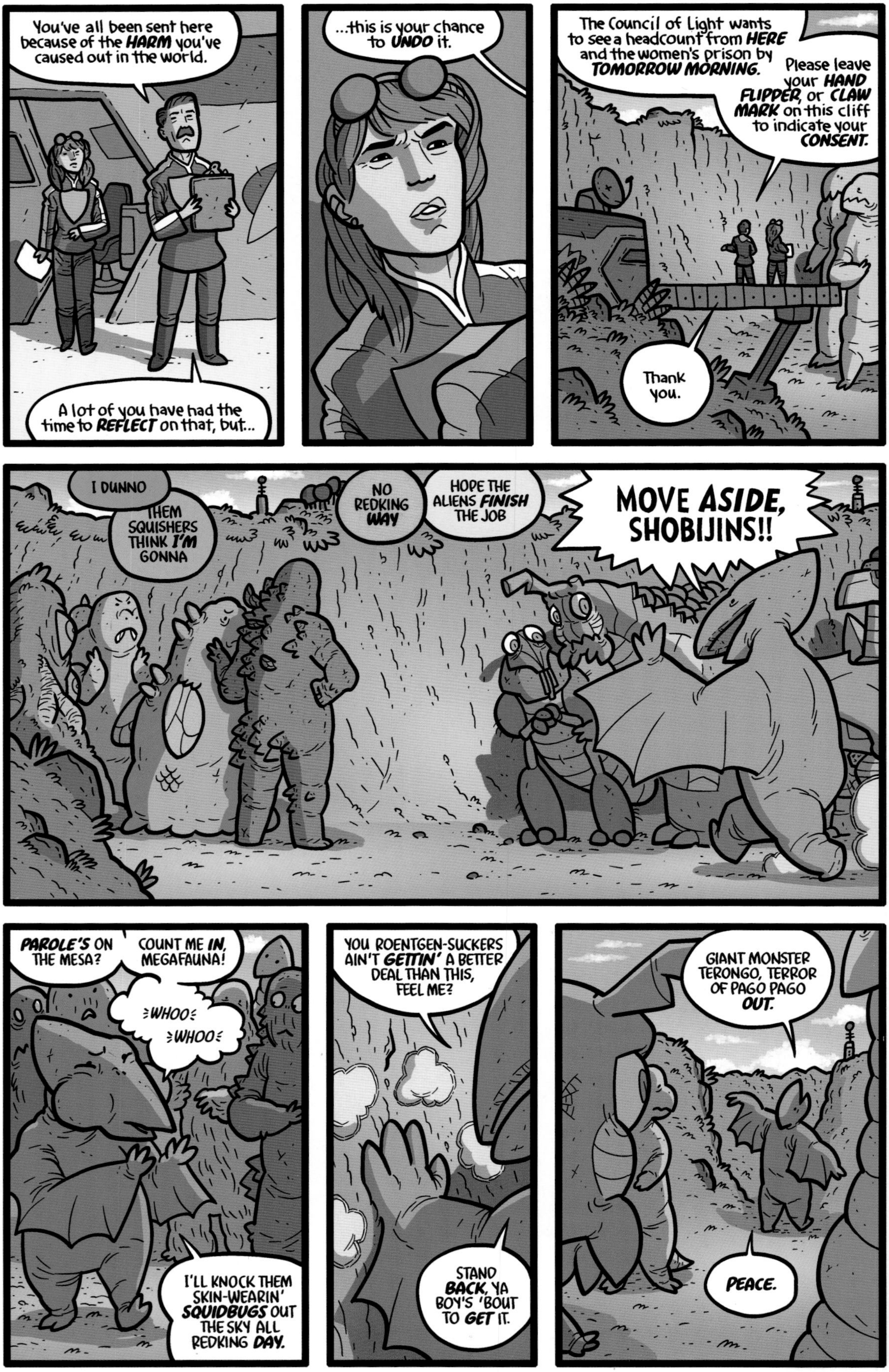

You've all been sent here because of the HARM you've caused out in the world.
A lot of you have had the time to REFLECT on that, but...
...this is your chance to UNDO it.
The Council of Light wants to see a headcount from HERE and the women's prison by TOMORROW MORNING.
Please leave your HAND FLIPPER, or CLAW MARK on this cliff to indicate your CONSENT.
Thank you.
I DUNNO
THEM SQUISHERS THINK I'M GONNA
NO REDKING WAY
HOPE THE ALIENS FINISH THE JOB
MOVE ASIDE, SHOBIJINS!!
PAROLE'S ON THE MESA?
COUNT ME IN, MEGAFAUNA!
WHOO
WHOO
I'LL KNOCK THEM SKIN-WEARIN' SQUIDBUGS OUT THE SKY ALL REDKING DAY.
YOU ROENTGEN-SUCKERS AIN'T GETTIN' A BETTER DEAL THAN THIS, FEEL ME?
STAND BACK, YA BOY'S 'BOUT TO GET IT.
GIANT MONSTER TERONGO, TERROR OF PAGO PAGO OUT.
PEACE.

DAD, I-IT'S TOO **DANGEROUS**, BUT...

IT **IS**, YOU'RE **RIGHT**. I CAN'T HAVE **YOU** GO, BUT...

HE SAID THE **WOMEN'S** PRISON.

TORGAX WILL BE THERE. I **KNOW** IT.

AND IF THERE'S A CHANCE I CAN SEE YOUR **SISTER**, WORK THINGS **OUT**, AFTER EVERYTHING...

I **HAVE** TO TAKE IT.

LOOK AT **THAT**. SHIPPING **OUT**, SEA BUG?

Huh. I'LL **NEVER** UNDERSTAND YOU LIZZERS.

FIGHTIN' A **DISASTER** FOR THE SQUISHERS WHO HATE YOUR SLIMY WHITE **GUTS**?

YOU WON'T FIND NO **CRYPTIDS** DOING THAT.

ALIEN INVASIONS COME AND **GO**. CLEAR AWAY DEAD CIVILIZATIONS. IT'S **NATURAL**.

LIFE **HERE'S** GOTTA **CONTINUE**.

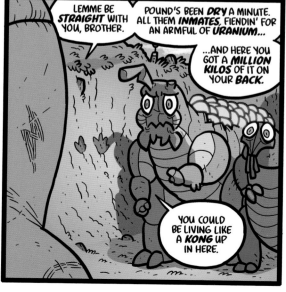

LEMME BE **STRAIGHT** WITH YOU, BROTHER.

POUND'S BEEN **DRY** A MINUTE. ALL THEM **INMATES**, FIENDIN' FOR AN ARMFUL OF **URANIUM**...

...AND HERE YOU GOT A **MILLION KILOS** OF IT ON YOUR **BACK**.

YOU COULD BE LIVING LIKE A **KONG** UP IN HERE.

I TOLD YOU, I AIN'T *SELLING.* PISS *OFF.*

YOU TRYIN' TO STAND UP TO THE *CRYPTIDS?*

THAT AIN'T *HEALTHY* FOR YOU AND YOUR FAMILY IF--

LEMME STOP YOUR LITTLE THREAT RIGHT *THERE.*

YOU *TRIED* ALREADY, "BROTHER."

AND *NOW* YOU CAN ONLY COLLAPSE *HALF* AS MANY BRIDGES.

PUT *THAT* IN YOUR CANDLE AND FLY TO IT.

LO, DID YA *GET* IT?

SHUT UP.

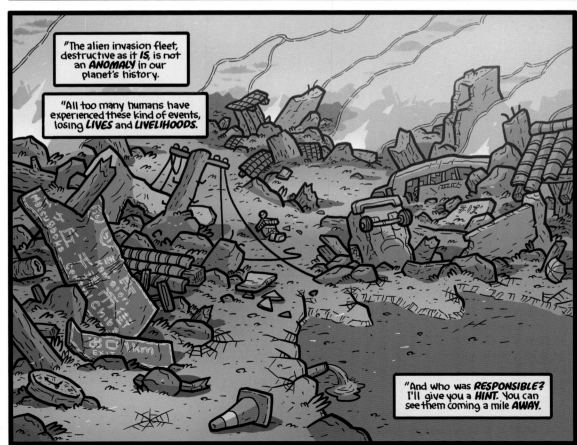

"The alien invasion fleet, destructive as it *IS,* is not an *ANOMALY* in our planet's history.

"All too many humans have experienced these kind of events, losing *LIVES* and *LIVELIHOODS.*

"And who was *RESPONSIBLE?* I'll give you a *HINT.* You can see them coming a mile *AWAY.*

"**COUNTLESS** cities now have scars that will never **HEAL.** If there's anything we can all agree on, it's **THIS:**

"The **PERPETRATORS** of these destructive acts have a lot to **ATONE** for."

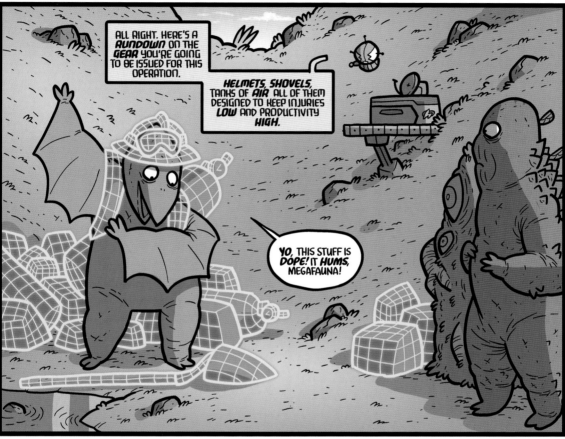

ALL RIGHT. HERE'S A **RUNDOWN** ON THE **GEAR** YOU'RE GOING TO BE ISSUED FOR THIS OPERATION.

HELMETS, SHOVELS, TANKS OF **AIR** ALL OF THEM DESIGNED TO KEEP INJURIES **LOW** AND PRODUCTIVITY **HIGH.**

YO, THIS STUFF IS **DOPE!** IT **HUMS,** MEGAFAUNA!

≷ ahem ≷ THAT'S **RIGHT.**

THEY'VE BEEN SPECIALLY DESIGNED BY **GRIDBOT,** SO THEY'RE EXPENSIVE. THE BUREAU OF PRISONS HAS A LOT OF MONEY SUNK INTO THIS.

SO ONCE YOU'VE BEEN ISSUED YOUR GEAR, THAT'S **IT.** YOU PROTECT IT WITH YOUR **LIFE.**

YO, WAIT-- THIS **PROTECTIVE EQUIPMENT...**

...**WE'RE** SUPPOSED TO PROTECT **IT?**

LISTEN, SMARTASS...

THE GENIUS **AIs** AT **GRIDBOT** DIDN'T GET TO WHERE THEY ARE BY THROWING MONEY AWAY ON DUMB 'NILLAS LIKE **YOU** BREAKING THEIR **STUFF.**

SO STOP PLAYING THE **VICTIMS** AND SUIT UP.

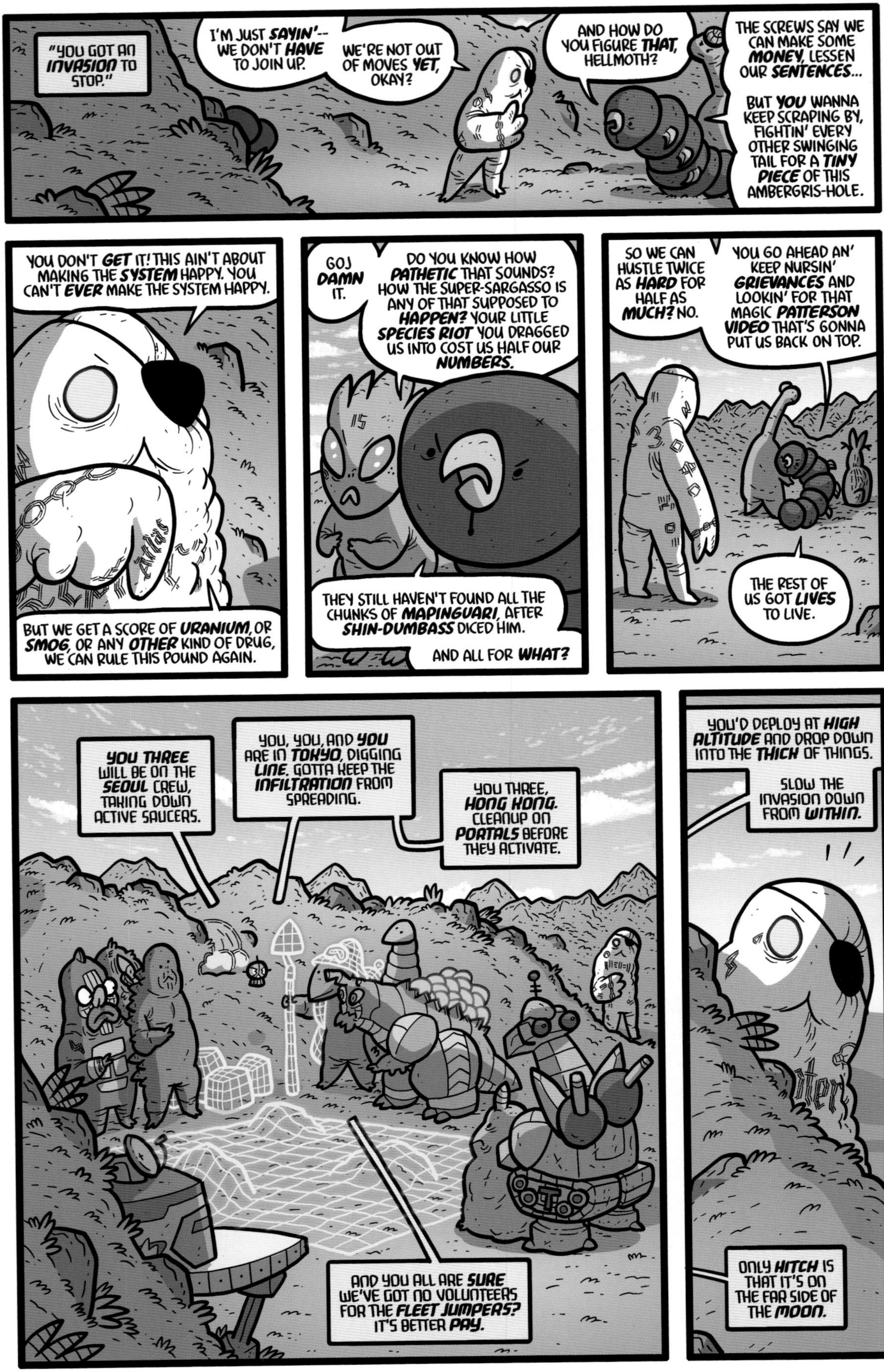
"YOU GOT AN INVASION TO STOP."
I'M JUST SAYIN'-- WE DON'T HAVE TO JOIN UP.
WE'RE NOT OUT OF MOVES YET, OKAY?
AND HOW DO YOU FIGURE THAT, HELLMOTH?
THE SCREWS SAY WE CAN MAKE SOME MONEY, LESSEN OUR SENTENCES...
BUT YOU WANNA KEEP SCRAPING BY, FIGHTIN' EVERY OTHER SWINGING TAIL FOR A TINY PIECE OF THIS AMBERGRIS-HOLE.
YOU DON'T GET IT! THIS AIN'T ABOUT MAKING THE SYSTEM HAPPY. YOU CAN'T EVER MAKE THE SYSTEM HAPPY.
BUT WE GET A SCORE OF URANIUM, OR SMOG, OR ANY OTHER KIND OF DRUG, WE CAN RULE THIS POUND AGAIN.
GOJ DAMN IT.
DO YOU KNOW HOW PATHETIC THAT SOUNDS? HOW THE SUPER-SARGASSO IS ANY OF THAT SUPPOSED TO HAPPEN? YOUR LITTLE SPECIES RIOT YOU DRAGGED US INTO COST US HALF OUR NUMBERS.
THEY STILL HAVEN'T FOUND ALL THE CHUNKS OF MAPINGUARI, AFTER SHIN-DUMBASS DICED HIM.
AND ALL FOR WHAT?
SO WE CAN HUSTLE TWICE AS HARD FOR HALF AS MUCH? NO.
YOU GO AHEAD AN' KEEP NURSIN' GRIEVANCES AND LOOKIN' FOR THAT MAGIC PATTERSON VIDEO THAT'S GONNA PUT US BACK ON TOP.
THE REST OF US GOT LIVES TO LIVE.
YOU THREE WILL BE ON THE SEOUL CREW, TAKING DOWN ACTIVE SAUCERS.
YOU, YOU, AND YOU ARE IN TOKYO, DIGGING LINE. GOTTA KEEP THE INFILTRATION FROM SPREADING.
YOU THREE, HONG KONG. CLEANUP ON PORTALS BEFORE THEY ACTIVATE.
AND YOU ALL ARE SURE WE'VE GOT NO VOLUNTEERS FOR THE FLEET JUMPERS? IT'S BETTER PAY.
YOU'D DEPLOY AT HIGH ALTITUDE AND DROP DOWN INTO THE THICK OF THINGS.
SLOW THE INVASION DOWN FROM WITHIN.
ONLY HITCH IS THAT IT'S ON THE FAR SIDE OF THE MOON.

"Perhaps some of these **PERPETRATORS** feel remorse now.

"Perhaps they finally wish to **HELP.**

"To finally take **PRIDE** in the planet they live on.

≥nnf≤

Ow!

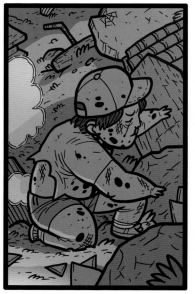

"Maybe even find **COMMON CAUSE** with us humans."

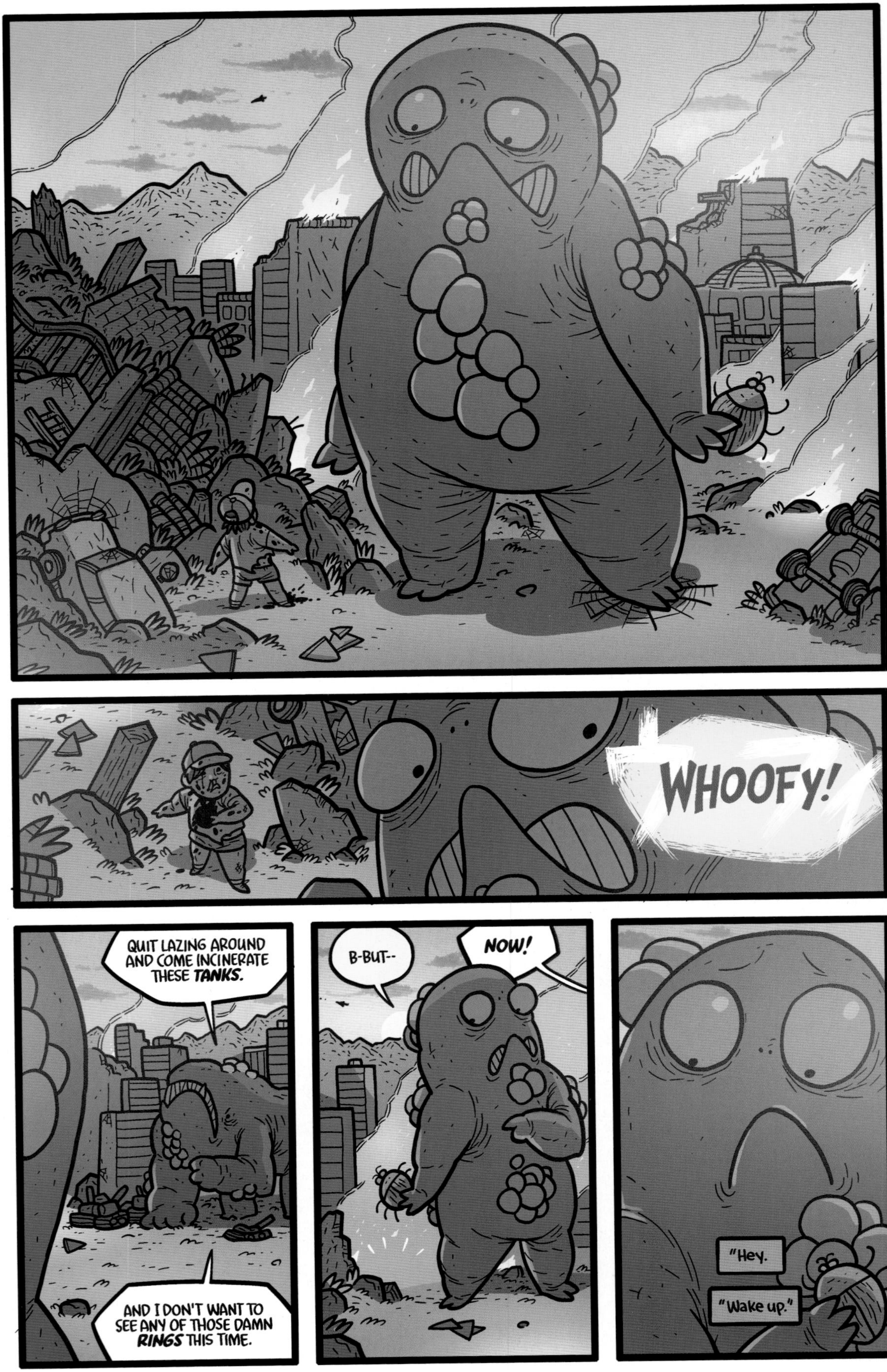
WHOOFY!
QUIT LAZING AROUND AND COME INCINERATE THESE TANKS.
AND I DON'T WANT TO SEE ANY OF THOSE DAMN RINGS THIS TIME.
B-BUT--
NOW!
"Hey.
"Wake up."

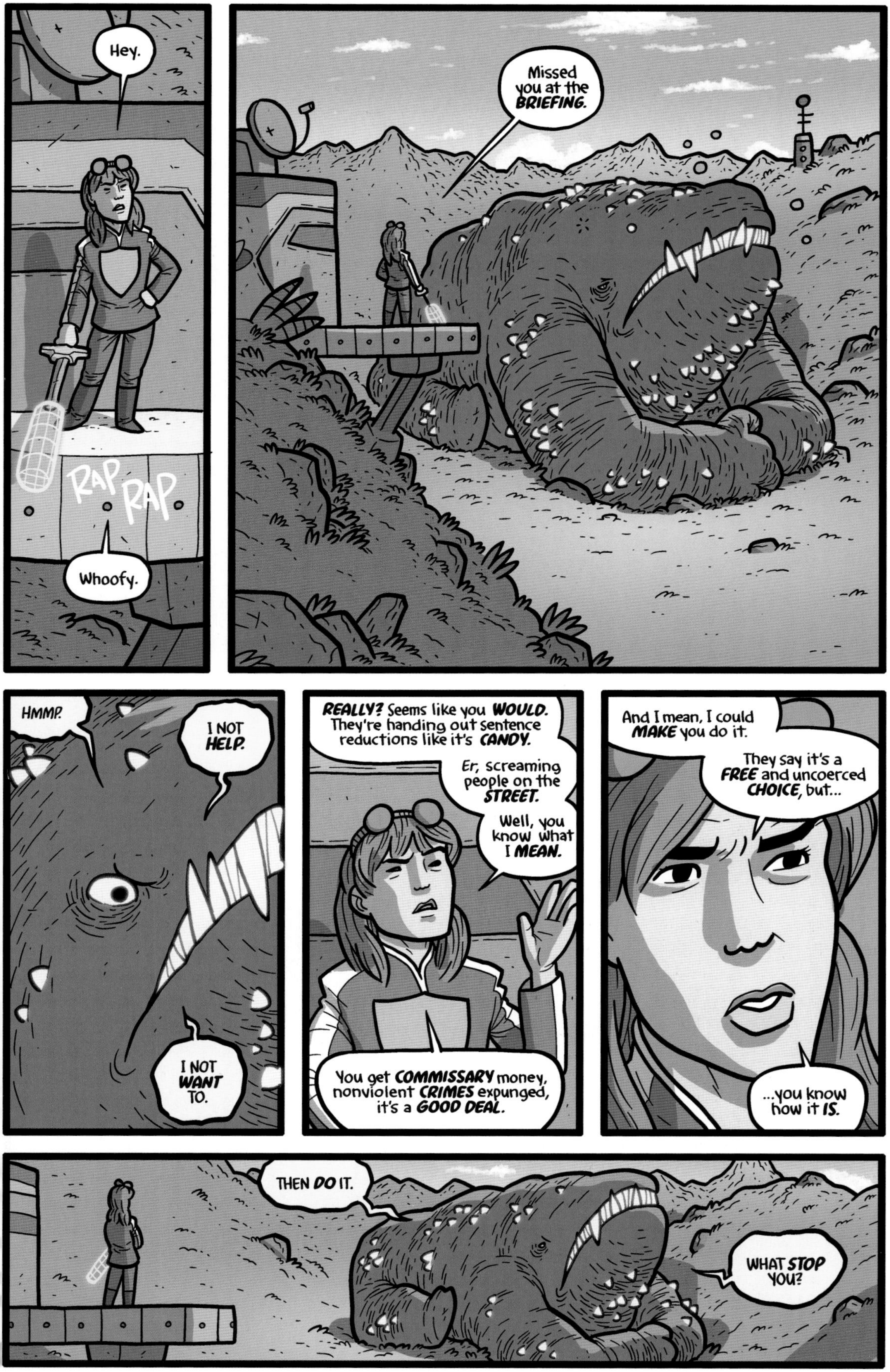
Hey.
RAP RAP
Whoofy.
Missed you at the BRIEFING.
HMMP.
I NOT HELP.
I NOT WANT TO.
REALLY? Seems like you WOULD. They're handing out sentence reductions like it's CANDY.
Er, screaming people on the STREET.
Well, you know what I MEAN.
You get COMMISSARY money, nonviolent CRIMES expunged, it's a GOOD DEAL.
And I mean, I could MAKE you do it.
They say it's a FREE and uncoerced CHOICE, but...
...you know how it IS.
THEN DO IT.
WHAT STOP YOU?

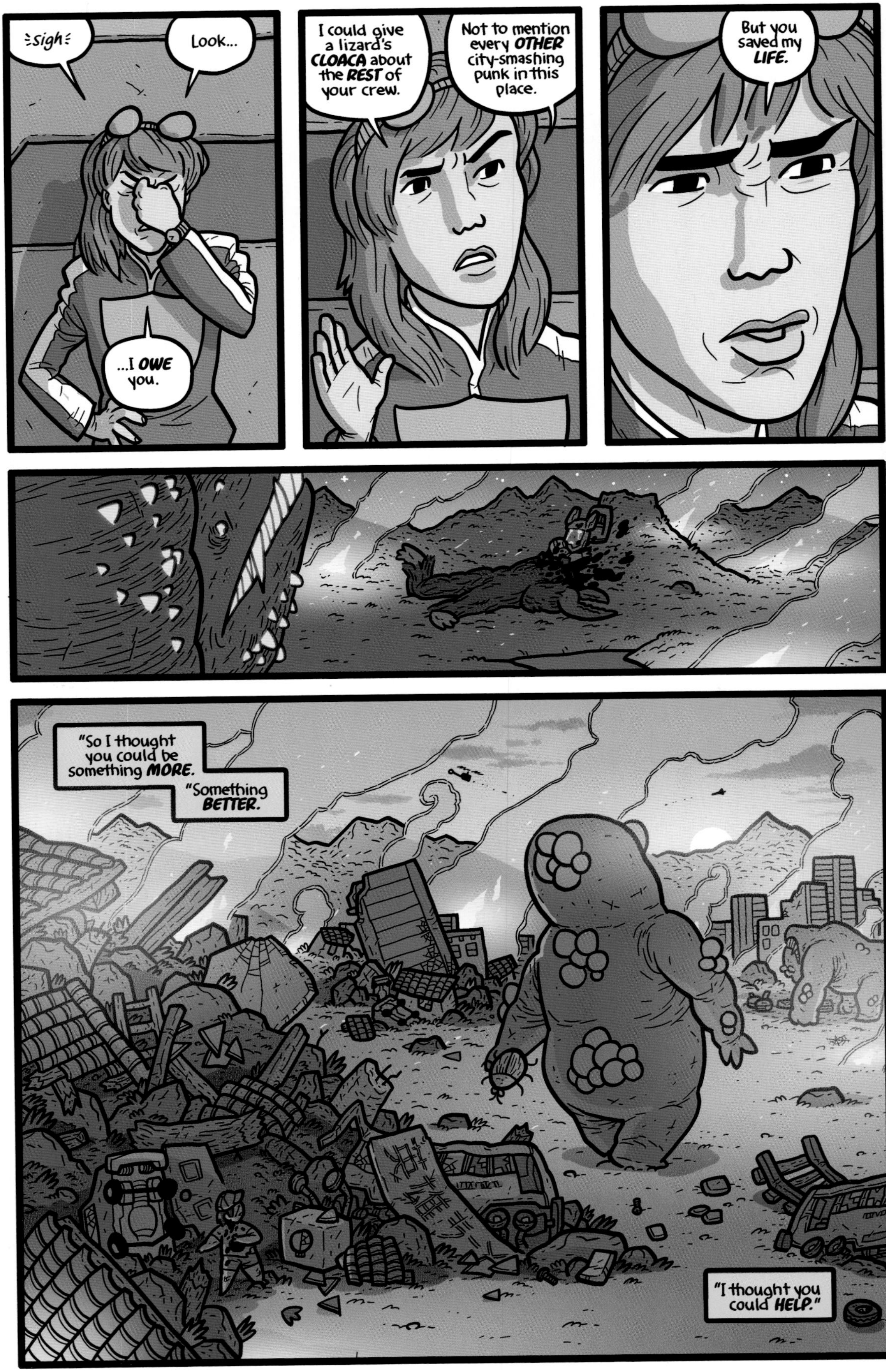

sigh
Look...
...I **OWE** you.
I could give a lizard's **CLOACA** about the **REST** of your crew.
Not to mention every **OTHER** city-smashing punk in this place.
But you saved my **LIFE.**
"So I thought you could be something **MORE.**
"Something **BETTER.**
"I thought you could **HELP.**"

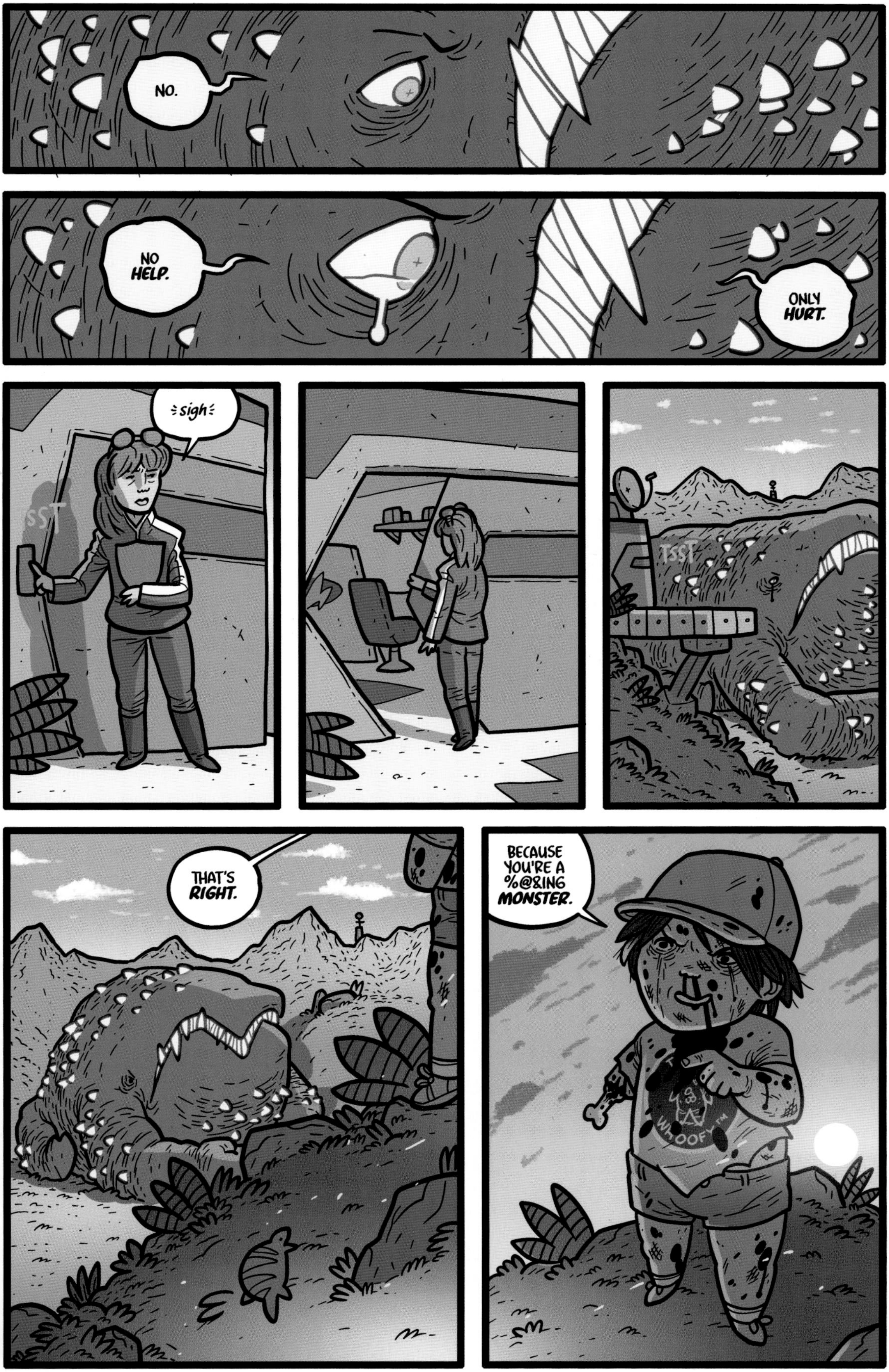
NO.
NO HELP.
ONLY HURT.
sigh
TSST
TSST
THAT'S RIGHT.
BECAUSE YOU'RE A %@&ING MONSTER.
WOOFY™

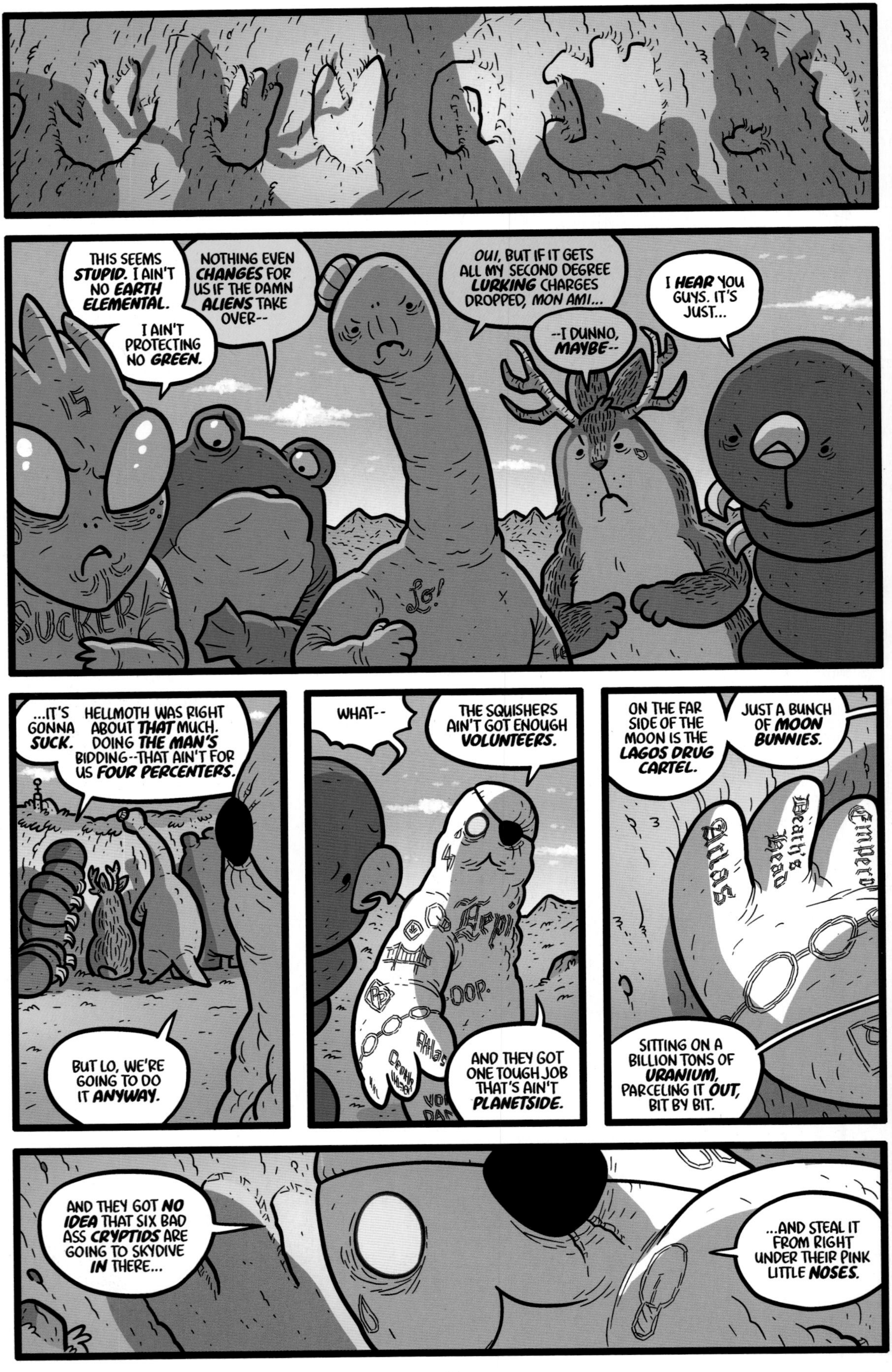

THIS SEEMS STUPID. I AIN'T NO EARTH ELEMENTAL.
I AIN'T PROTECTING NO GREEN.
NOTHING EVEN CHANGES FOR US IF THE DAMN ALIENS TAKE OVER--
OUI, BUT IF IT GETS ALL MY SECOND DEGREE LURKING CHARGES DROPPED, MON AMI...
--I DUNNO, MAYBE--
I HEAR YOU GUYS. IT'S JUST...
SUCKER
Lo!
...IT'S GONNA SUCK.
HELLMOTH WAS RIGHT ABOUT THAT MUCH. DOING THE MAN'S BIDDING--THAT AIN'T FOR US FOUR PERCENTERS.
BUT LO, WE'RE GOING TO DO IT ANYWAY.
WHAT--
THE SQUISHERS AIN'T GOT ENOUGH VOLUNTEERS.
AND THEY GOT ONE TOUGH JOB THAT'S AIN'T PLANETSIDE.
ON THE FAR SIDE OF THE MOON IS THE LAGOS DRUG CARTEL.
JUST A BUNCH OF MOON BUNNIES.
Atlas
Death's Head
Emperor
SITTING ON A BILLION TONS OF URANIUM, PARCELING IT OUT, BIT BY BIT.
AND THEY GOT NO IDEA THAT SIX BAD ASS CRYPTIDS ARE GOING TO SKYDIVE IN THERE...
...AND STEAL IT FROM RIGHT UNDER THEIR PINK LITTLE NOSES.

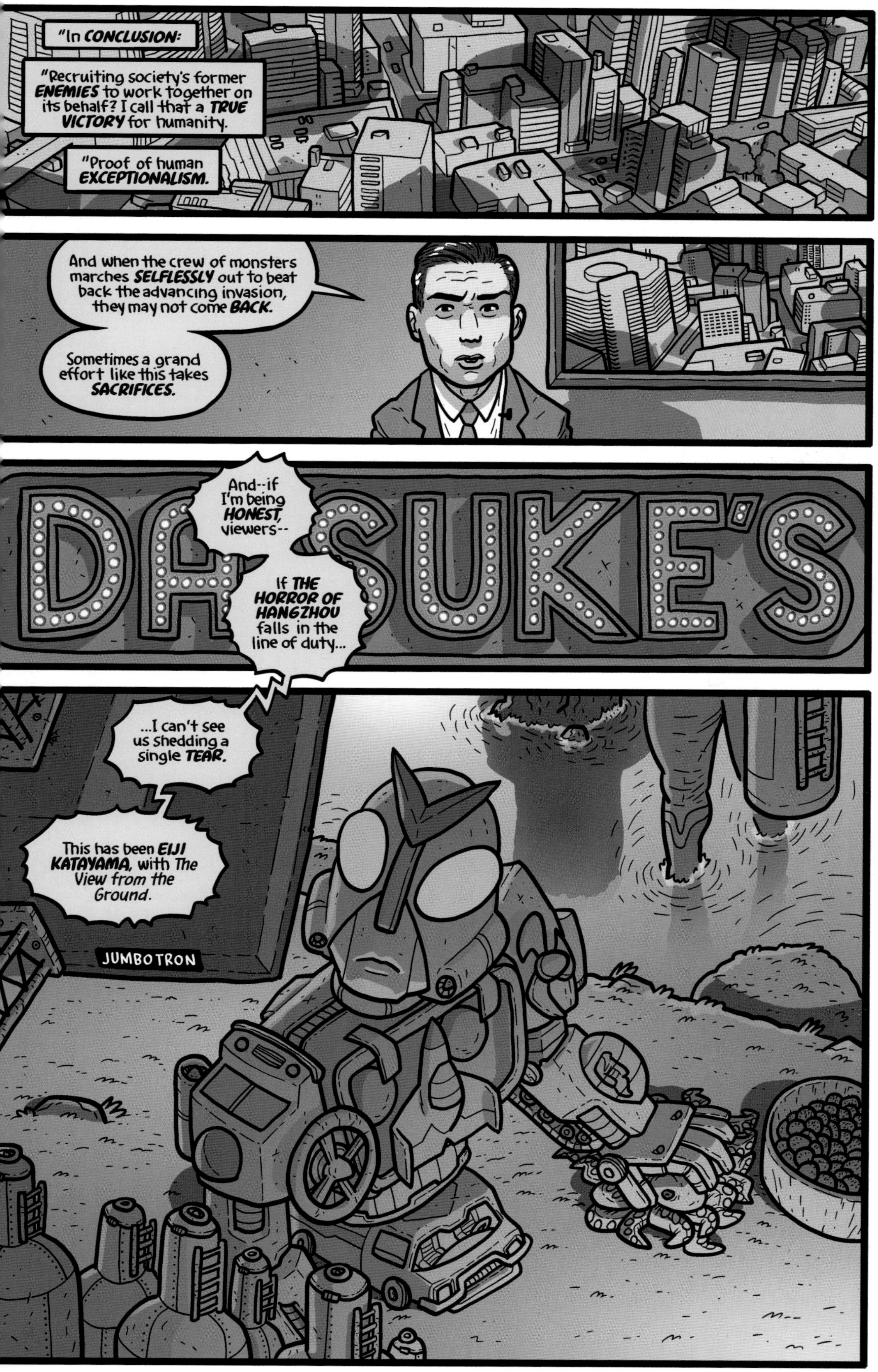
"In CONCLUSION:
"Recruiting society's former ENEMIES to work together on its behalf? I call that a TRUE VICTORY for humanity.
"Proof of human EXCEPTIONALISM.
And when the crew of monsters marches SELFLESSLY out to beat back the advancing invasion, they may not come BACK.
Sometimes a grand effort like this takes SACRIFICES.
And--if I'm being HONEST, viewers--
If THE HORROR OF HANGZHOU falls in the line of duty...
...I can't see us shedding a single TEAR.
This has been EIJI KATAYAMA, with The View from the Ground.
JUMBOTRON

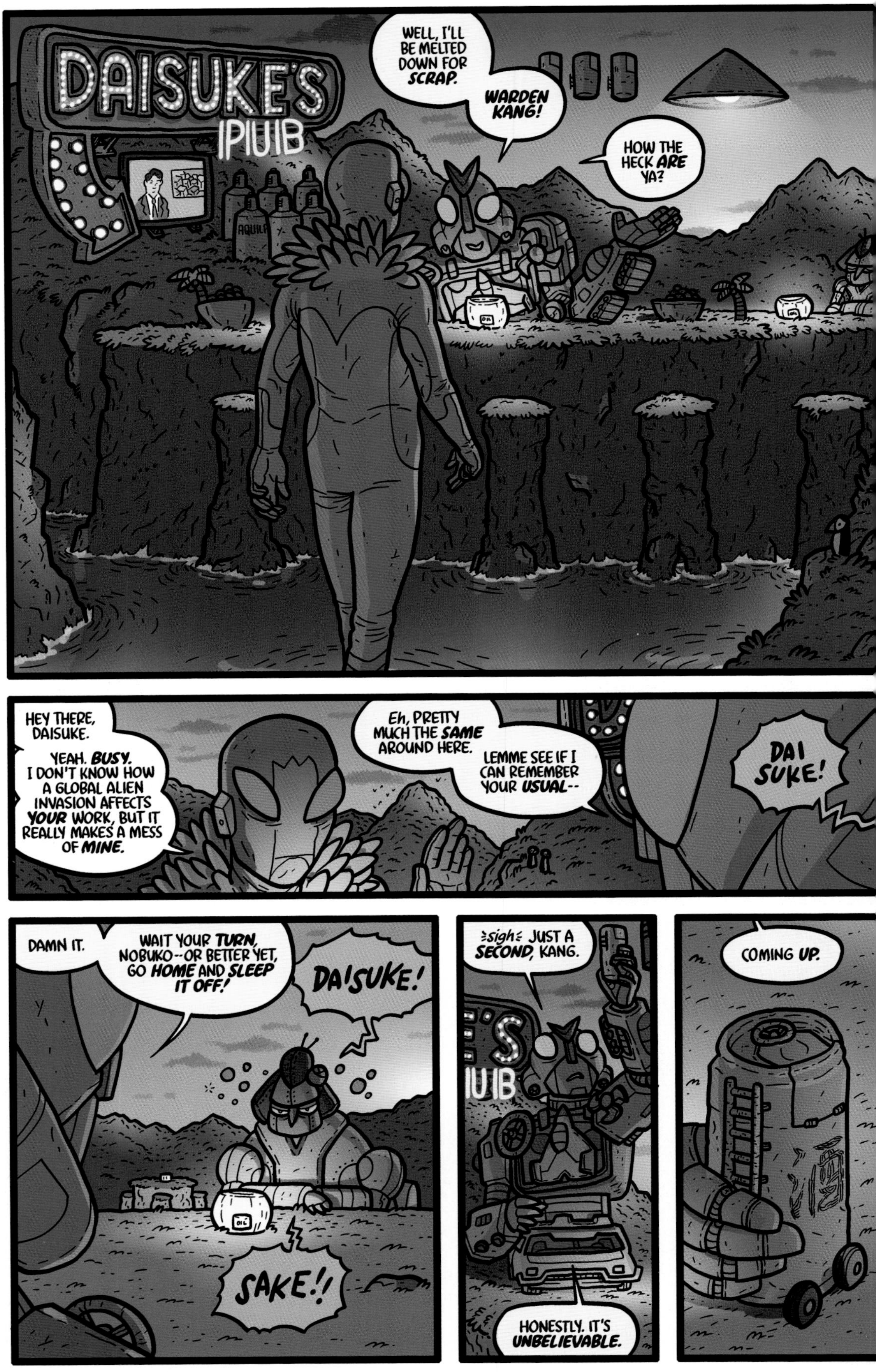

DAISUKE'S PUB
WELL, I'LL BE MELTED DOWN FOR SCRAP.
WARDEN KANG!
HOW THE HECK ARE YA?
HEY THERE, DAISUKE.
YEAH. BUSY. I DON'T KNOW HOW A GLOBAL ALIEN INVASION AFFECTS YOUR WORK, BUT IT REALLY MAKES A MESS OF MINE.
Eh, PRETTY MUCH THE SAME AROUND HERE.
LEMME SEE IF I CAN REMEMBER YOUR USUAL--
DAI SUKE!
DAMN IT.
WAIT YOUR TURN, NOBUKO--OR BETTER YET, GO HOME AND SLEEP IT OFF!
DAISUKE!
SAKE!!
sigh JUST A SECOND, KANG.
HONESTLY. IT'S UNBELIEVABLE.
COMING UP.

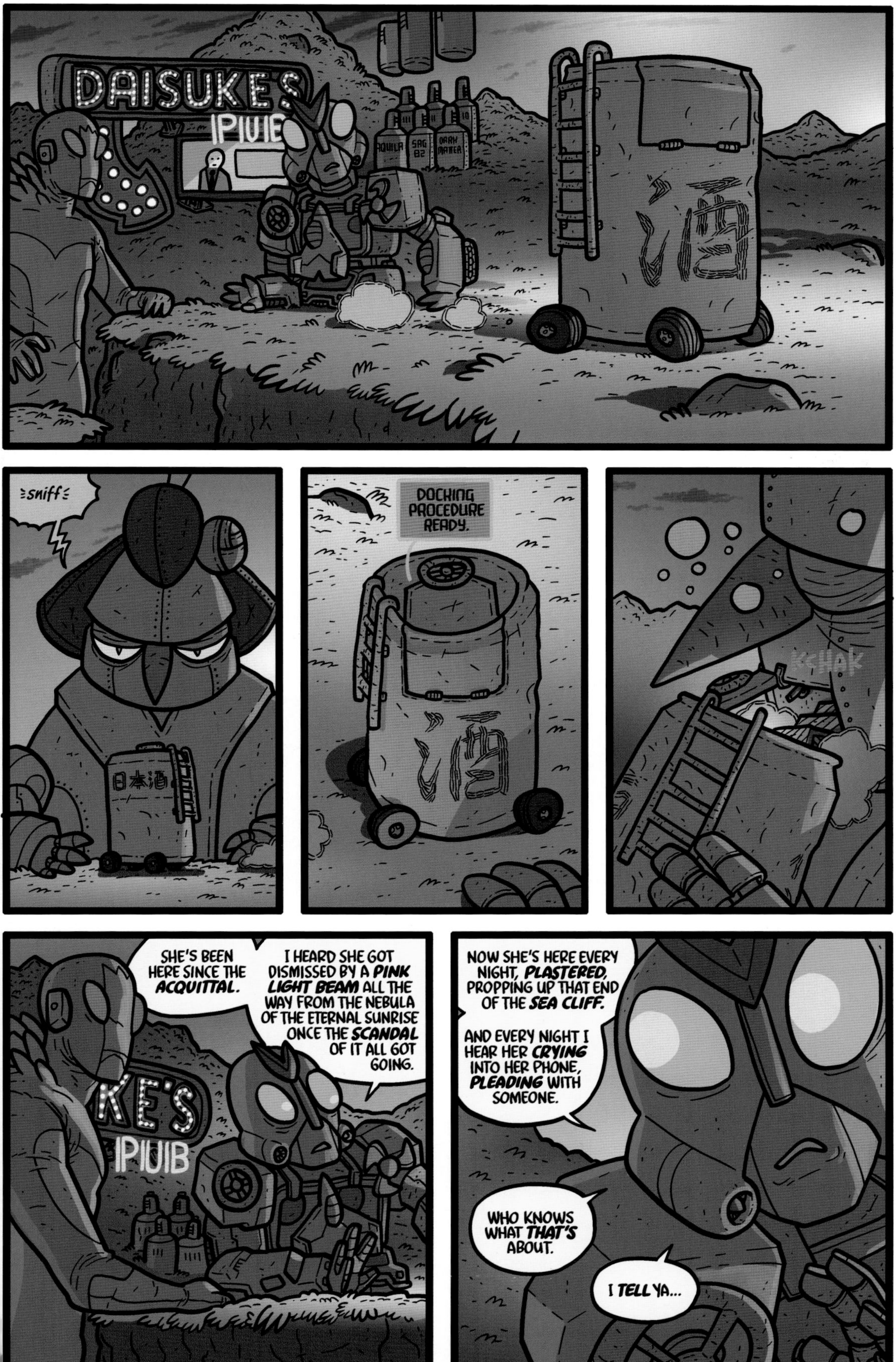
DAISUKE'S
PUB
酒
sniff
日本酒
DOCKING PROCEDURE READY.
酒
KCHAK
SHE'S BEEN HERE SINCE THE ACQUITTAL.
I HEARD SHE GOT DISMISSED BY A PINK LIGHT BEAM ALL THE WAY FROM THE NEBULA OF THE ETERNAL SUNRISE ONCE THE SCANDAL OF IT ALL GOT GOING.
KE'S
PUB
NOW SHE'S HERE EVERY NIGHT, PLASTERED, PROPPING UP THAT END OF THE SEA CLIFF.
AND EVERY NIGHT I HEAR HER CRYING INTO HER PHONE, PLEADING WITH SOMEONE.
WHO KNOWS WHAT THAT'S ABOUT.
I TELL YA...

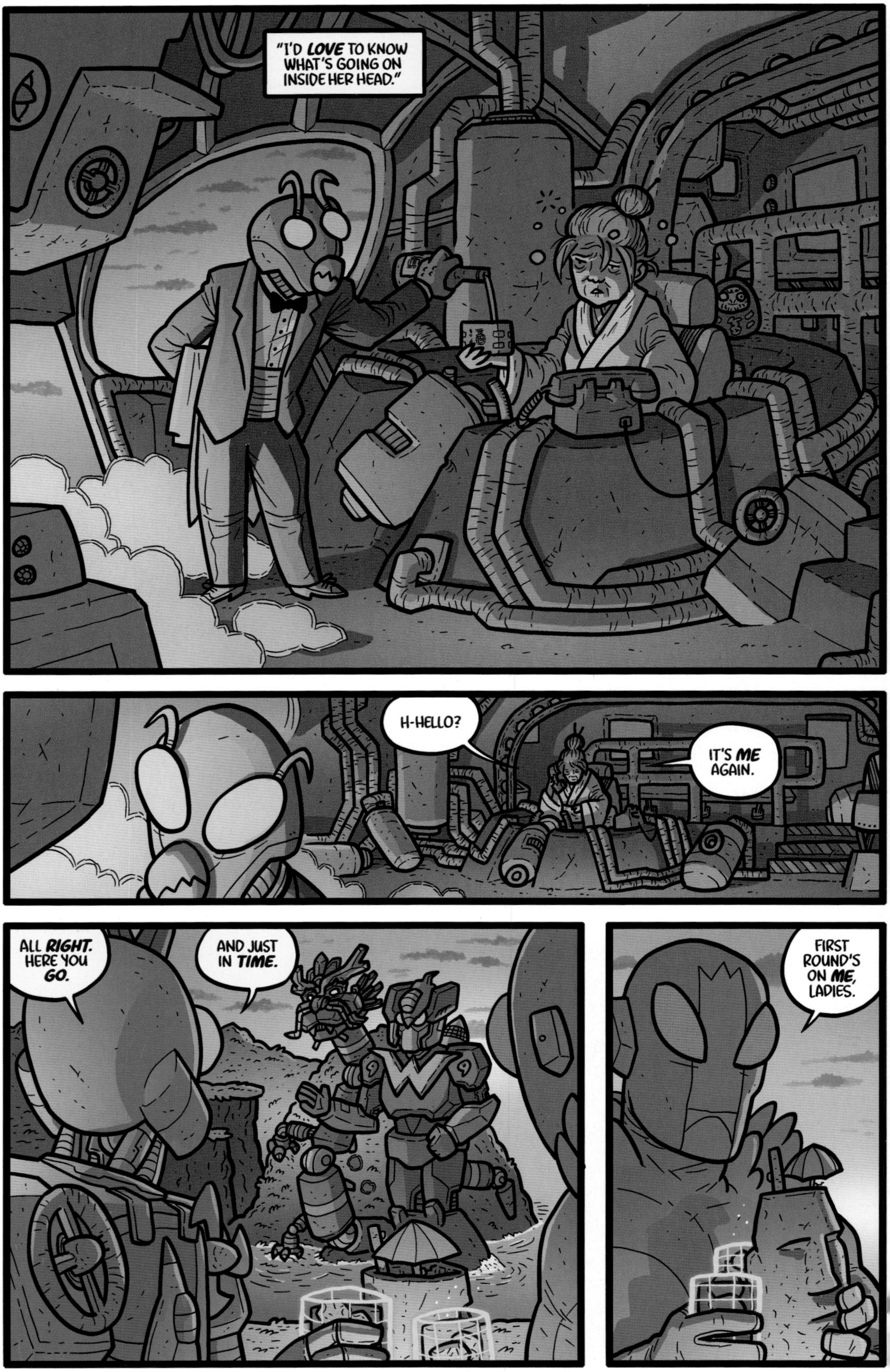
"I'D LOVE TO KNOW WHAT'S GOING ON INSIDE HER HEAD."
H-HELLO?
IT'S ME AGAIN.
ALL RIGHT. HERE YOU GO.
AND JUST IN TIME.
FIRST ROUND'S ON ME, LADIES.

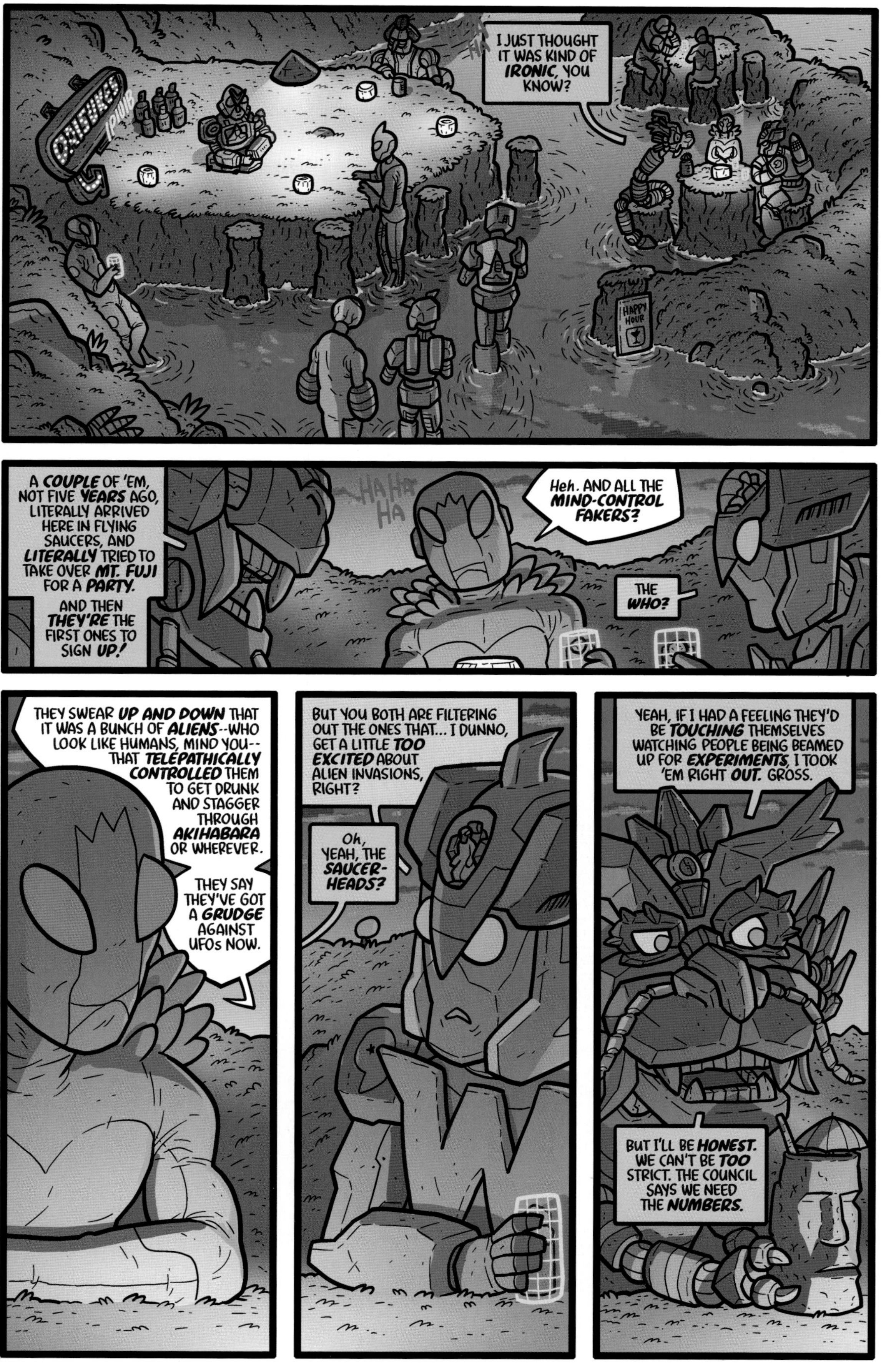
HA HA HA
I JUST THOUGHT IT WAS KIND OF IRONIC, YOU KNOW?
HAPPY HOUR
A COUPLE OF 'EM, NOT FIVE YEARS AGO, LITERALLY ARRIVED HERE IN FLYING SAUCERS, AND LITERALLY TRIED TO TAKE OVER MT. FUJI FOR A PARTY.
AND THEN THEY'RE THE FIRST ONES TO SIGN UP!
HA HA HA
Heh. AND ALL THE MIND-CONTROL FAKERS?
THE WHO?
THEY SWEAR UP AND DOWN THAT IT WAS A BUNCH OF ALIENS--WHO LOOK LIKE HUMANS, MIND YOU-- THAT TELEPATHICALLY CONTROLLED THEM TO GET DRUNK AND STAGGER THROUGH AKIHABARA OR WHEREVER.
THEY SAY THEY'VE GOT A GRUDGE AGAINST UFOs NOW.
BUT YOU BOTH ARE FILTERING OUT THE ONES THAT... I DUNNO, GET A LITTLE TOO EXCITED ABOUT ALIEN INVASIONS, RIGHT?
Oh, YEAH, THE SAUCER-HEADS?
YEAH, IF I HAD A FEELING THEY'D BE TOUCHING THEMSELVES WATCHING PEOPLE BEING BEAMED UP FOR EXPERIMENTS, I TOOK 'EM RIGHT OUT. GROSS.
BUT I'LL BE HONEST. WE CAN'T BE TOO STRICT. THE COUNCIL SAYS WE NEED THE NUMBERS.

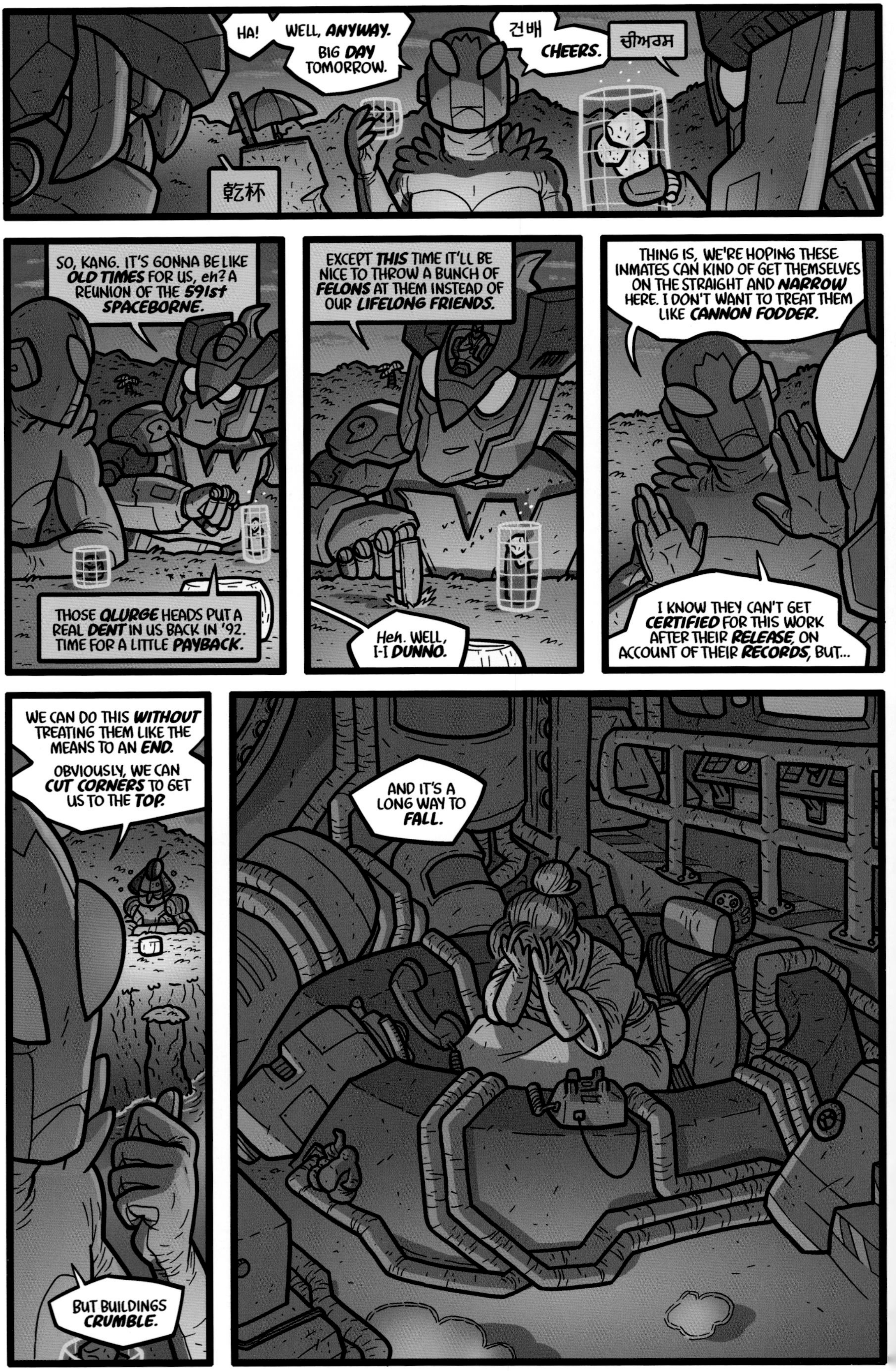
HA!
WELL, ANYWAY. BIG DAY TOMORROW.
건배
CHEERS.
ਚੀਅਰਸ
乾杯
SO, KANG. IT'S GONNA BE LIKE OLD TIMES FOR US, eh? A REUNION OF THE 591st SPACEBORNE.
THOSE QLURGE HEADS PUT A REAL DENT IN US BACK IN '92. TIME FOR A LITTLE PAYBACK.
EXCEPT THIS TIME IT'LL BE NICE TO THROW A BUNCH OF FELONS AT THEM INSTEAD OF OUR LIFELONG FRIENDS.
Heh. WELL, I-I DUNNO.
THING IS, WE'RE HOPING THESE INMATES CAN KIND OF GET THEMSELVES ON THE STRAIGHT AND NARROW HERE. I DON'T WANT TO TREAT THEM LIKE CANNON FODDER.
I KNOW THEY CAN'T GET CERTIFIED FOR THIS WORK AFTER THEIR RELEASE, ON ACCOUNT OF THEIR RECORDS, BUT...
WE CAN DO THIS WITHOUT TREATING THEM LIKE THE MEANS TO AN END.
OBVIOUSLY, WE CAN CUT CORNERS TO GET US TO THE TOP.
BUT BUILDINGS CRUMBLE.
AND IT'S A LONG WAY TO FALL.

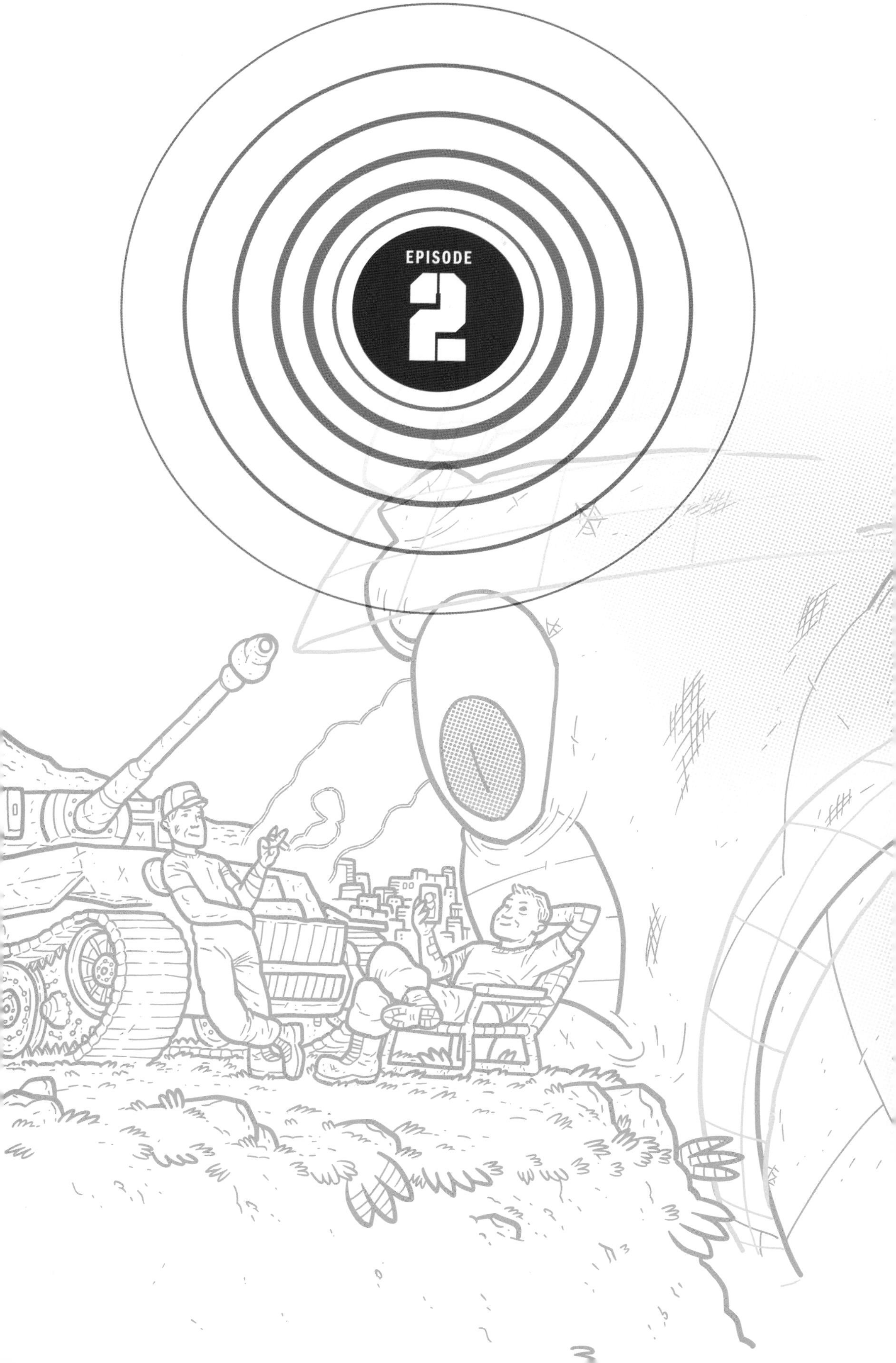
EPISODE
2

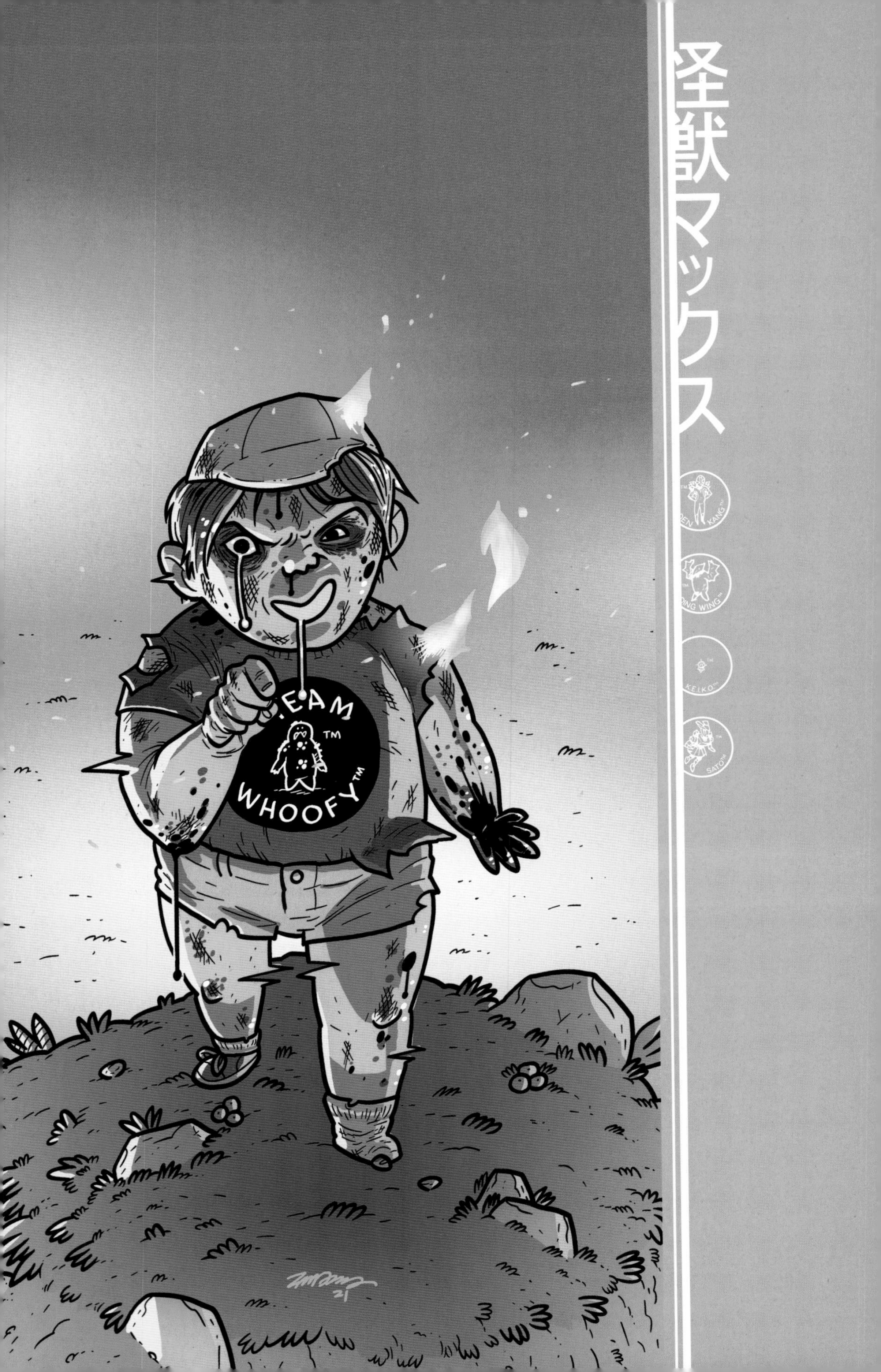

怪獣マックス
WHOOFY™
KANG™
K.E.I.K.O.™
SATO™

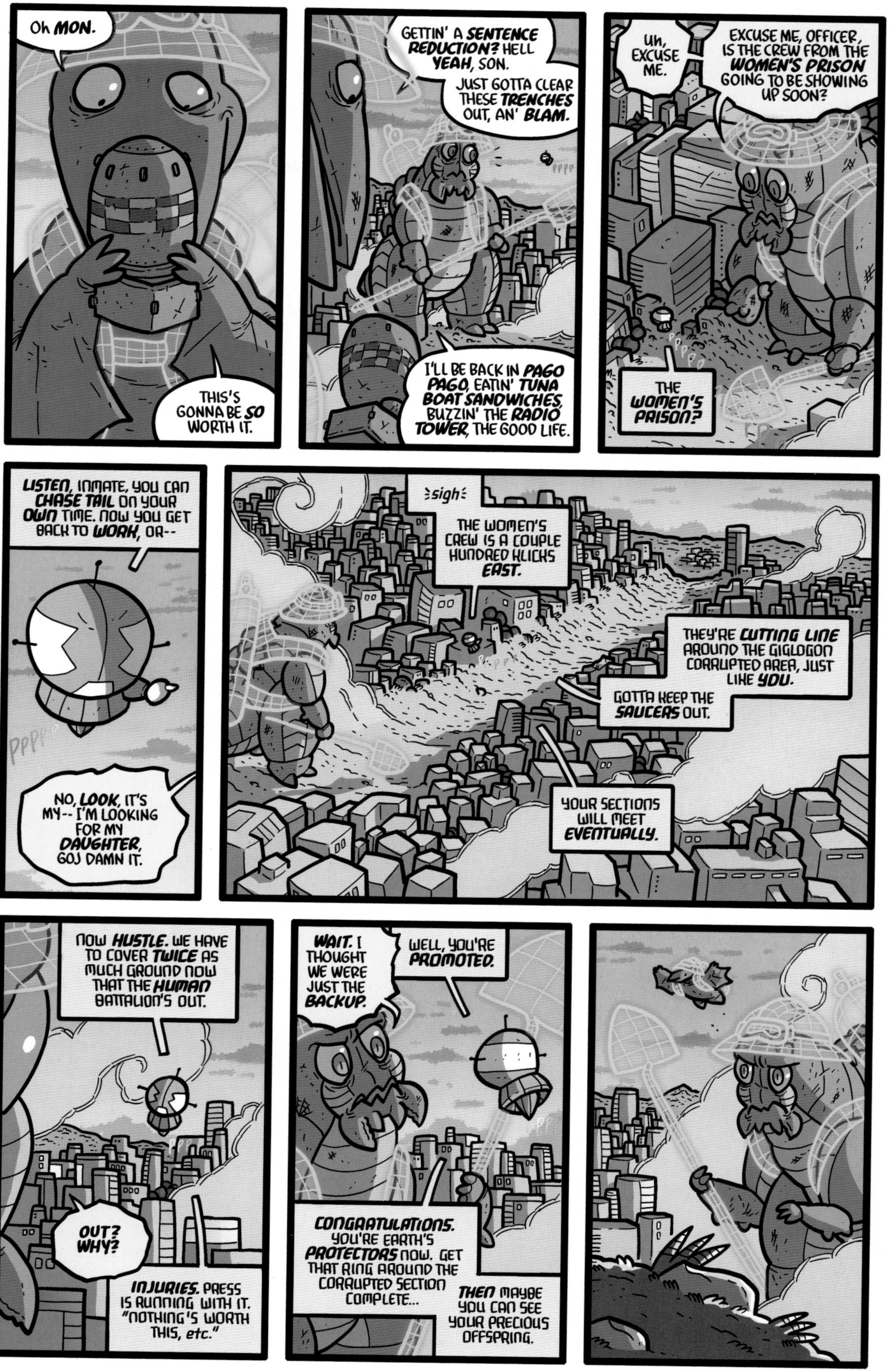
Oh MON.
THIS'S GONNA BE SO WORTH IT.
GETTIN' A SENTENCE REDUCTION? HELL YEAH, SON.
JUST GOTTA CLEAR THESE TRENCHES OUT, AN' BLAM.
I'LL BE BACK IN PAGO PAGO, EATIN' TUNA BOAT SANDWICHES, BUZZIN' THE RADIO TOWER, THE GOOD LIFE.
Uh, EXCUSE ME.
EXCUSE ME, OFFICER, IS THE CREW FROM THE WOMEN'S PRISON GOING TO BE SHOWING UP SOON?
THE WOMEN'S PRISON?
LISTEN, INMATE, YOU CAN CHASE TAIL ON YOUR OWN TIME. NOW YOU GET BACK TO WORK, OR--
NO, LOOK, IT'S MY-- I'M LOOKING FOR MY DAUGHTER, GOJ DAMN IT.
sigh
THE WOMEN'S CREW IS A COUPLE HUNDRED KLICKS EAST.
THEY'RE CUTTING LINE AROUND THE GIGLOGON CORRUPTED AREA, JUST LIKE YOU.
GOTTA KEEP THE SAUCERS OUT.
YOUR SECTIONS WILL MEET EVENTUALLY.
NOW HUSTLE. WE HAVE TO COVER TWICE AS MUCH GROUND NOW THAT THE HUMAN BATTALION'S OUT.
OUT? WHY?
INJURIES. PRESS IS RUNNING WITH IT. "NOTHING'S WORTH THIS, etc."
WAIT. I THOUGHT WE WERE JUST THE BACKUP.
WELL, YOU'RE PROMOTED.
CONGRATULATIONS. YOU'RE EARTH'S PROTECTORS NOW. GET THAT RING AROUND THE CORRUPTED SECTION COMPLETE...
THEN MAYBE YOU CAN SEE YOUR PRECIOUS OFFSPRING.

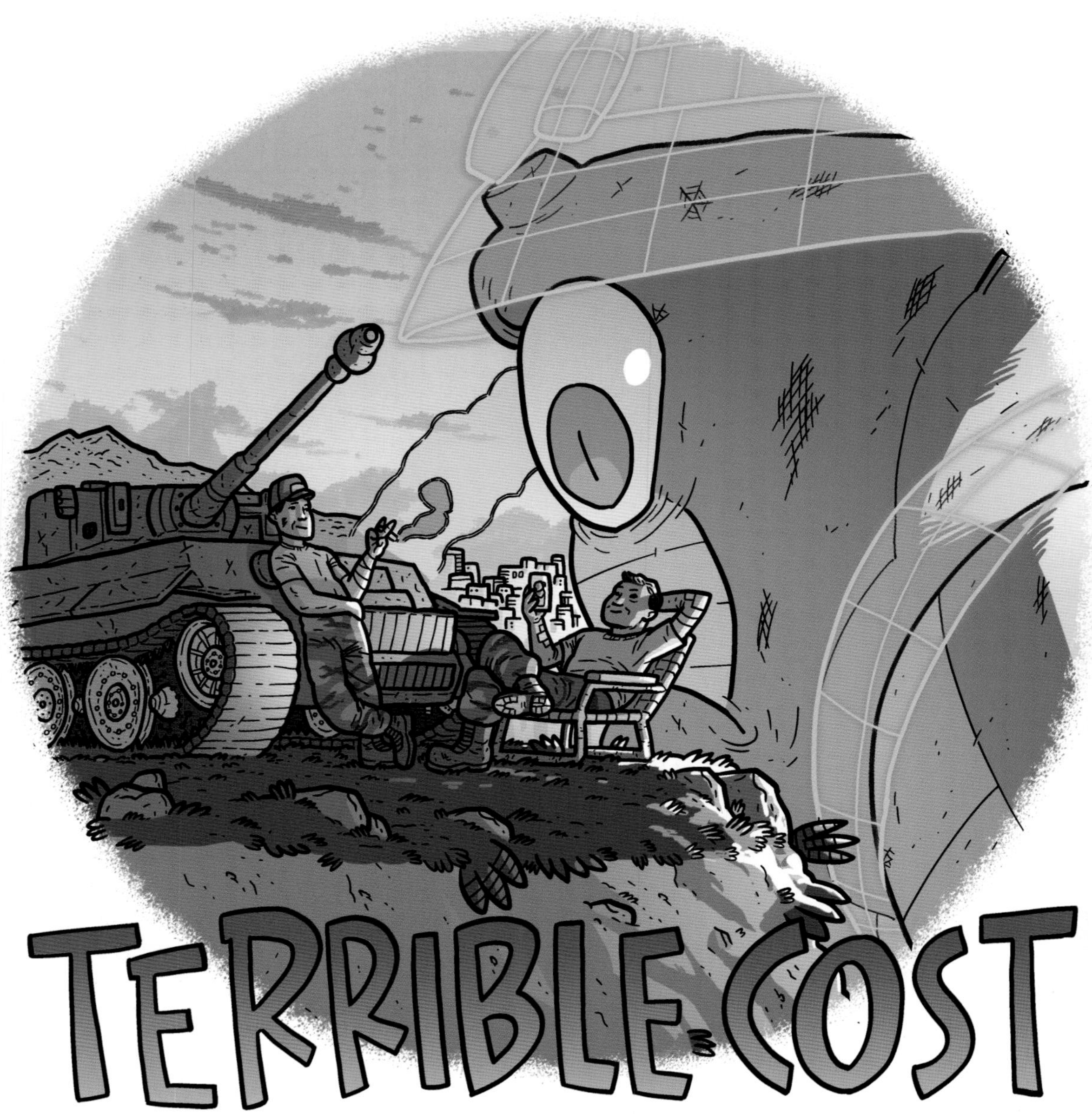

TERRIBLE COST

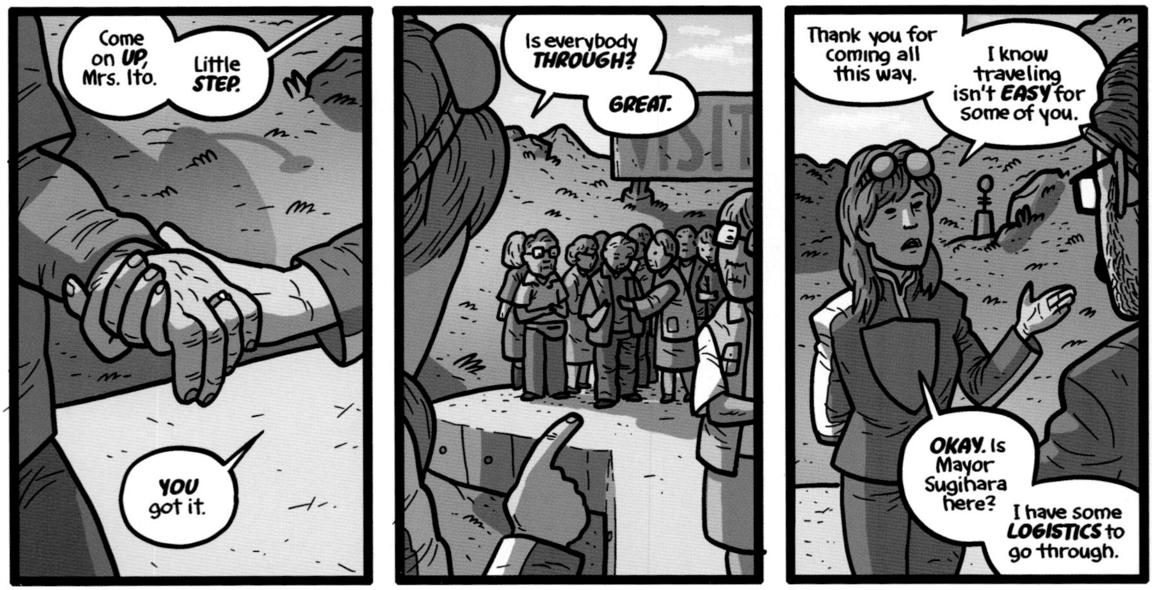
Come on UP, Mrs. Ito.
Little STEP.
YOU got it.
Is everybody THROUGH?
GREAT.
VISIT
Thank you for coming all this way.
I know traveling isn't EASY for some of you.
OKAY. Is Mayor Sugihara here?
I have some LOGISTICS to go through.

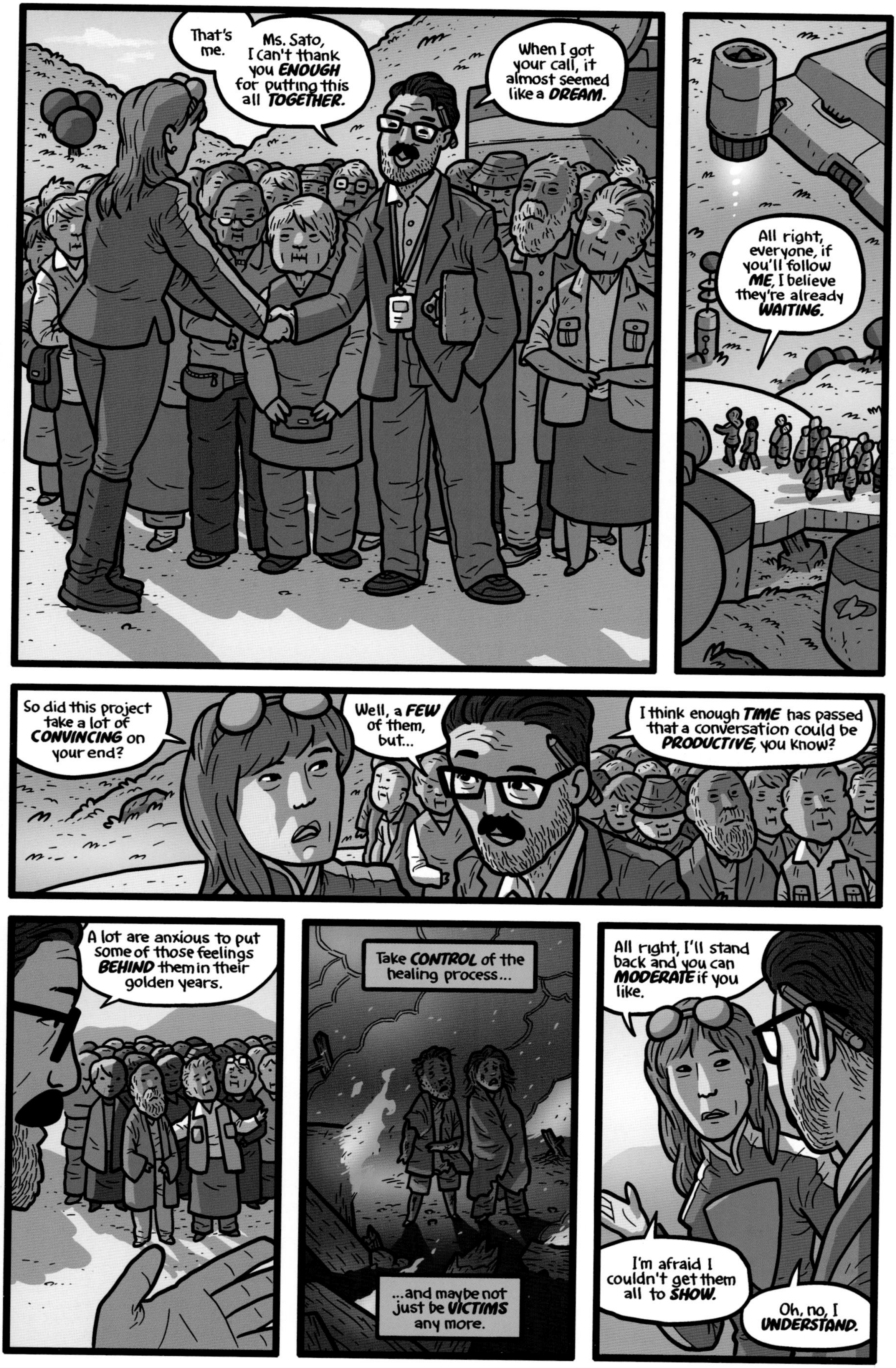
That's me.
Ms. Sato, I can't thank you ENOUGH for putting this all TOGETHER.
When I got your call, it almost seemed like a DREAM.
All right, everyone, if you'll follow ME, I believe they're already WAITING.
So did this project take a lot of CONVINCING on your end?
Well, a FEW of them, but...
I think enough TIME has passed that a conversation could be PRODUCTIVE, you know?
A lot are anxious to put some of those feelings BEHIND them in their golden years.
Take CONTROL of the healing process...
...and maybe not just be VICTIMS any more.
All right, I'll stand back and you can MODERATE if you like.
I'm afraid I couldn't get them all to SHOW.
Oh, no, I UNDERSTAND.

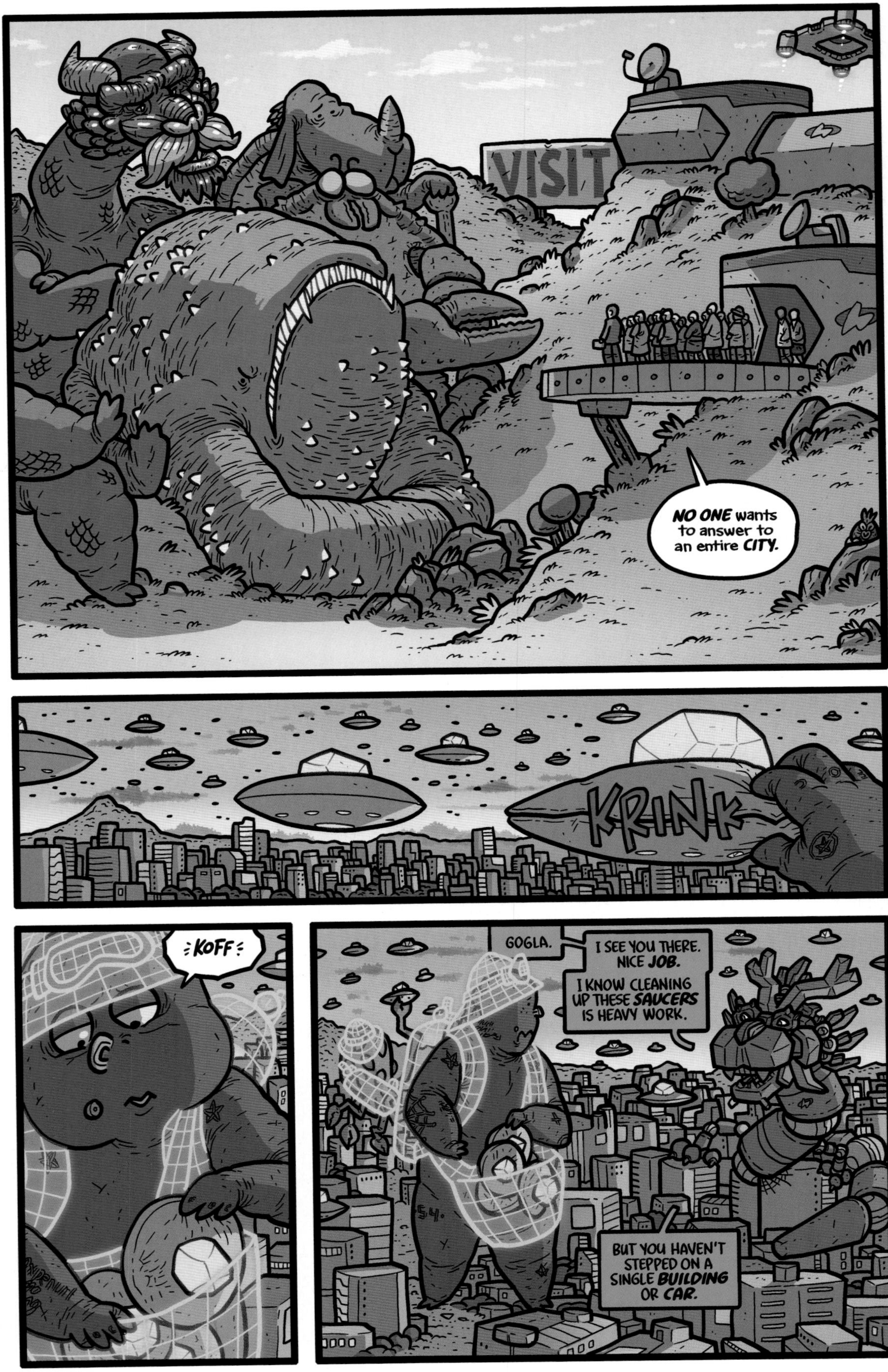
VISIT
NO ONE wants to answer to an entire CITY.
KRINK
KOFF
GOGLA.
I SEE YOU THERE. NICE JOB.
I KNOW CLEANING UP THESE SAUCERS IS HEAVY WORK.
BUT YOU HAVEN'T STEPPED ON A SINGLE BUILDING OR CAR.

Uh, YEAH. THANKS, WARDEN.

I'M *FROM* HERE. I NEVER WANTED TO MAKE A *MESS* OF IT OR NOTHIN'.

WELL, IT SHOWS.

I SUPPOSE BEING BACK IN SEOUL IS A BIT OF A TRIP DOWN *MEMORY LANE.*

EVERYTHING REMINDING YOU OF OLD *TIMES?*

Er, I DON'T KNOW ABOUT *THAT.* I DON'T WANT TO THINK ABOUT OLD JUNK *TOO* MUCH.

Hmm. FAIR *ENOUGH.*

Ah!

THERE WE GO. THE REST OF THE CREW FROM THE *MEN'S PRISON.*

THAT OUGHT TO LIGHTEN YOUR LOAD A BIT.

WELCOME TO SEOUL, EVERYO AS YOU CAN *SEE,* WE'RE PULLING *KOBLOID SAUCE* DOWN FROM THE SKY AN STORING THEM IN OUR

YOU CAME TO THE *WRONG* GOJ DAMN *CITY,* MEGAFAUNA.

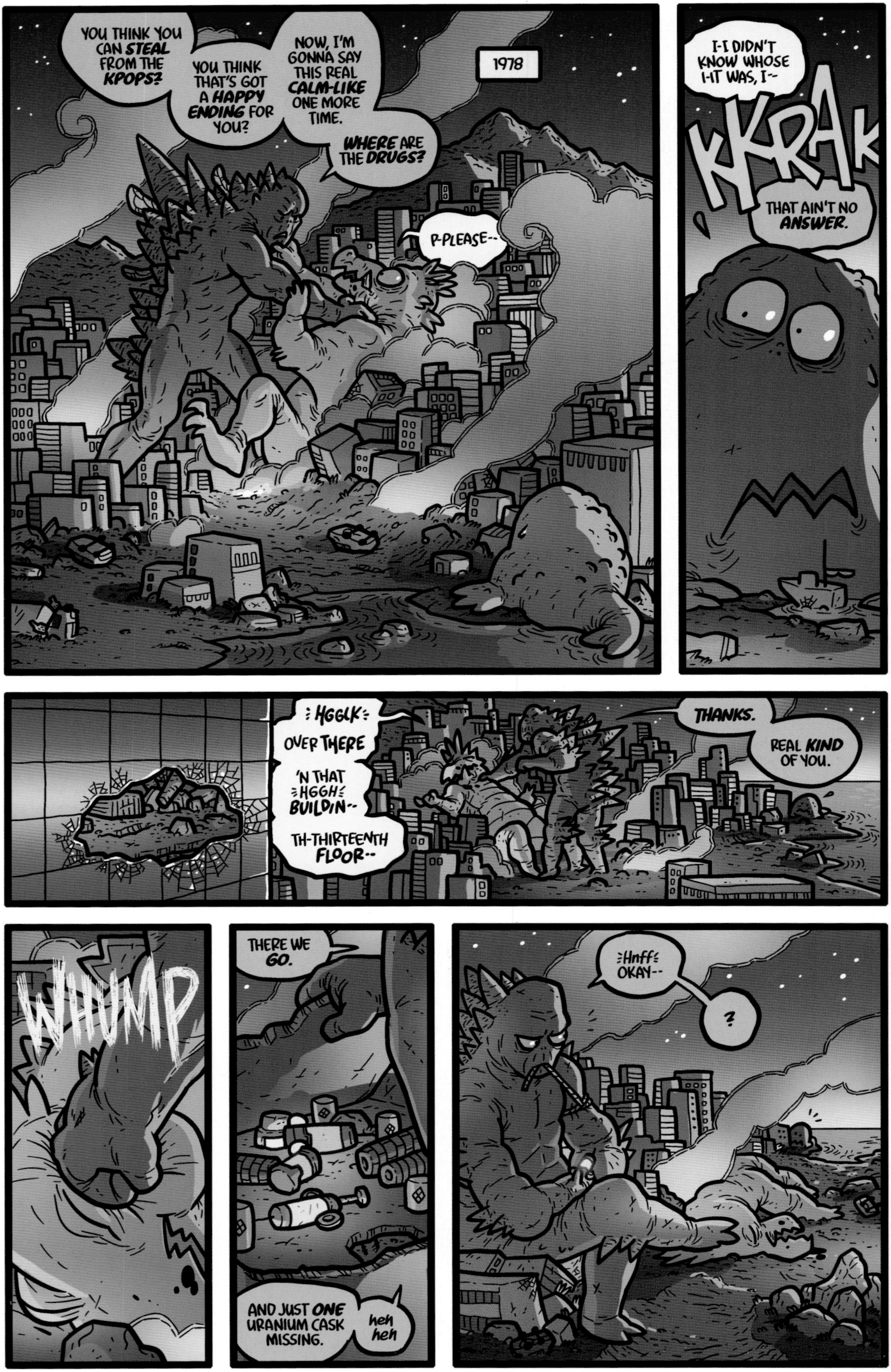
1978
YOU THINK YOU CAN STEAL FROM THE KPOPS?
YOU THINK THAT'S GOT A HAPPY ENDING FOR YOU?
NOW, I'M GONNA SAY THIS REAL CALM-LIKE ONE MORE TIME.
WHERE ARE THE DRUGS?
P-PLEASE--
I-I DIDN'T KNOW WHOSE I-IT WAS, I--
KKRAK
THAT AIN'T NO ANSWER.
HGGLK
OVER THERE
'N THAT HGGH BUILDIN--
TH-THIRTEENTH FLOOR--
THANKS.
REAL KIND OF YOU.
WHUMP
THERE WE GO.
AND JUST ONE URANIUM CASK MISSING.
heh heh
Hnff OKAY--
?

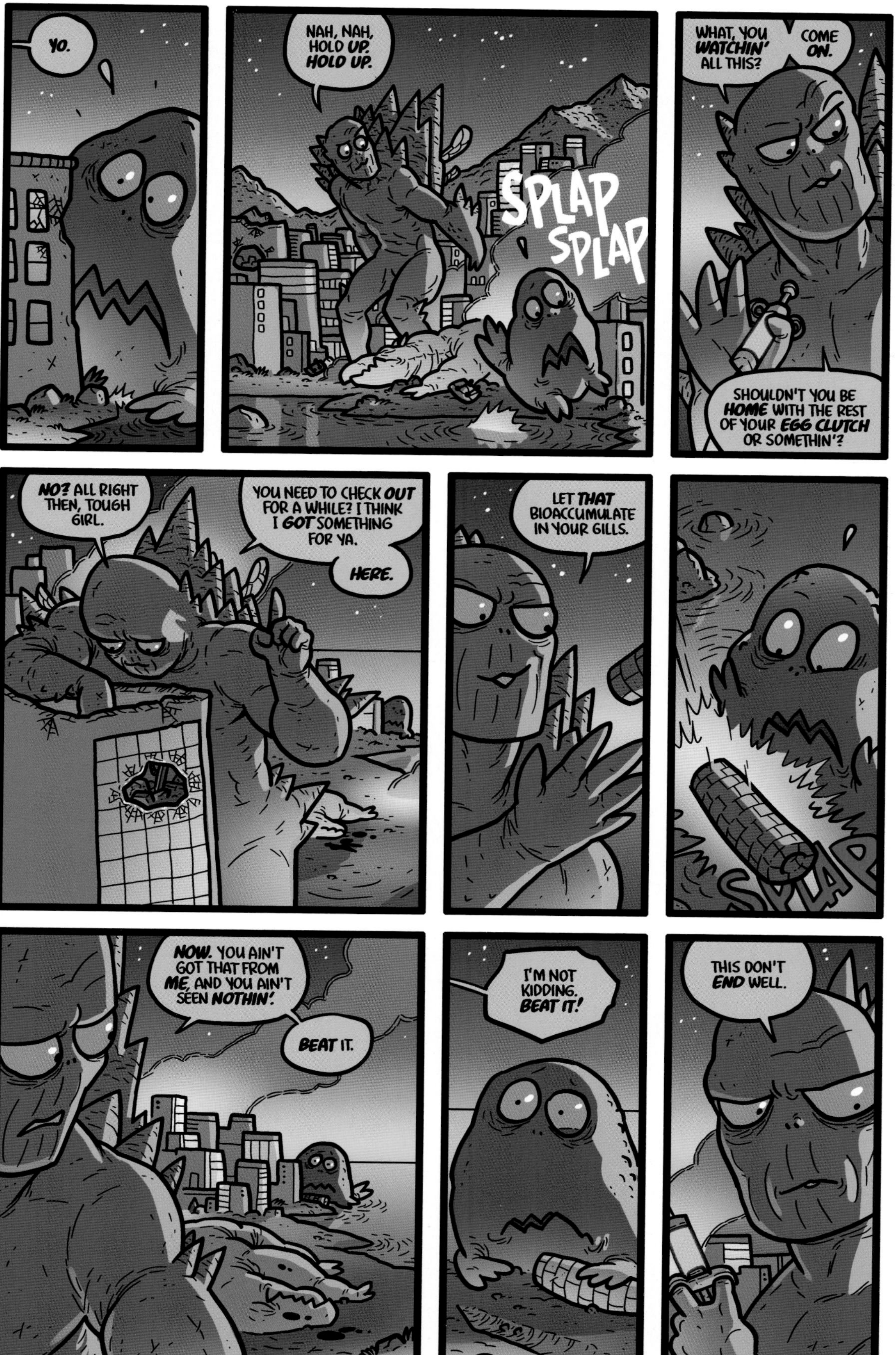
YO.
NAH, NAH, HOLD UP. HOLD UP.
SPLAP SPLAP
WHAT, YOU WATCHIN' ALL THIS?
COME ON.
SHOULDN'T YOU BE HOME WITH THE REST OF YOUR EGG CLUTCH OR SOMETHIN'?
NO? ALL RIGHT THEN, TOUGH GIRL.
YOU NEED TO CHECK OUT FOR A WHILE? I THINK I GOT SOMETHING FOR YA.
HERE.
LET THAT BIOACCUMULATE IN YOUR GILLS.
SPLAP
NOW. YOU AIN'T GOT THAT FROM ME, AND YOU AIN'T SEEN NOTHIN'.
BEAT IT.
I'M NOT KIDDING. BEAT IT!
THIS DON'T END WELL.

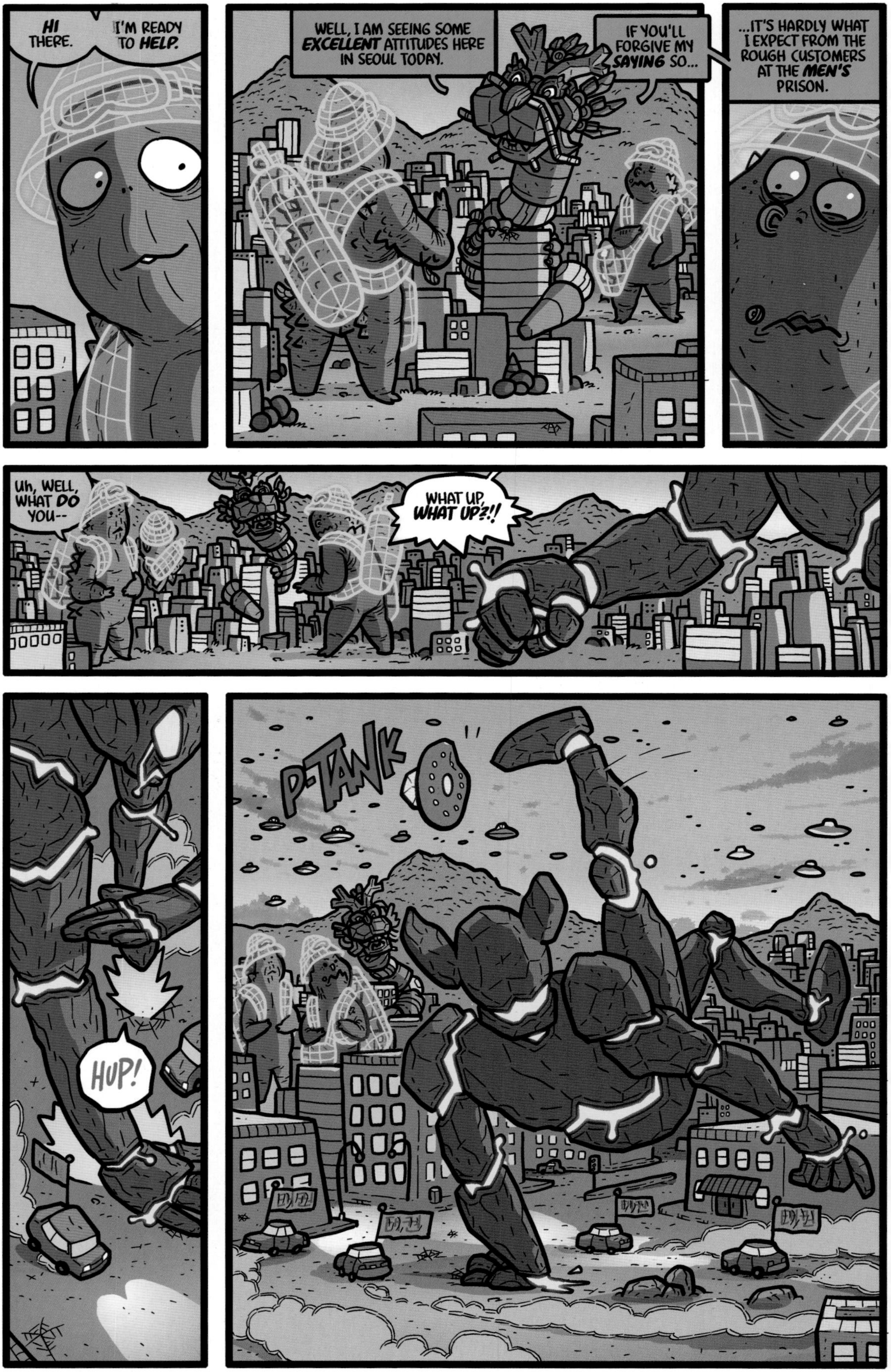
HI THERE.
I'M READY TO HELP.
WELL, I AM SEEING SOME EXCELLENT ATTITUDES HERE IN SEOUL TODAY.
IF YOU'LL FORGIVE MY SAYING SO...
...IT'S HARDLY WHAT I EXPECT FROM THE ROUGH CUSTOMERS AT THE MEN'S PRISON.
Uh, WELL, WHAT DO YOU--
WHAT UP, WHAT UP?!!
HUP!
P-TANK

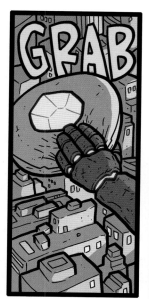

GRAB

FWEE

BOOM.

THAT'S WHAT I'M *TALKIN'* ABOUT. YA BOY *GEOKNIGHT TAEKWON* IN THE COMMERCIAL DISTRICT, SUCKA.

PLOOSH

GOD *DAMN* IT, TAEKWON. YOU'RE SUPPOSED TO *COLLECT* THEM IN THE *BAGS.*

AND YOU JUST STEPPED ON SOMEONE IN YOUR *ENTOURAGE.*

WHAT? BABE, *NO.*

HE'S *FINE.* THEY'LL GET HIM TO A HOSPITAL, *RIGHT,* GUYS?

You *BET,* G.K.T.!

Keep on *CRUSHING* it!

OH, MY *GOODNESS.* WE'RE CERTAINLY HONORED TO HAVE *YOU* HELPING US, *MR. TAEKWON.*

A *CELEBRITY* PITCHING IN WHEN THINGS ARE *DIRE?* JUST WHAT THE WORLD NEEDS TO *SEE,* I THINK.

THAT *SAID,* IT'S TRUE WE SHOULDN'T THROW THEM IN THE OCEAN, AS *UNDERSEA CIVILIZATIONS* HAVE BEEN A PROBLEM IN THE PAST, AND--

OH HOLY *AMBERGRIS.*

YOU.

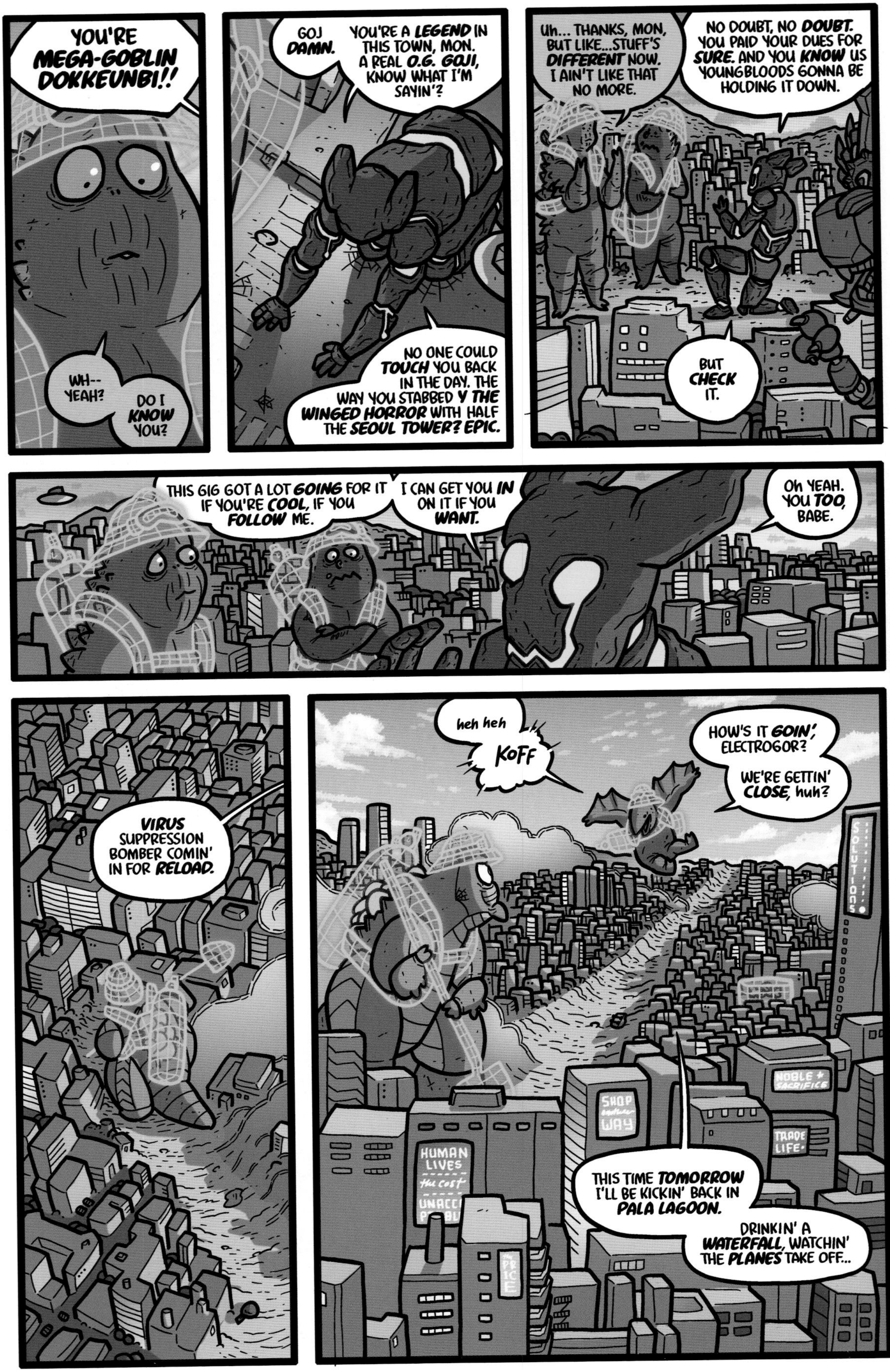
YOU'RE MEGA-GOBLIN DOKKEUNBI!!
WH-- YEAH?
DO I KNOW YOU?
GOJ DAMN.
YOU'RE A LEGEND IN THIS TOWN, MON. A REAL O.G. GOJI, KNOW WHAT I'M SAYIN'?
NO ONE COULD TOUCH YOU BACK IN THE DAY. THE WAY YOU STABBED Y THE WINGED HORROR WITH HALF THE SEOUL TOWER? EPIC.
Uh... THANKS, MON, BUT LIKE...STUFF'S DIFFERENT NOW. I AIN'T LIKE THAT NO MORE.
NO DOUBT, NO DOUBT. YOU PAID YOUR DUES FOR SURE. AND YOU KNOW US YOUNGBLOODS GONNA BE HOLDING IT DOWN.
BUT CHECK IT.
THIS GIG GOT A LOT GOING FOR IT IF YOU'RE COOL, IF YOU FOLLOW ME.
I CAN GET YOU IN ON IT IF YOU WANT.
Oh YEAH. YOU TOO, BABE.
VIRUS SUPPRESSION BOMBER COMIN' IN FOR RELOAD.
heh heh
KOFF
HOW'S IT GOIN', ELECTROGOR?
WE'RE GETTIN' CLOSE, huh?
SOLUTIONS
NOBLE + SACRIFICE
TRADE LIFE
HUMAN LIVES
the cost
THIS TIME TOMORROW I'LL BE KICKIN' BACK IN PALA LAGOON.
DRINKIN' A WATERFALL, WATCHIN' THE PLANES TAKE OFF...

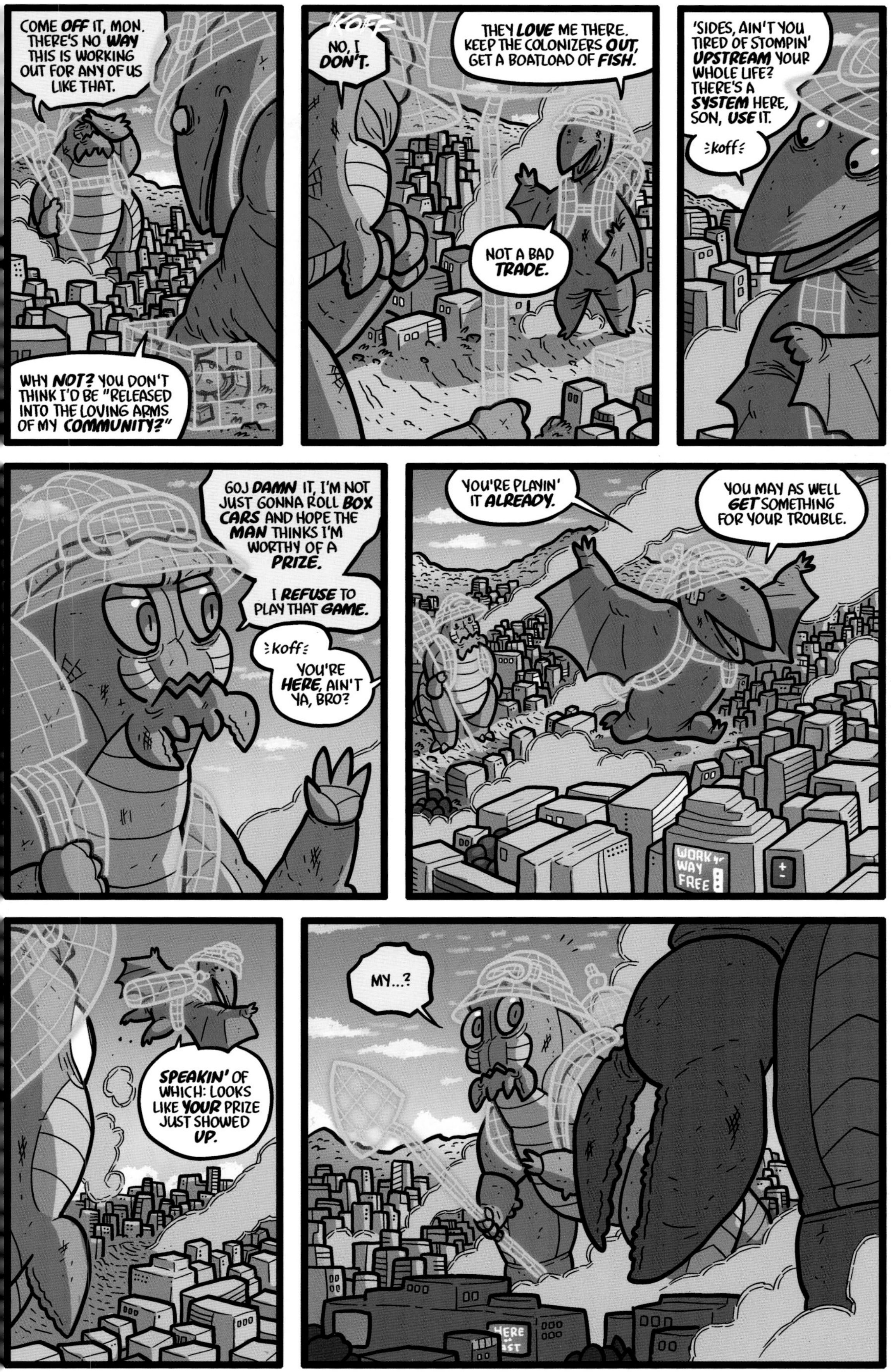
COME OFF IT, MON. THERE'S NO WAY THIS IS WORKING OUT FOR ANY OF US LIKE THAT.
WHY NOT? YOU DON'T THINK I'D BE "RELEASED INTO THE LOVING ARMS OF MY COMMUNITY?"
KOFF
NO, I DON'T.
THEY LOVE ME THERE. KEEP THE COLONIZERS OUT, GET A BOATLOAD OF FISH.
NOT A BAD TRADE.
'SIDES, AIN'T YOU TIRED OF STOMPIN' UPSTREAM YOUR WHOLE LIFE? THERE'S A SYSTEM HERE, SON, USE IT.
koff
GOJ DAMN IT, I'M NOT JUST GONNA ROLL BOX CARS AND HOPE THE MAN THINKS I'M WORTHY OF A PRIZE.
I REFUSE TO PLAY THAT GAME.
koff
YOU'RE HERE, AIN'T YA, BRO?
YOU'RE PLAYIN' IT ALREADY.
YOU MAY AS WELL GET SOMETHING FOR YOUR TROUBLE.
WORK WAY FREE
SPEAKIN' OF WHICH: LOOKS LIKE YOUR PRIZE JUST SHOWED UP.
MY...?
HERE

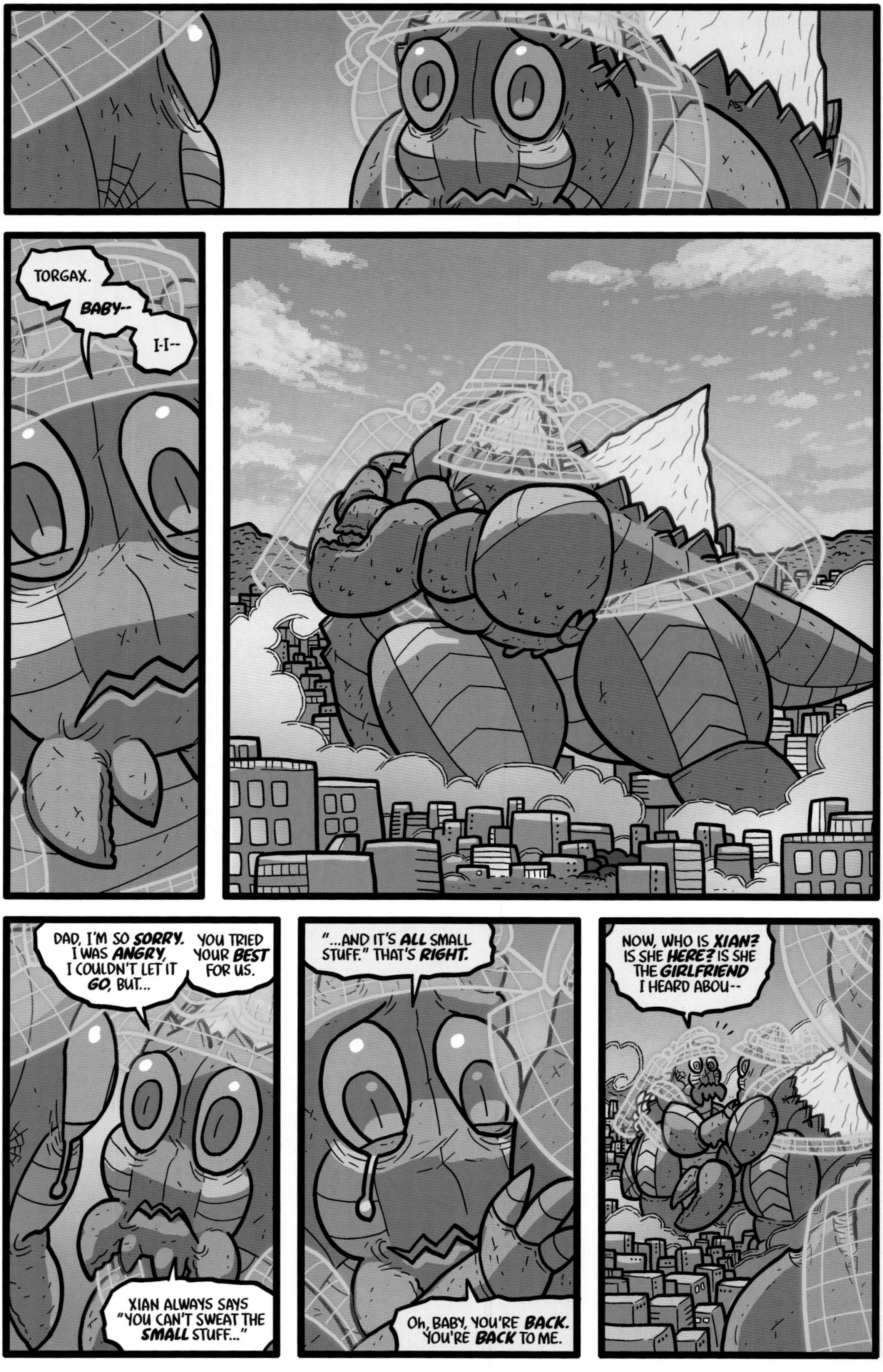
TORGAX.
BABY--
I-I--
DAD, I'M SO SORRY. I WAS ANGRY, I COULDN'T LET IT GO, BUT...
YOU TRIED YOUR BEST FOR US.
XIAN ALWAYS SAYS "YOU CAN'T SWEAT THE SMALL STUFF..."
"...AND IT'S ALL SMALL STUFF." THAT'S RIGHT.
Oh, BABY, YOU'RE BACK. YOU'RE BACK TO ME.
NOW, WHO IS XIAN? IS SHE HERE? IS SHE THE GIRLFRIEND I HEARD ABOU--

NO--

NO

NO

NO

NO

NO

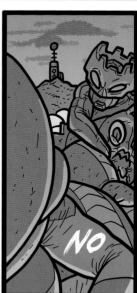

NO

NO

TORGAX. TELL ME THIS ISN'T RIGHT.

TELL ME SHE'S NOT--

ELECTROGOR--

45

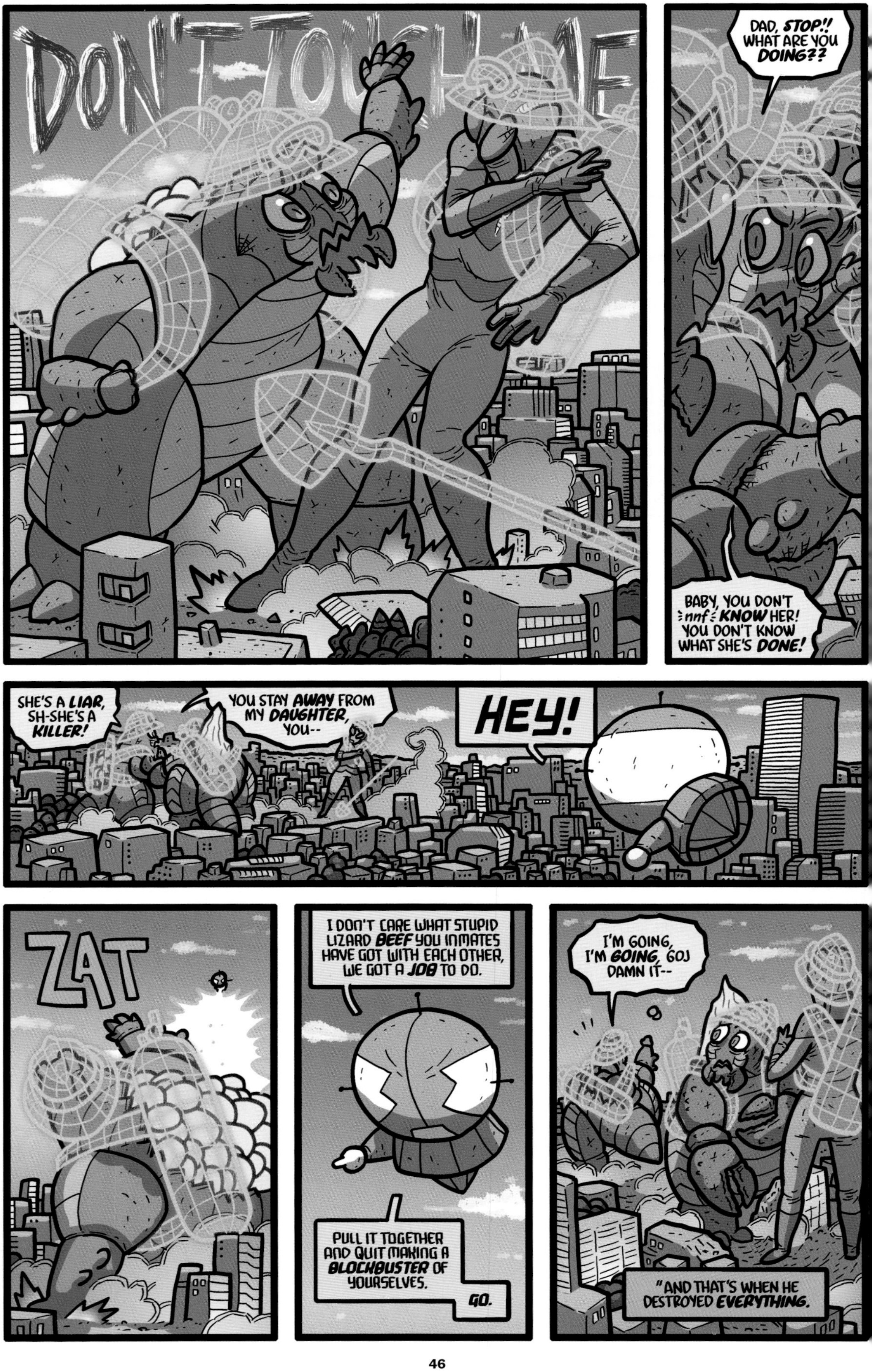
DON'T TOUCH ME
DAD, STOP!! WHAT ARE YOU DOING??
BABY, YOU DON'T nnf KNOW HER! YOU DON'T KNOW WHAT SHE'S DONE!
SHE'S A LIAR, SH-SHE'S A KILLER!
YOU STAY AWAY FROM MY DAUGHTER, YOU--
HEY!
ZAT
I DON'T CARE WHAT STUPID LIZARD BEEF YOU INMATES HAVE GOT WITH EACH OTHER, WE GOT A JOB TO DO.
PULL IT TOGETHER AND QUIT MAKING A BLOCKBUSTER OF YOURSELVES.
GO.
I'M GOING, I'M GOING, GOJ DAMN IT--
"AND THAT'S WHEN HE DESTROYED EVERYTHING.

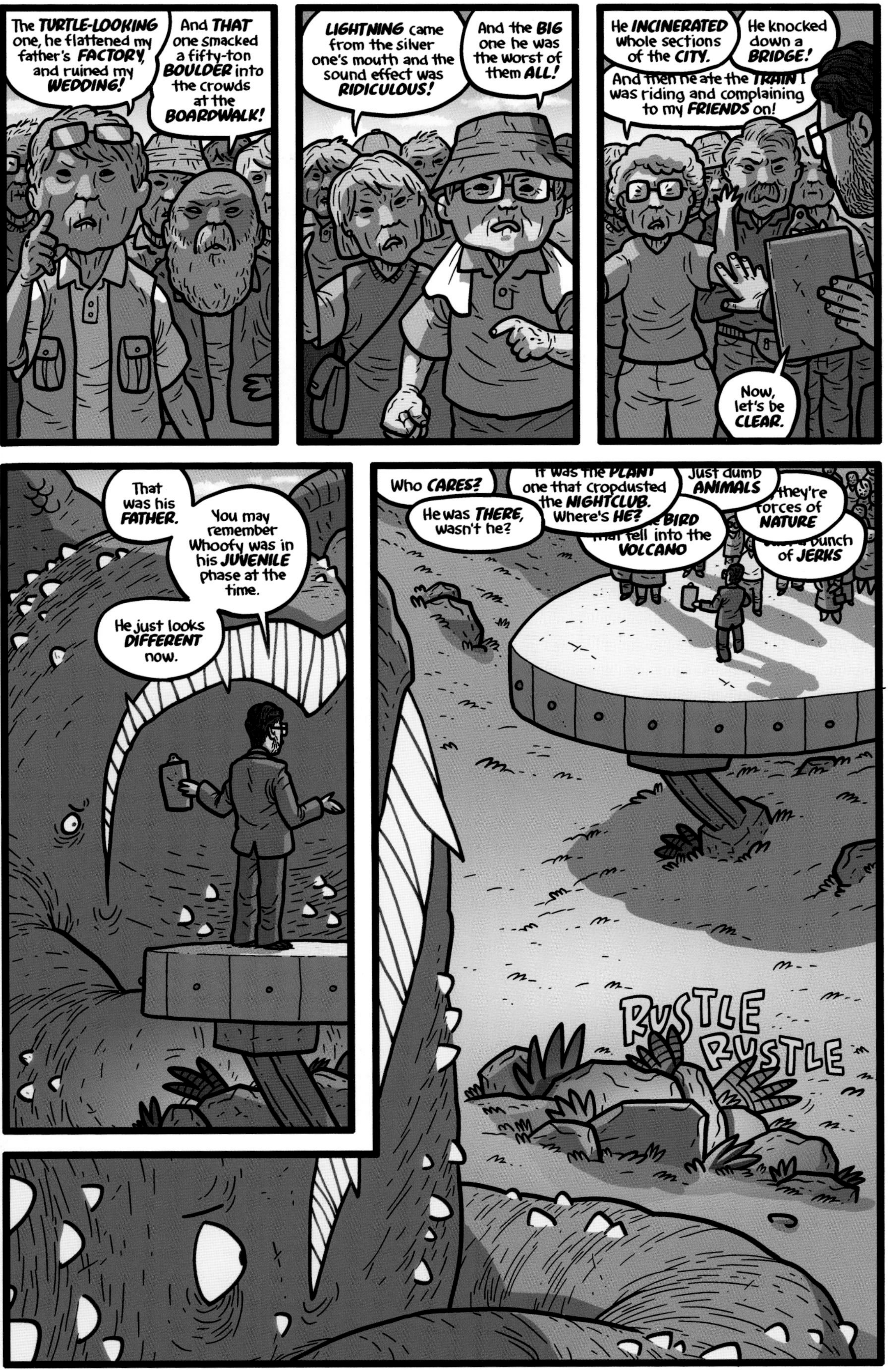

The TURTLE-LOOKING one, he flattened my father's FACTORY, and ruined my WEDDING!
And THAT one smacked a fifty-ton BOULDER into the crowds at the BOARDWALK!
LIGHTNING came from the silver one's mouth and the sound effect was RIDICULOUS!
And the BIG one he was the worst of them ALL!
He INCINERATED whole sections of the CITY.
He knocked down a BRIDGE!
And then he ate the TRAIN I was riding and complaining to my FRIENDS on!
Now, let's be CLEAR.
That was his FATHER.
You may remember Whoofy was in his JUVENILE phase at the time.
He just looks DIFFERENT now.
Who CARES?
He was THERE, wasn't he?
one that cropdusted the NIGHTCLUB. Where's HE?
BIRD
fell into the VOLCANO
Just dumb ANIMALS
they're forces of NATURE
bunch of JERKS
RUSTLE RUSTLE

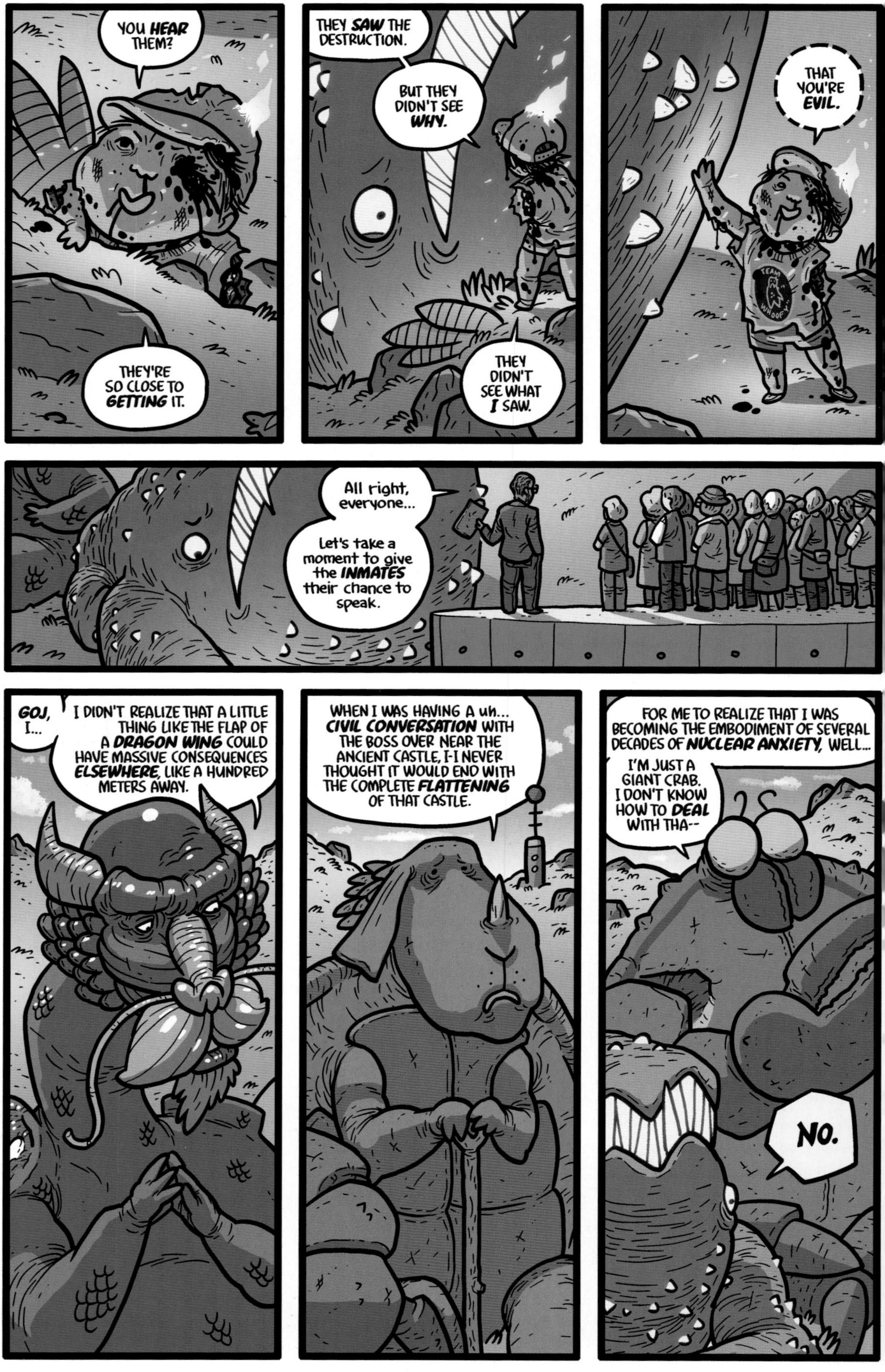

YOU HEAR THEM?
THEY'RE SO CLOSE TO GETTING IT.
THEY SAW THE DESTRUCTION.
BUT THEY DIDN'T SEE WHY.
THEY DIDN'T SEE WHAT I SAW.
THAT YOU'RE EVIL.
All right, everyone...
Let's take a moment to give the INMATES their chance to speak.
GOJ, I...
I DIDN'T REALIZE THAT A LITTLE THING LIKE THE FLAP OF A DRAGON WING COULD HAVE MASSIVE CONSEQUENCES ELSEWHERE, LIKE A HUNDRED METERS AWAY.
WHEN I WAS HAVING A uh... CIVIL CONVERSATION WITH THE BOSS OVER NEAR THE ANCIENT CASTLE, I-I NEVER THOUGHT IT WOULD END WITH THE COMPLETE FLATTENING OF THAT CASTLE.
FOR ME TO REALIZE THAT I WAS BECOMING THE EMBODIMENT OF SEVERAL DECADES OF NUCLEAR ANXIETY, WELL...
I'M JUST A GIANT CRAB. I DON'T KNOW HOW TO DEAL WITH THA--
NO.

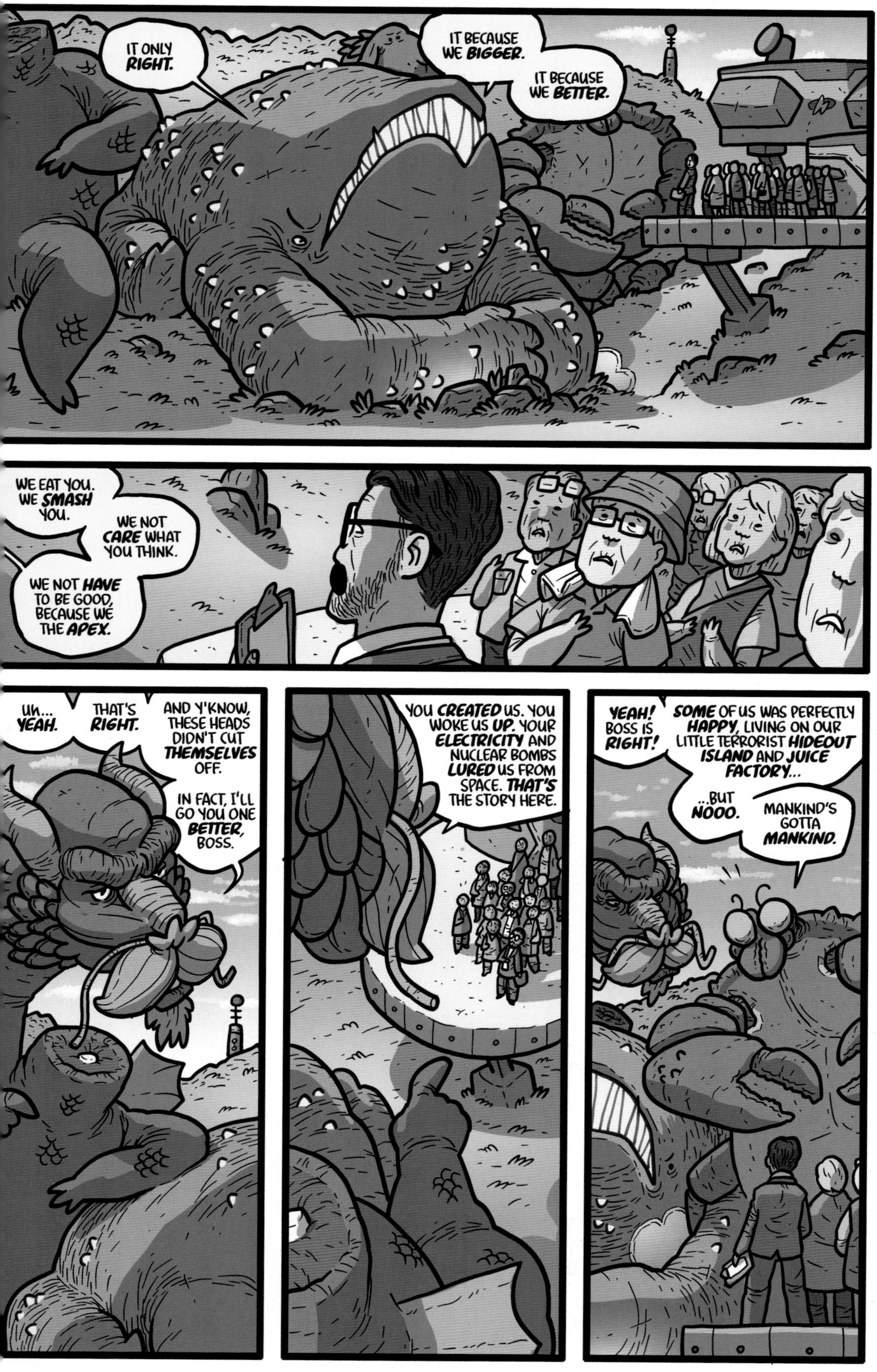
IT ONLY **RIGHT.**
IT BECAUSE WE **BIGGER.**
IT BECAUSE WE **BETTER.**
WE EAT YOU. WE **SMASH** YOU.
WE NOT **CARE** WHAT YOU THINK.
WE NOT **HAVE** TO BE GOOD, BECAUSE WE THE **APEX.**
UH... **YEAH.**
THAT'S **RIGHT.**
AND Y'KNOW, THESE HEADS DIDN'T CUT **THEMSELVES** OFF.
IN FACT, I'LL GO YOU ONE **BETTER,** BOSS.
YOU **CREATED** US. YOU WOKE US **UP.** YOUR **ELECTRICITY** AND NUCLEAR BOMBS **LURED** US FROM SPACE. **THAT'S** THE STORY HERE.
YEAH! BOSS IS **RIGHT!**
SOME OF US WAS PERFECTLY **HAPPY,** LIVING ON OUR LITTLE TERRORIST **HIDEOUT ISLAND** AND **JUICE FACTORY...**
...BUT **NOOO.**
MANKIND'S GOTTA **MANKIND.**

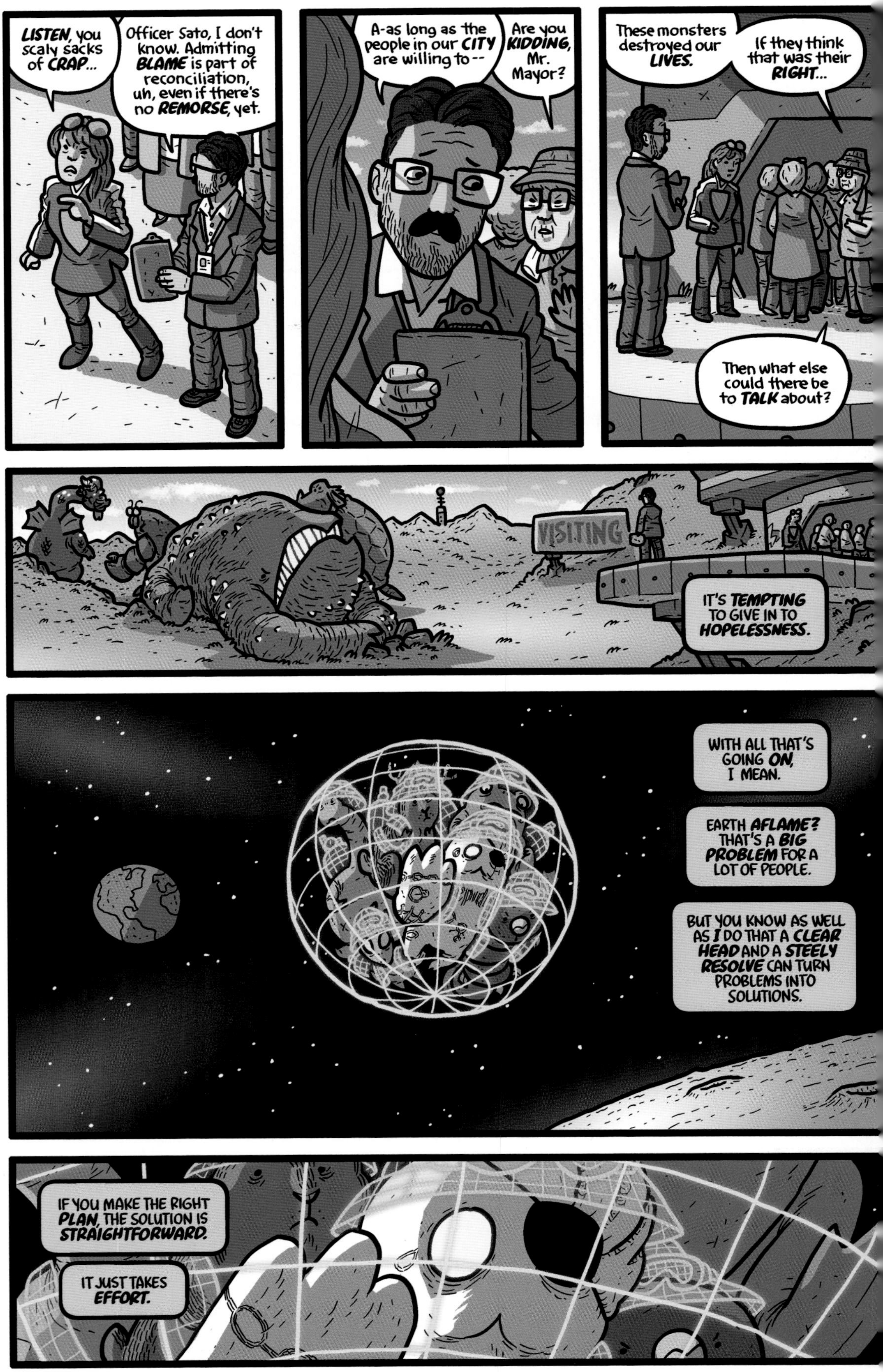
LISTEN, you scaly sacks of CRAP...
Officer Sato, I don't know. Admitting BLAME is part of reconciliation, uh, even if there's no REMORSE, yet.
A-as long as the people in our CITY are willing to --
Are you KIDDING, Mr. Mayor?
These monsters destroyed our LIVES.
If they think that was their RIGHT...
Then what else could there be to TALK about?
VISITING
IT'S TEMPTING TO GIVE IN TO HOPELESSNESS.
WITH ALL THAT'S GOING ON, I MEAN.
EARTH AFLAME? THAT'S A BIG PROBLEM FOR A LOT OF PEOPLE.
BUT YOU KNOW AS WELL AS I DO THAT A CLEAR HEAD AND A STEELY RESOLVE CAN TURN PROBLEMS INTO SOLUTIONS.
IF YOU MAKE THE RIGHT PLAN, THE SOLUTION IS STRAIGHTFORWARD.
IT JUST TAKES EFFORT.

IT'S HOW WE'VE ENDED UP SELLING TO EVERYONE FROM THE **MILITARY** TO THIS CORNER **PUB**.

SEEING WHAT'S POSSIBLE AND **DOING** IT.

YOU'VE SEEN IT. SOMEONE WITH **YOUR** SKILLS AND EXPERIENCE? IT'S THE SAME **THING**.

THE **PIVOT** AFTER THE **SETBACK**.

WE CAN **ALWAYS** USE SOMEONE WHO CAN SEE THE OPPORTUNITY IN A **CRISIS**.

I MEAN...

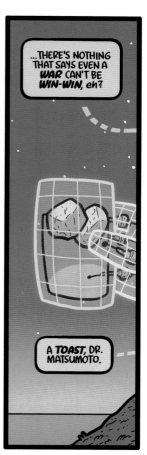

...THERE'S NOTHING THAT SAYS EVEN A **WAR** CAN'T BE **WIN-WIN**, eh?

A **TOAST**, DR. MATSUMOTO.

TO THE PRIVATE **SECTOR**.

ANYWAY, HERE'S MY **CARD**. THAT'LL GET YOU RIGHT THROUGH TO MY **DIRECT LINE**.

THINK ABOUT IT.

GRIDBOT
THE SEPTAGON, TOKYO
"it's Heptagonal"

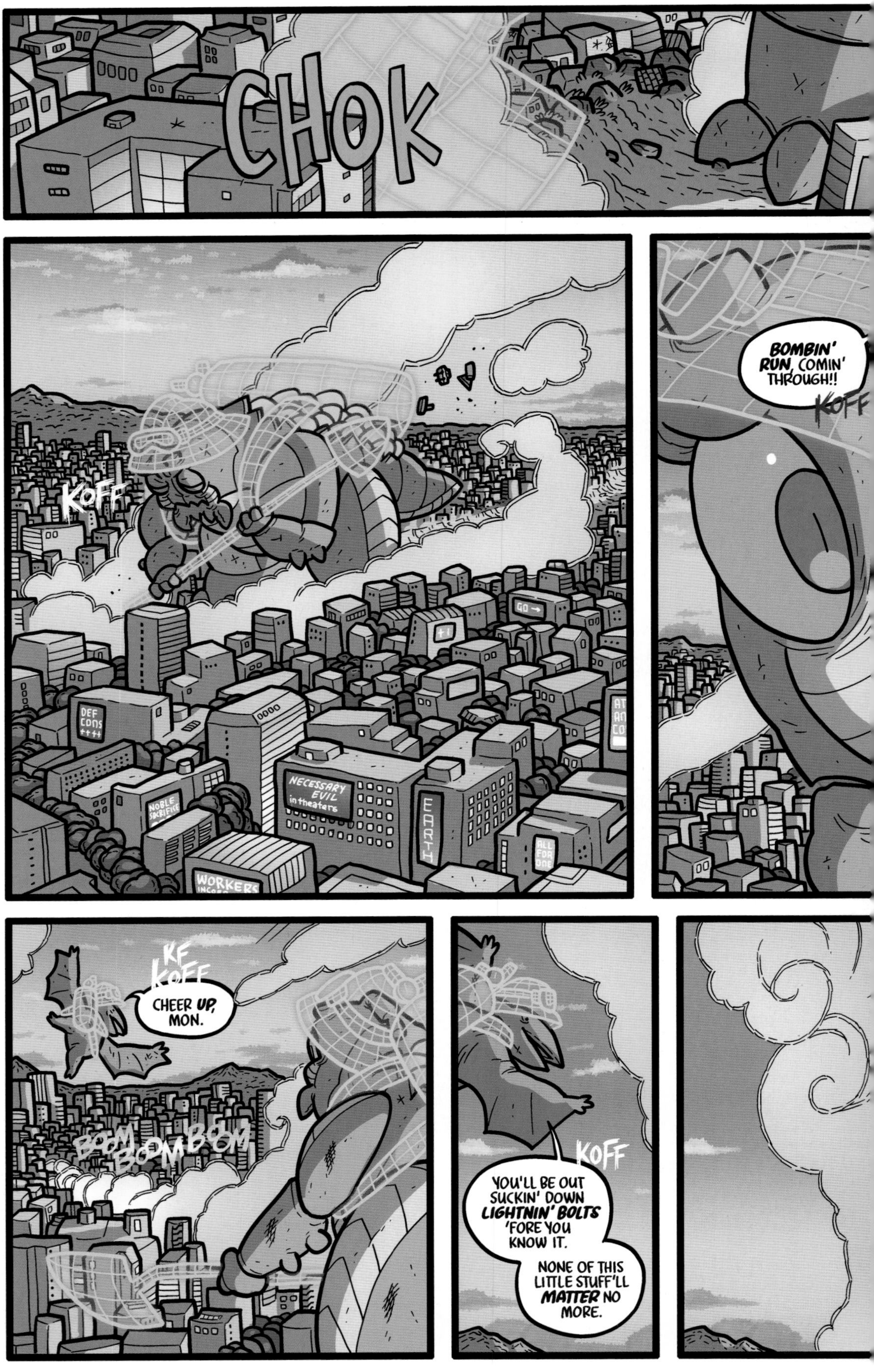
CHOK
KOFF
DEF CON 5
NOBLE SACRIFICE
NECESSARY EVIL in theaters
EARTH
ALL FOR ONE
WORKERS
GO →
BOMBIN' RUN, COMIN' THROUGH!!
KOFF
KF KOFF
CHEER UP, MON.
BOOM BOOM BOOM
KOFF
YOU'LL BE OUT SUCKIN' DOWN LIGHTNIN' BOLTS 'FORE YOU KNOW IT.
NONE OF THIS LITTLE STUFF'LL MATTER NO MORE.

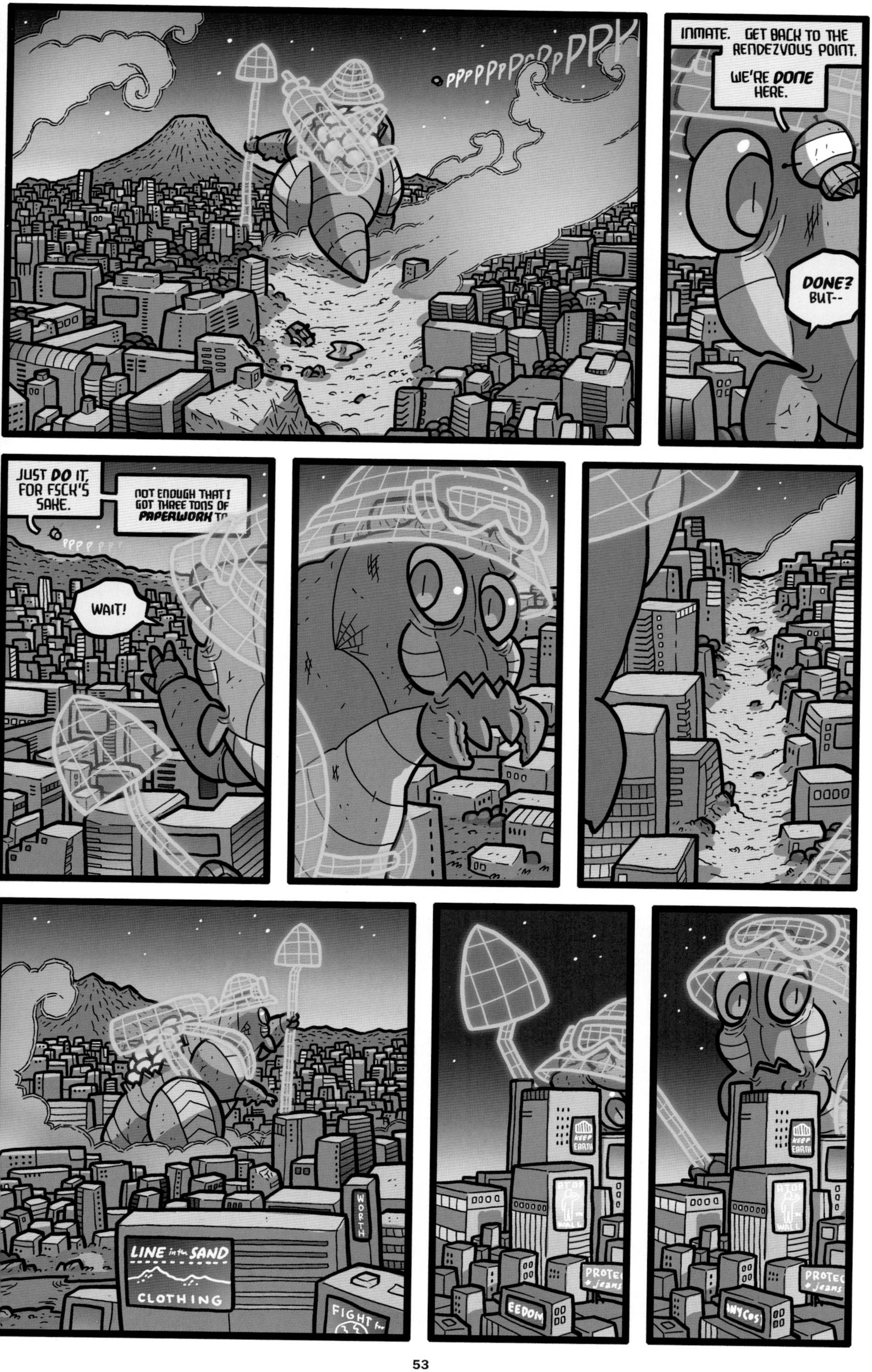
PPPPPPPPPPPK
INMATE. GET BACK TO THE RENDEZVOUS POINT.
WE'RE DONE HERE.
DONE? BUT--
JUST DO IT, FOR FSCK'S SAKE.
NOT ENOUGH THAT I GOT THREE TONS OF PAPERWORK TO
PPPPPPP
WAIT!
WORTH
LINE in the SAND
CLOTHING
FIGHT for
KEEP EARTH
PROTEC + jeans
EEDOM

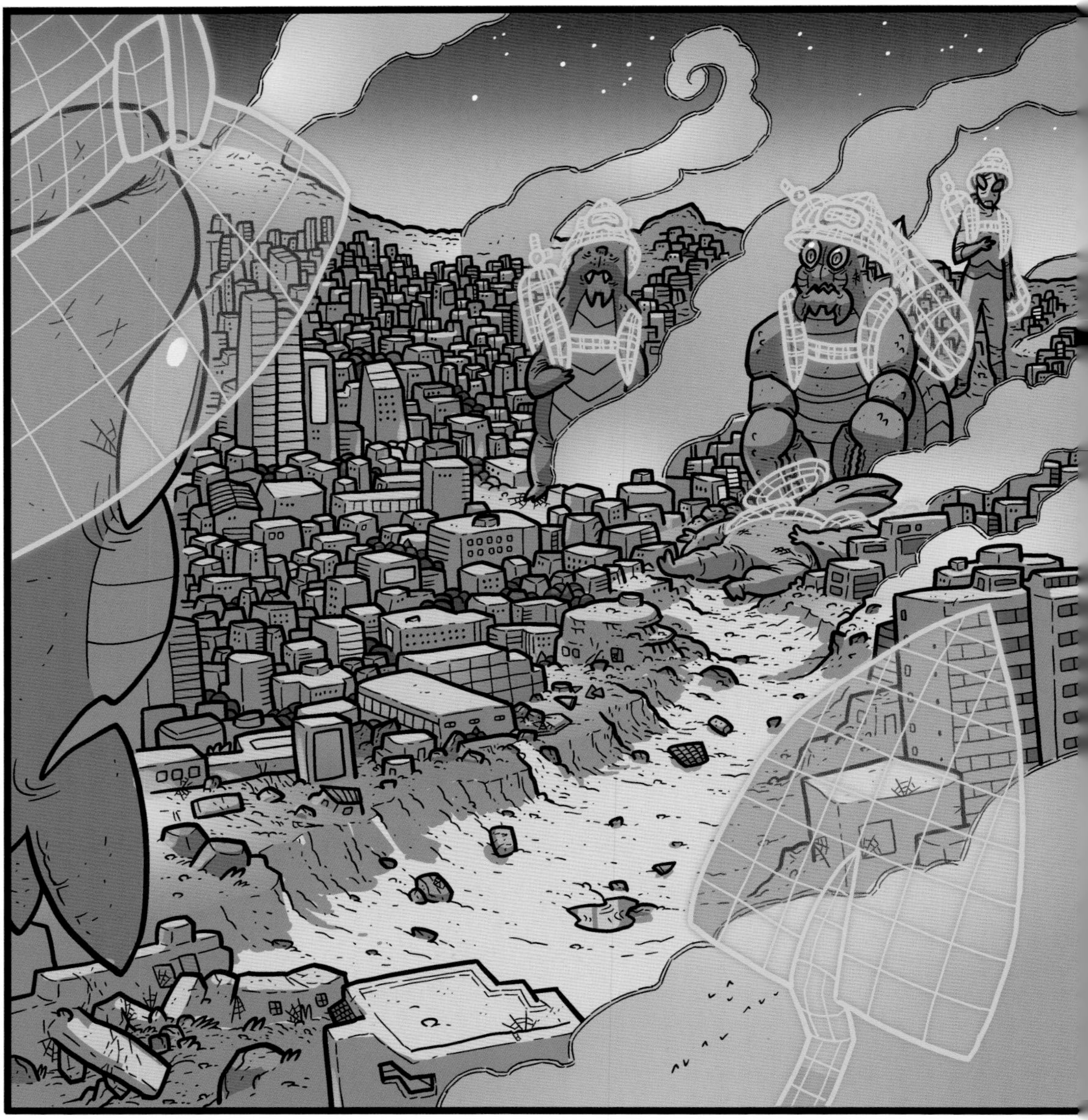

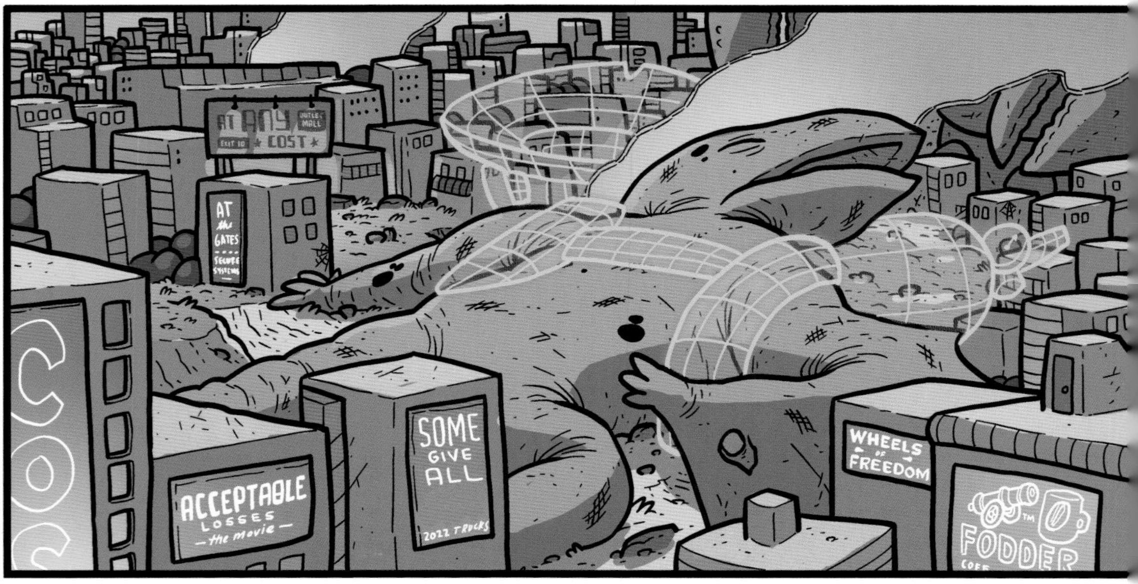
AT ANY COST
OUTLET MALL
EXIT 10
AT the GATES
SECURE SYSTEMS
ACCEPTABLE LOSSES
—the movie—
SOME GIVE ALL
2022 TRUCKS
WHEELS of FREEDOM
FODDER

EPISODE 3

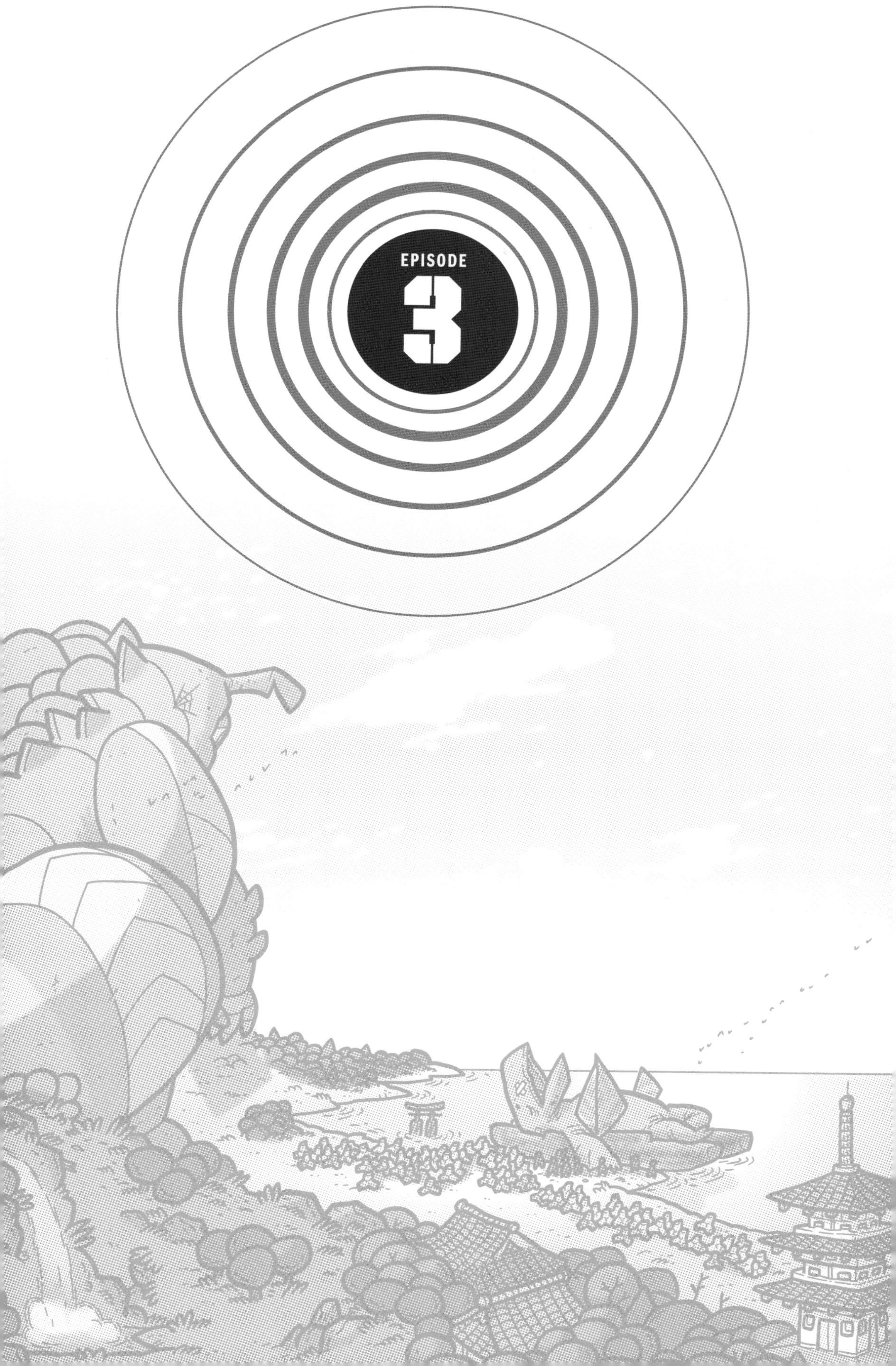

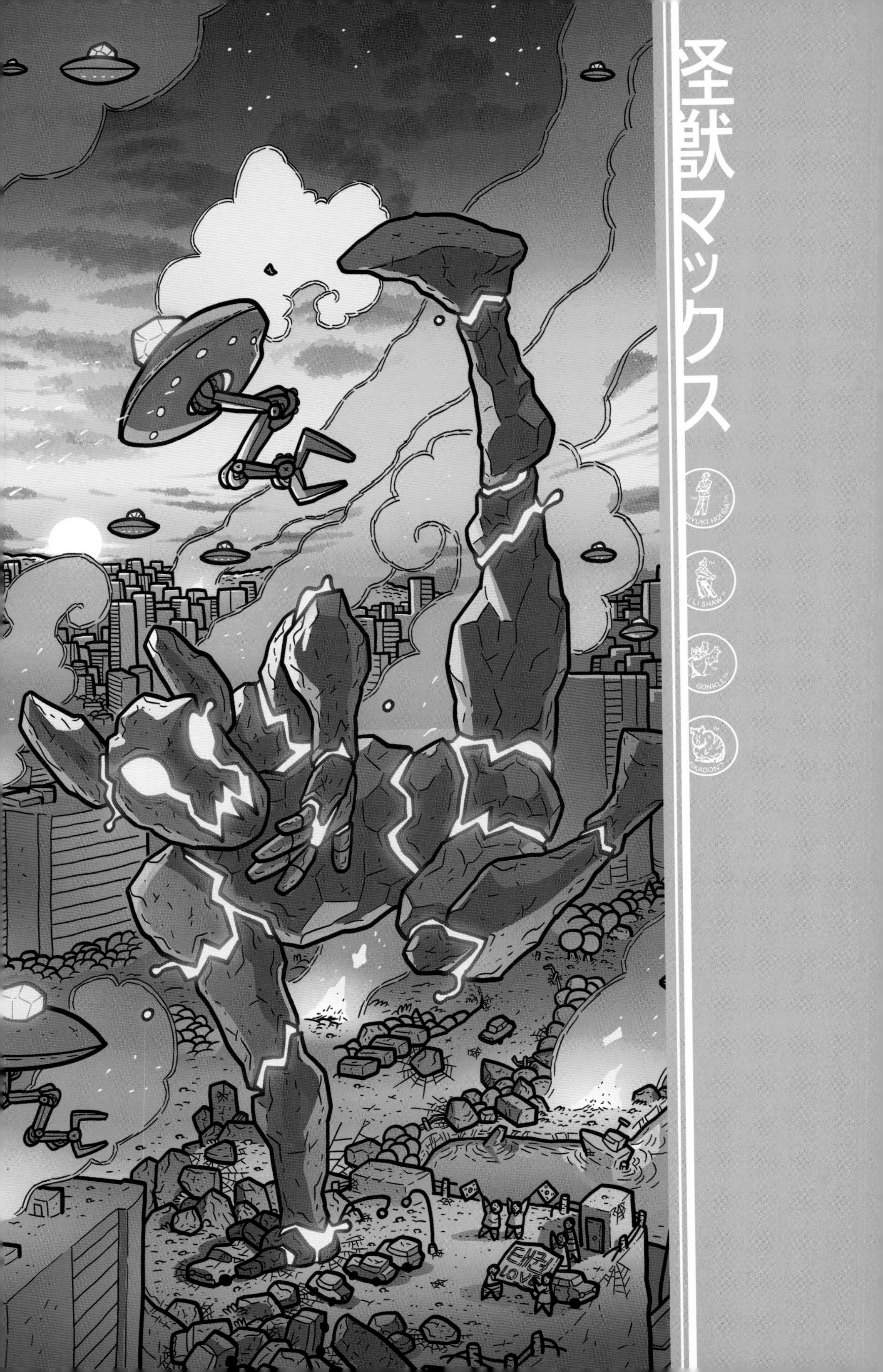
怪獣マックス
GONKLE™

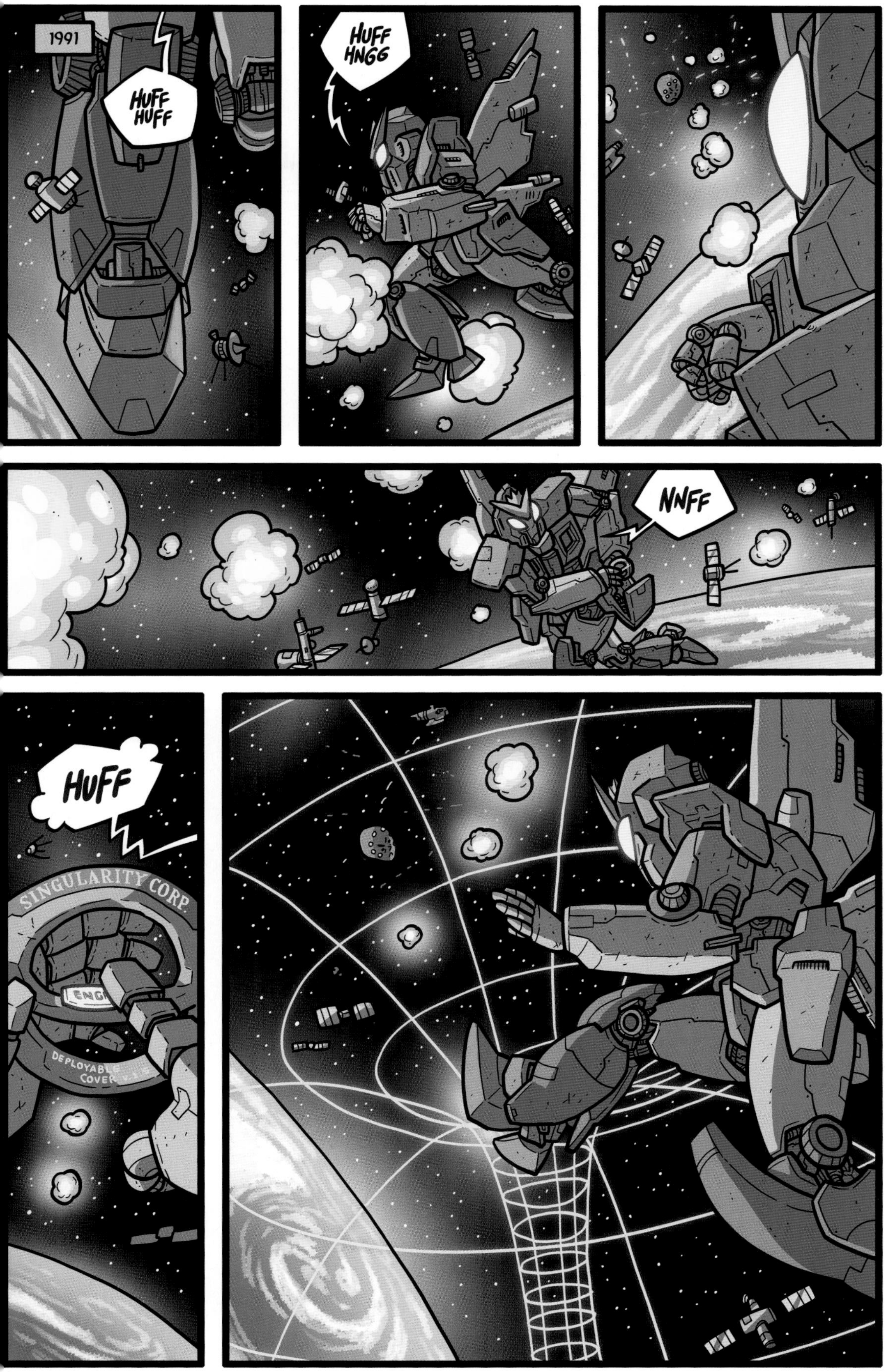
1991
HUFF HUFF
HUFF HNGG
NNFF
HUFF
SINGULARITY CORP.
ENG
DEPLOYABLE COVER v.1.5

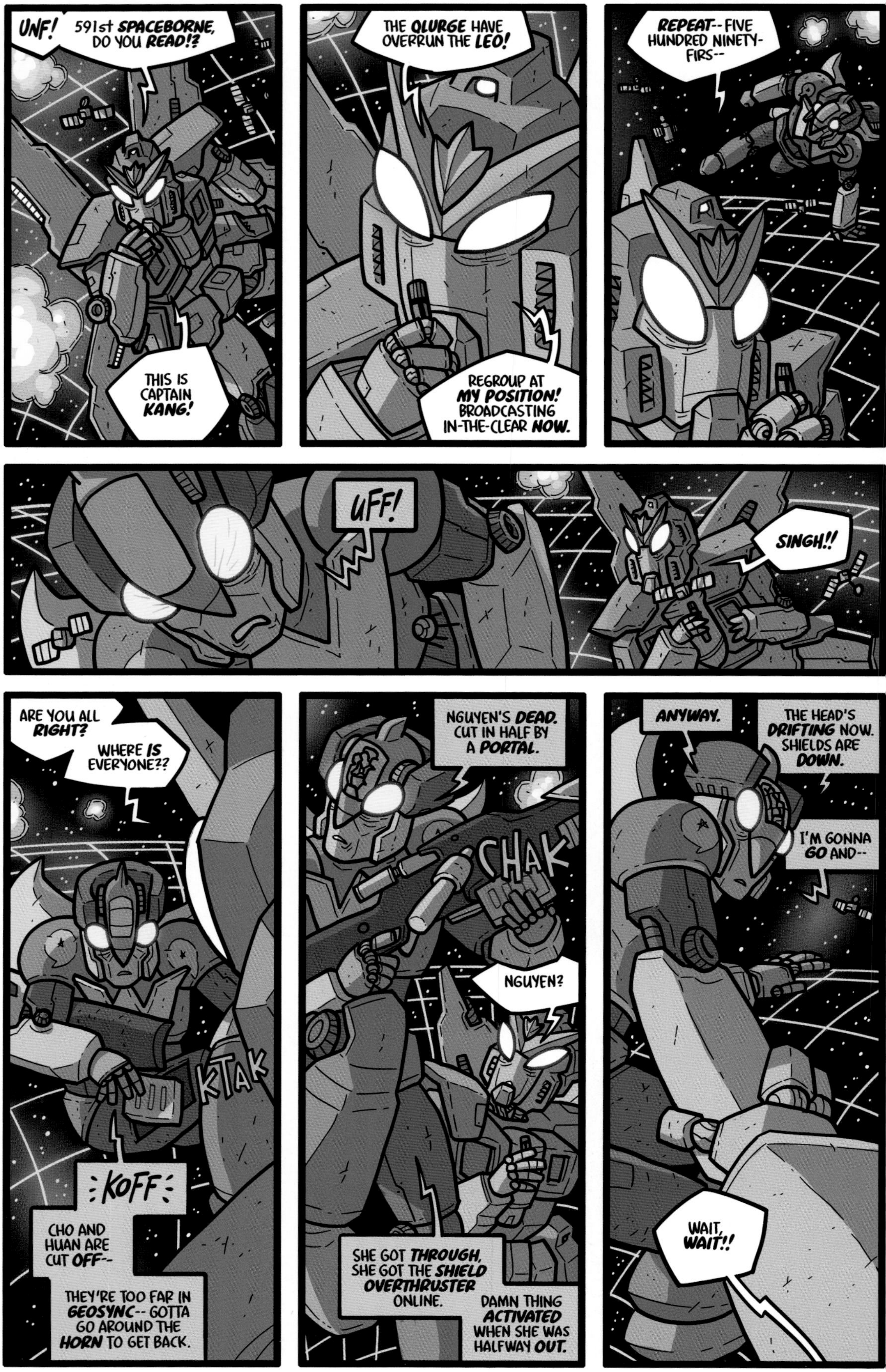
UNF!
591st SPACEBORNE, DO YOU READ!?
THIS IS CAPTAIN KANG!
THE QLURGE HAVE OVERRUN THE LEO!
REGROUP AT MY POSITION! BROADCASTING IN-THE-CLEAR NOW.
REPEAT-- FIVE HUNDRED NINETY-FIRS--
UFF!
SINGH!!
ARE YOU ALL RIGHT?
WHERE IS EVERYONE??
KTAK
KOFF
CHO AND HUAN ARE CUT OFF--
THEY'RE TOO FAR IN GEOSYNC-- GOTTA GO AROUND THE HORN TO GET BACK.
NGUYEN'S DEAD. CUT IN HALF BY A PORTAL.
CHAK
NGUYEN?
SHE GOT THROUGH, SHE GOT THE SHIELD OVERTHRUSTER ONLINE.
DAMN THING ACTIVATED WHEN SHE WAS HALFWAY OUT.
ANYWAY.
THE HEAD'S DRIFTING NOW. SHIELDS ARE DOWN.
I'M GONNA GO AND--
WAIT, WAIT!!

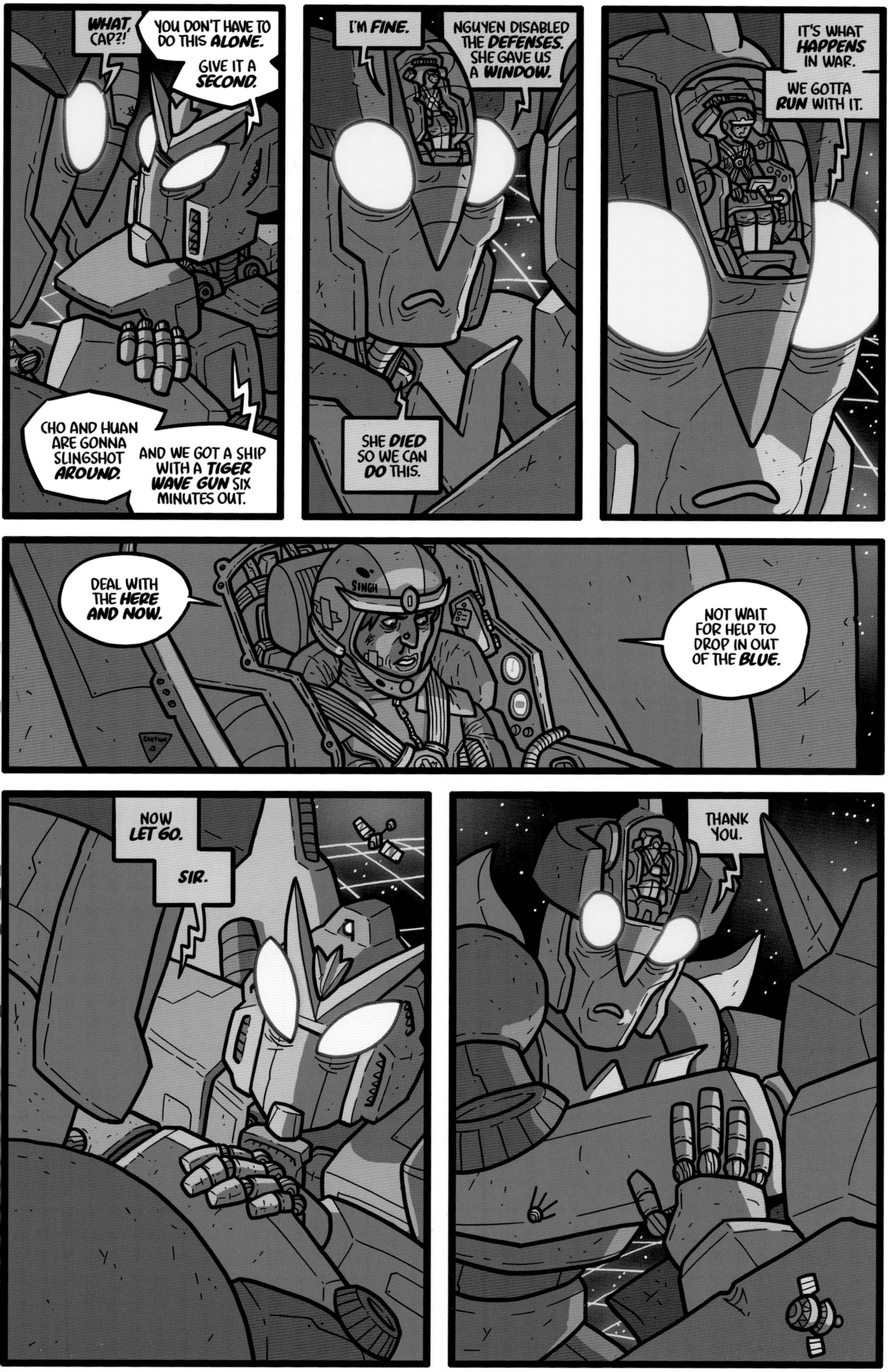
WHAT, CAP?!
YOU DON'T HAVE TO DO THIS ALONE.
GIVE IT A SECOND.
CHO AND HUAN ARE GONNA SLINGSHOT AROUND.
AND WE GOT A SHIP WITH A TIGER WAVE GUN SIX MINUTES OUT.
I'M FINE.
NGUYEN DISABLED THE DEFENSES. SHE GAVE US A WINDOW.
SHE DIED SO WE CAN DO THIS.
IT'S WHAT HAPPENS IN WAR.
WE GOTTA RUN WITH IT.
SINGH
DEAL WITH THE HERE AND NOW.
NOT WAIT FOR HELP TO DROP IN OUT OF THE BLUE.
CAUTION
NOW LET GO.
SIR.
THANK YOU.

NO ATHEISTS IN BLACK HOLES

NOW

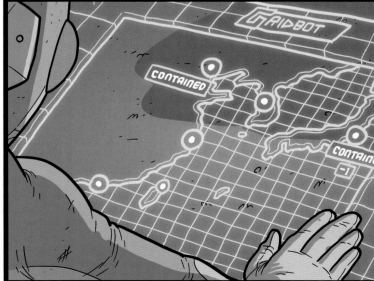

GRIDBOT

CONTAINED

CONTAINED

ALL RIGHT, SINGH. LOOKS LIKE THE *JAPAN CREW* COMPLETED THEIR RING AROUND *TOKYO* AND CONTAINED THE *GIGLOGON COMPUTER VIRUS.*

THEY LOST A *CREWMEMBER,* THOUGH. *SMOKE* INHALATION.

INMATE OR CIVILIAN?

INMATE.

WELL, SOUNDS LIKE IT WAS *WORTH* IT THEN.

WHAT DOES THAT *PUT* US AT, 20% CONTAINED?

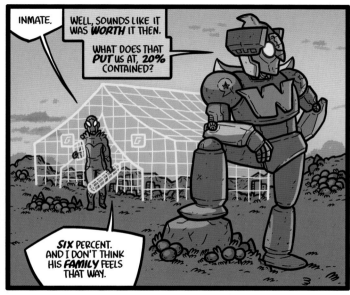

SIX PERCENT. AND I DON'T THINK HIS *FAMILY* FEELS THAT WAY.

Heh. *FIRST* OF ALL, *WHAT* FAMILY?

SECOND OF ALL, SEE HOW THEY FEEL ABOUT IT IN TWENTY YEARS WHEN HIS *GRAND-SPAWN* ARE STILL ROARING *EARTH LANGUAGES.*

OKAY. WELL, THEY *DID* DO A GREAT *JOB.*

ISOLATED THE *OUTBREAK.* KEPT THE SAUCERS FROM JUMPING THE *LINE.*

GOT A SMALL *DETACHMENT* DOING SOME *CLEANUP,* BUT THEY'RE ESSENTIALLY *DONE.*

SO. BOTTOM LINE: THAT CREW'S *AVAILABLE* TO ANY OTHER SITE THAT *NEEDS* IT.

WELL THEN, BAD *NEWS.*

THAT'S *US.*

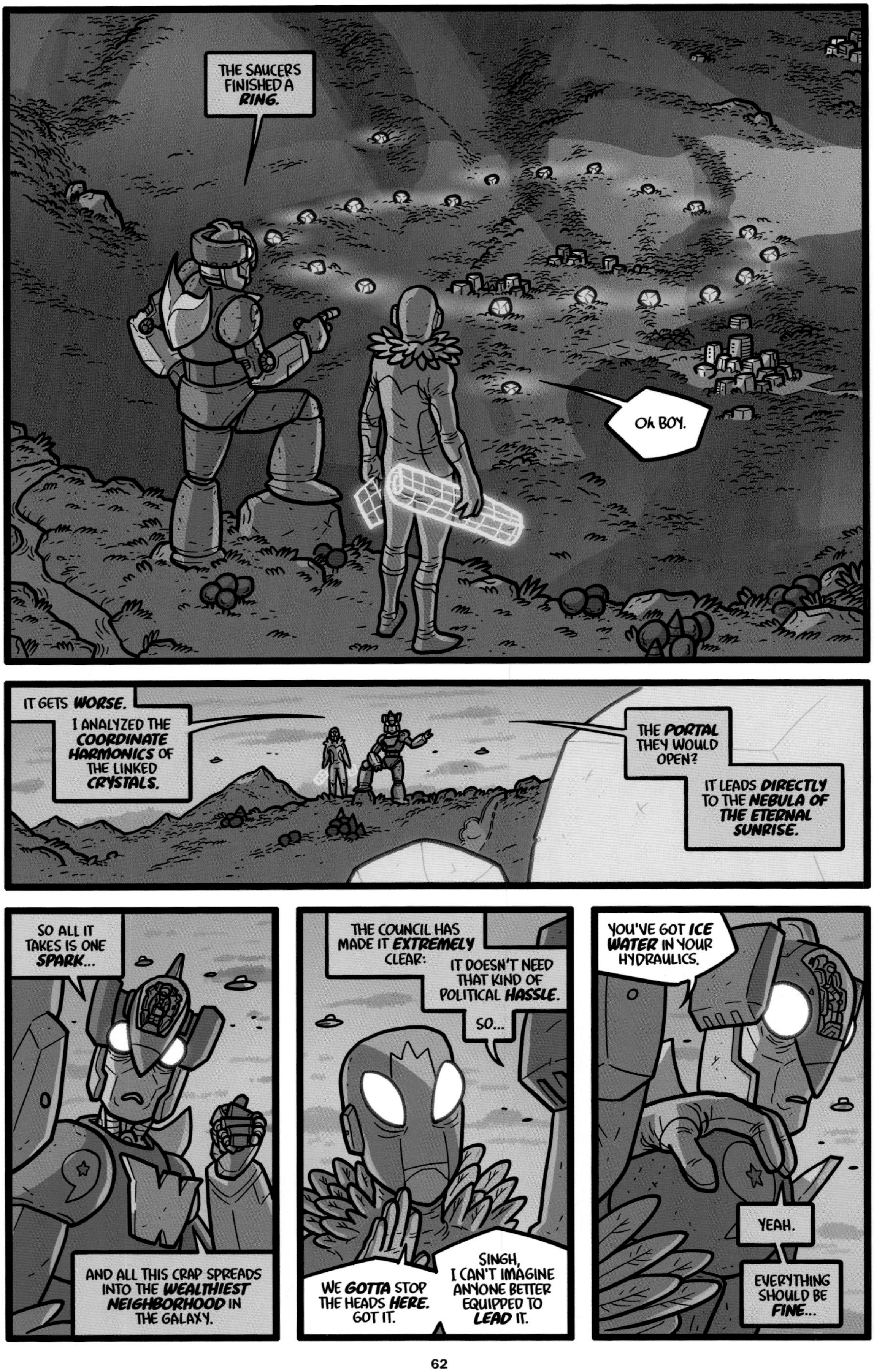
THE SAUCERS FINISHED A RING.
Oh BOY.
IT GETS WORSE.
I ANALYZED THE COORDINATE HARMONICS OF THE LINKED CRYSTALS.
THE PORTAL THEY WOULD OPEN?
IT LEADS DIRECTLY TO THE NEBULA OF THE ETERNAL SUNRISE.
SO ALL IT TAKES IS ONE SPARK...
AND ALL THIS CRAP SPREADS INTO THE WEALTHIEST NEIGHBORHOOD IN THE GALAXY.
THE COUNCIL HAS MADE IT EXTREMELY CLEAR:
IT DOESN'T NEED THAT KIND OF POLITICAL HASSLE.
SO...
WE GOTTA STOP THE HEADS HERE. GOT IT.
SINGH, I CAN'T IMAGINE ANYONE BETTER EQUIPPED TO LEAD IT.
YOU'VE GOT ICE WATER IN YOUR HYDRAULICS.
YEAH.
EVERYTHING SHOULD BE FINE...

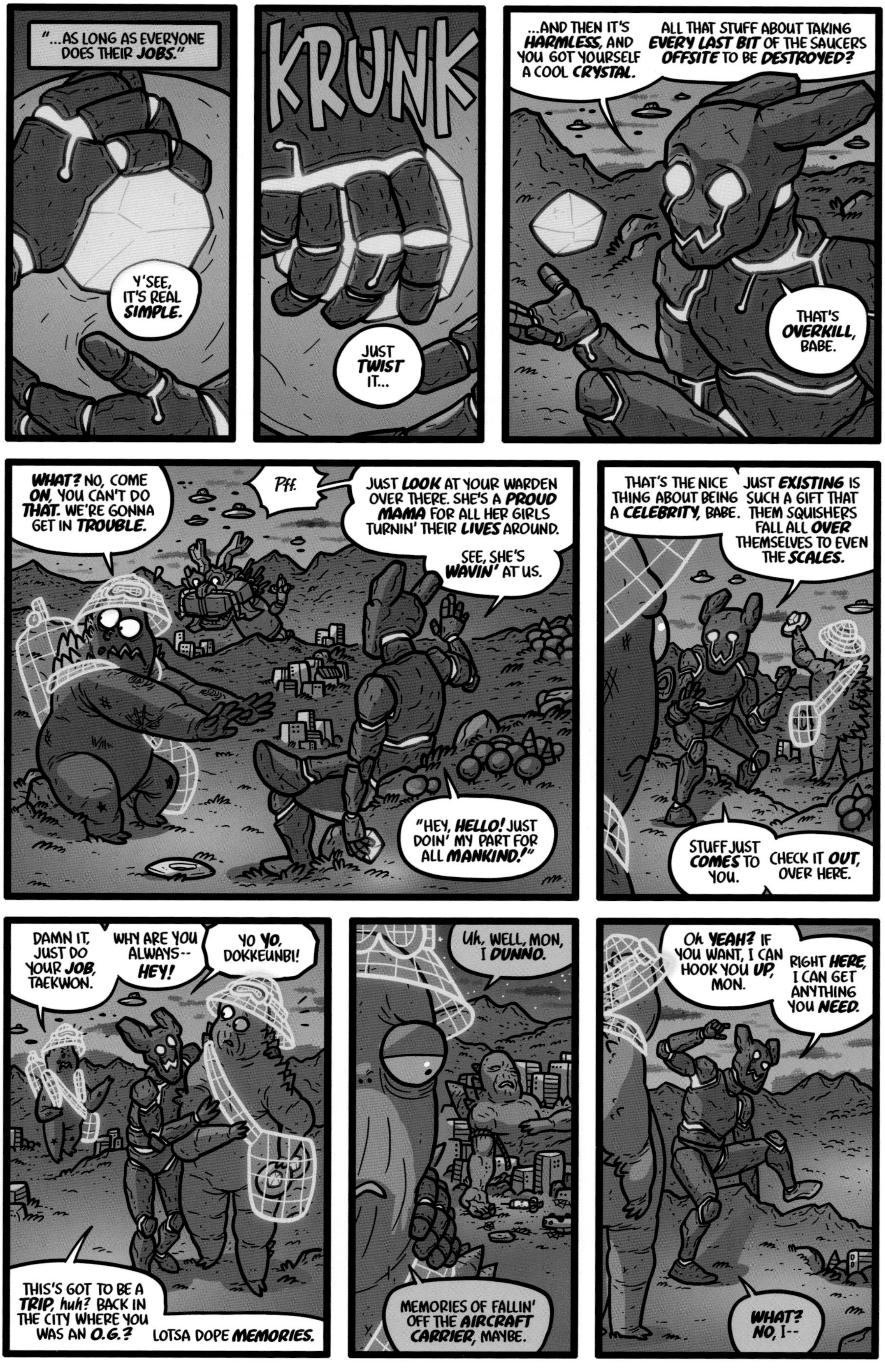
"...AS LONG AS EVERYONE DOES THEIR JOBS."
Y'SEE, IT'S REAL SIMPLE.
KRUNK
JUST TWIST IT...
...AND THEN IT'S HARMLESS, AND YOU GOT YOURSELF A COOL CRYSTAL.
ALL THAT STUFF ABOUT TAKING EVERY LAST BIT OF THE SAUCERS OFFSITE TO BE DESTROYED?
THAT'S OVERKILL, BABE.
WHAT? NO, COME ON, YOU CAN'T DO THAT. WE'RE GONNA GET IN TROUBLE.
Pff.
JUST LOOK AT YOUR WARDEN OVER THERE. SHE'S A PROUD MAMA FOR ALL HER GIRLS TURNIN' THEIR LIVES AROUND.
SEE, SHE'S WAVIN' AT US.
"HEY, HELLO! JUST DOIN' MY PART FOR ALL MANKIND!"
THAT'S THE NICE THING ABOUT BEING A CELEBRITY, BABE.
JUST EXISTING IS SUCH A GIFT THAT THEM SQUISHERS FALL ALL OVER THEMSELVES TO EVEN THE SCALES.
STUFF JUST COMES TO YOU.
CHECK IT OUT, OVER HERE.
DAMN IT, JUST DO YOUR JOB, TAEKWON.
WHY ARE YOU ALWAYS-- HEY!
YO YO, DOKKEUNBI!
THIS'S GOT TO BE A TRIP, huh? BACK IN THE CITY WHERE YOU WAS AN O.G.?
LOTSA DOPE MEMORIES.
Uh, WELL, MON, I DUNNO.
MEMORIES OF FALLIN' OFF THE AIRCRAFT CARRIER, MAYBE.
Oh YEAH? IF YOU WANT, I CAN HOOK YOU UP, MON.
RIGHT HERE, I CAN GET ANYTHING YOU NEED.
WHAT? NO, I--

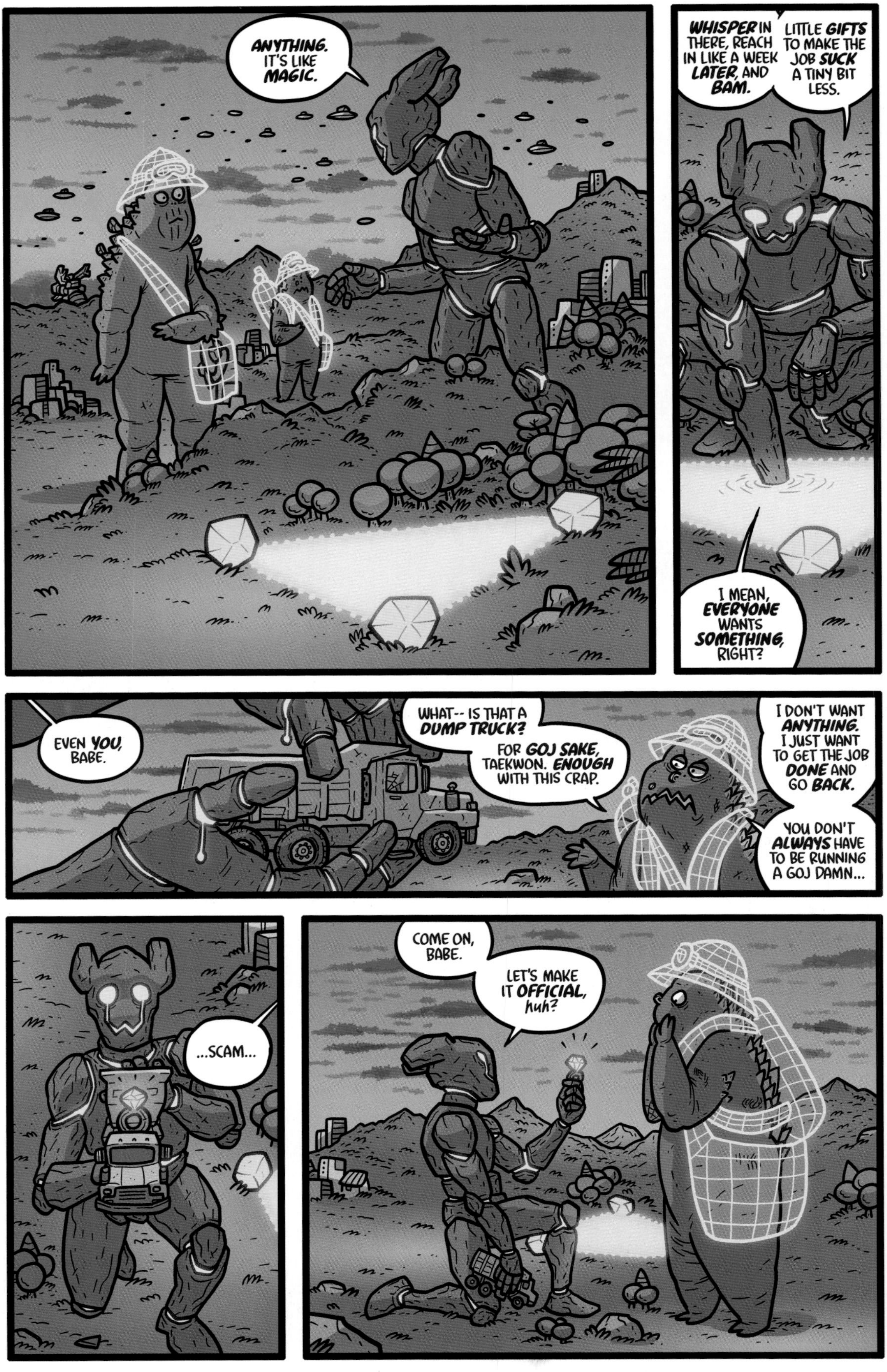
ANYTHING. IT'S LIKE MAGIC.
WHISPER IN THERE, REACH IN LIKE A WEEK LATER, AND BAM.
LITTLE GIFTS TO MAKE THE JOB SUCK A TINY BIT LESS.
I MEAN, EVERYONE WANTS SOMETHING, RIGHT?
EVEN YOU, BABE.
WHAT-- IS THAT A DUMP TRUCK?
FOR GOJ SAKE, TAEKWON. ENOUGH WITH THIS CRAP.
I DON'T WANT ANYTHING. I JUST WANT TO GET THE JOB DONE AND GO BACK.
YOU DON'T ALWAYS HAVE TO BE RUNNING A GOJ DAMN...
...SCAM...
COME ON, BABE.
LET'S MAKE IT OFFICIAL, huh?

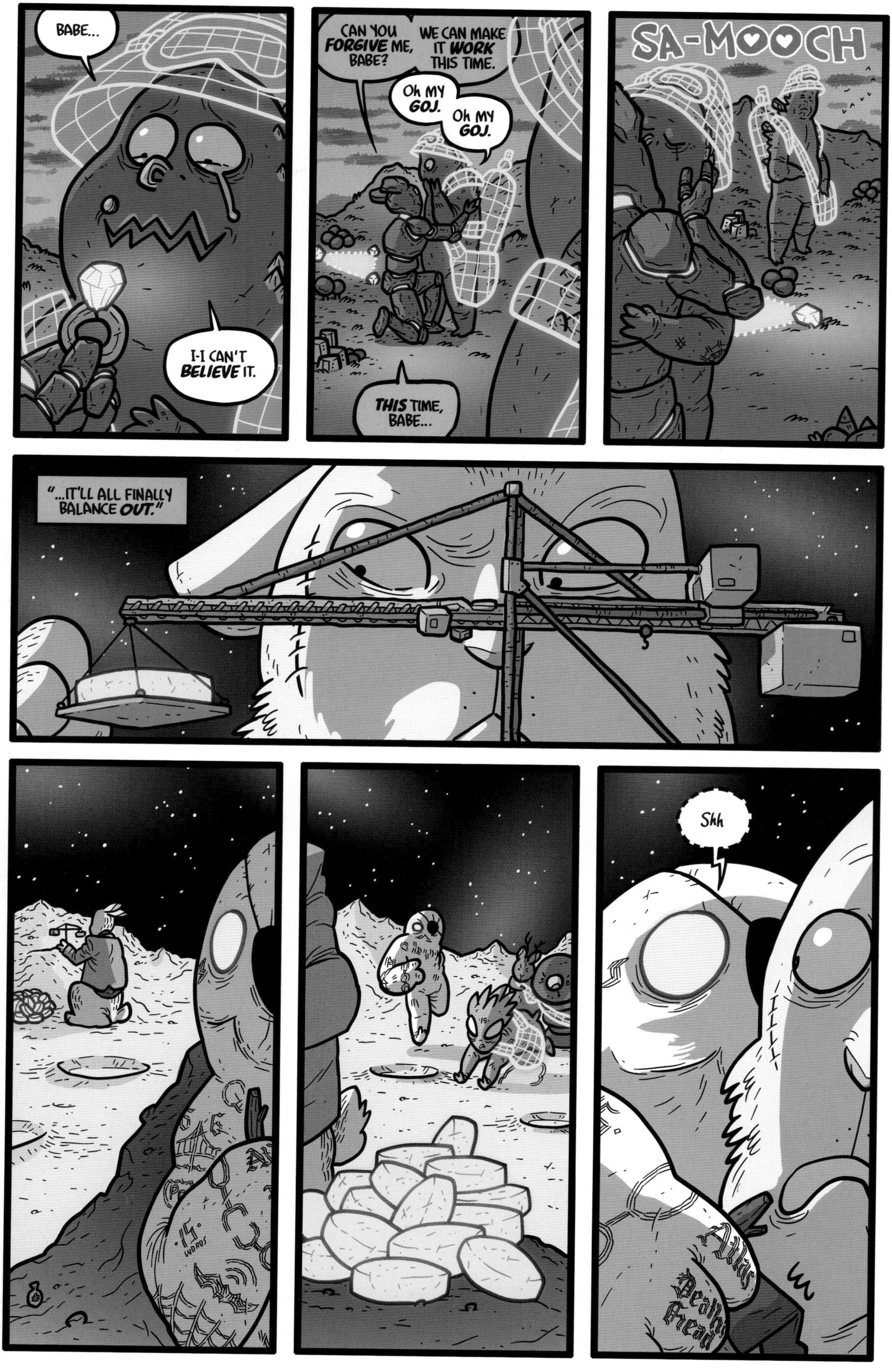
BABE...
I-I CAN'T **BELIEVE** IT.
CAN YOU **FORGIVE** ME, BABE?
WE CAN MAKE IT **WORK** THIS TIME.
Oh MY **GOJ.**
Oh MY **GOJ.**
THIS TIME, BABE...
SA-MOOCH
"...IT'LL ALL FINALLY BALANCE **OUT.**"
Shh

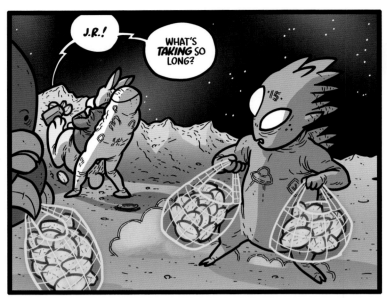

J.R.!

WHAT'S *TAKING* SO LONG?

ANSWER *RIGHT*, OR YOU'RE *DEAD*.

I--

B-BE THERE IN JUST A *SEC.*

ALL RIGHT. *HURRY.* WE GOT A DELIVERY DUE AT *PERIGEE.*

THANKS.

GLORK

LO, HELLMÓTH, WHAT WAS *THAT?*

HE DID EVERYTHING *RIGHT.*

AN' WE'RE GONNA BE BLASTIN' *OUT* OF HERE IN JUST A *SECOND.*

FOR FORT'S *SAKE--*

WHY'D YOU HAVE TO *KILL* HIM?

HE'S AN *ENEMY.*

HE WOULD HAVE HAD THAT WARREN ALL *OVER* US IN TWO TWITCHES OF HIS *NOSE.*

IT'S *EXPEDIENT.*

YOU WANT ME TO FEEL *BAD* FOR THAT?

NOT *LIKELY.*

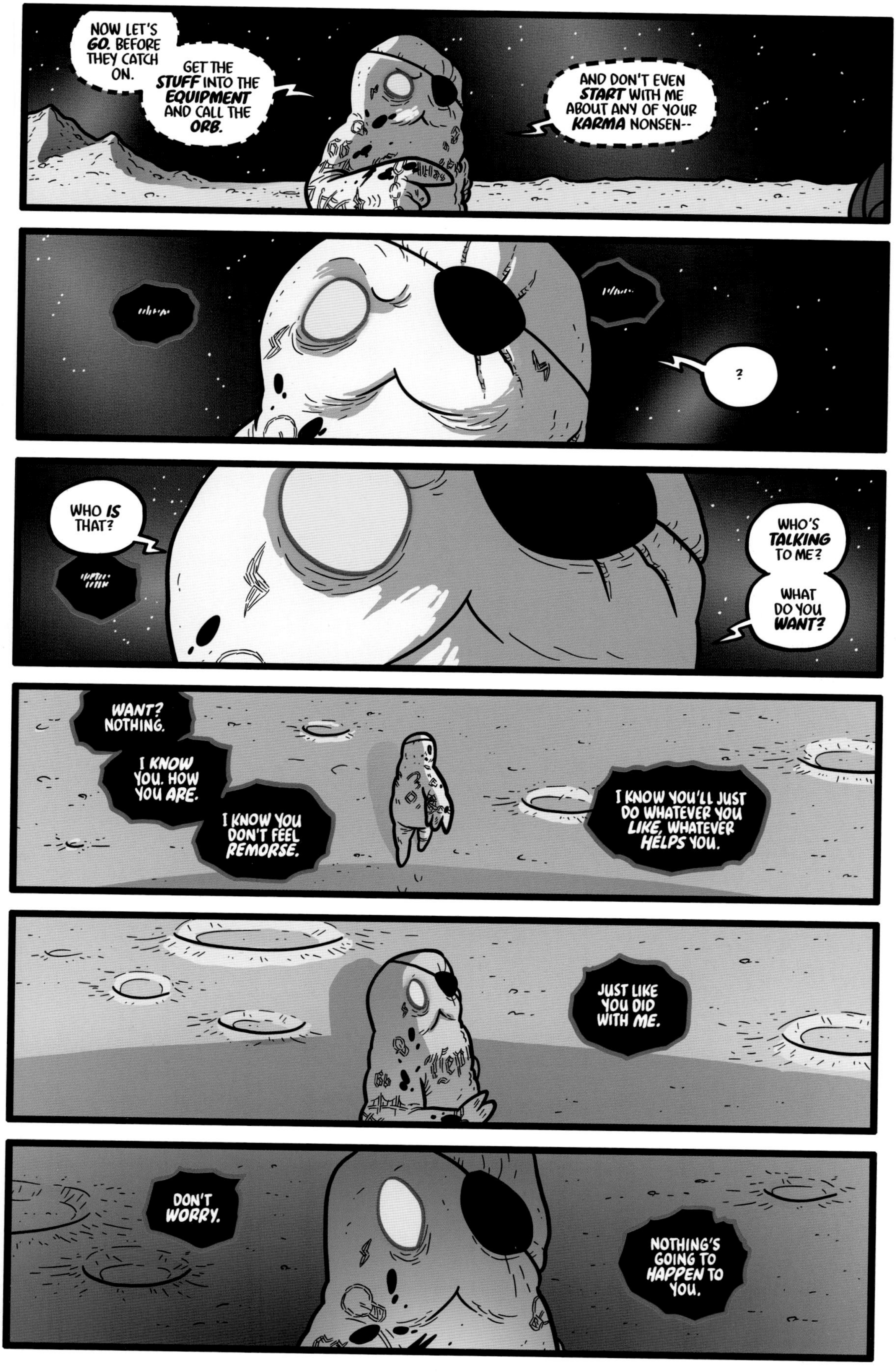
NOW LET'S GO. BEFORE THEY CATCH ON.
GET THE STUFF INTO THE EQUIPMENT AND CALL THE ORB.
AND DON'T EVEN START WITH ME ABOUT ANY OF YOUR KARMA NONSEN--
?
WHO IS THAT?
WHO'S TALKING TO ME?
WHAT DO YOU WANT?
WANT? NOTHING.
I KNOW YOU. HOW YOU ARE.
I KNOW YOU DON'T FEEL REMORSE.
I KNOW YOU'LL JUST DO WHATEVER YOU LIKE, WHATEVER HELPS YOU.
JUST LIKE YOU DID WITH ME.
DON'T WORRY.
NOTHING'S GOING TO HAPPEN TO YOU.

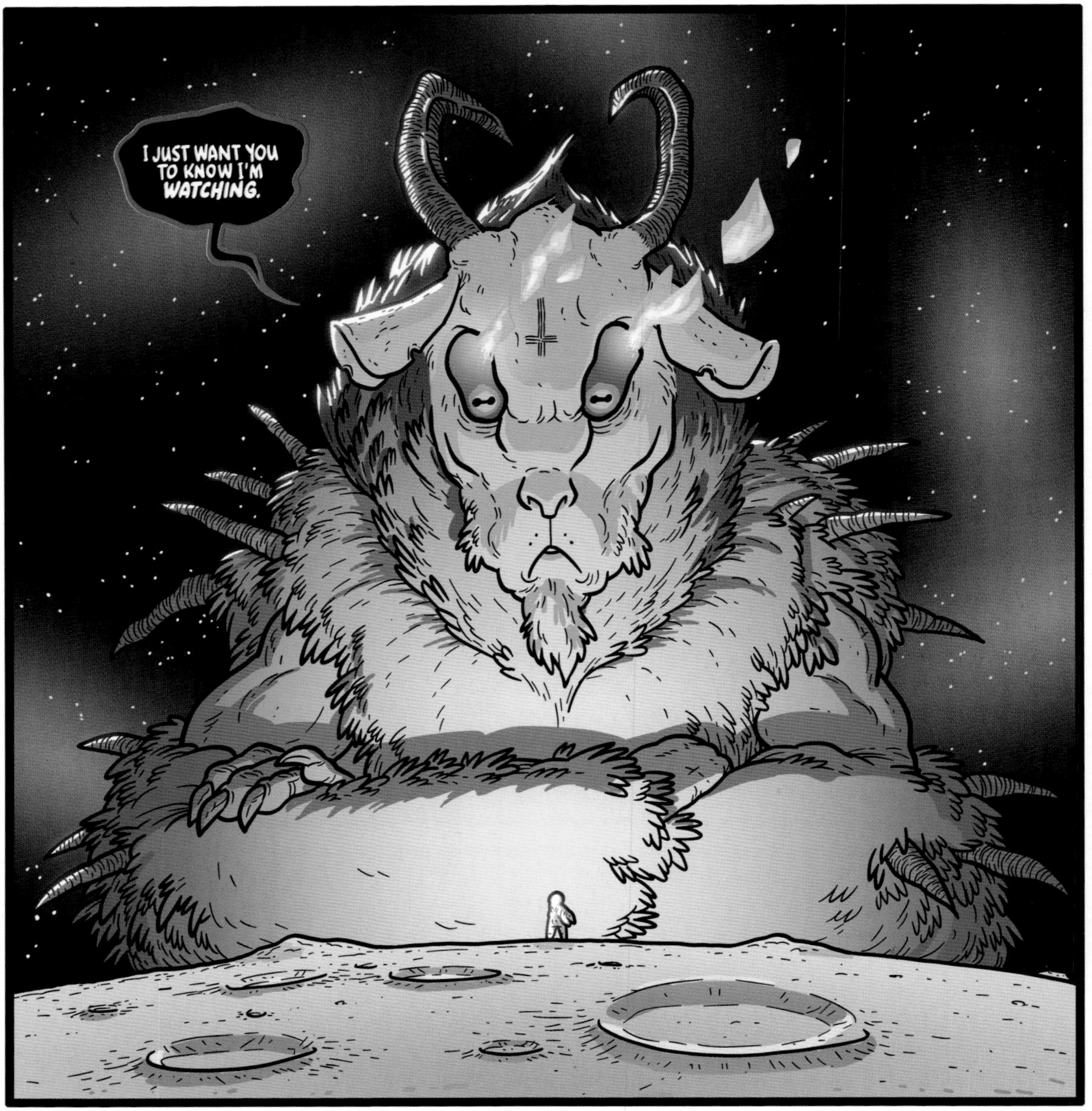
I JUST WANT YOU TO KNOW I'M WATCHING.

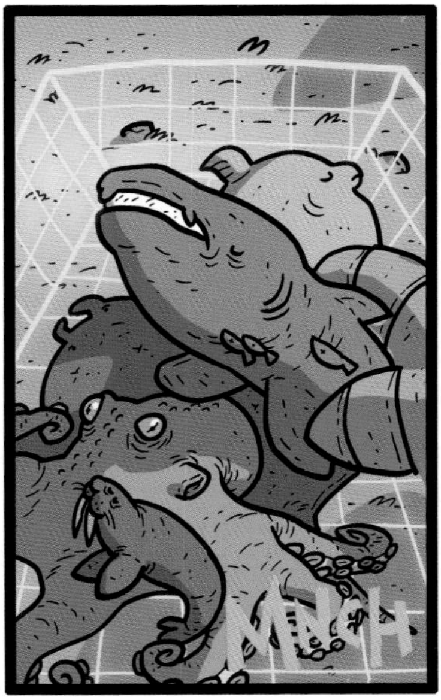
MNCH

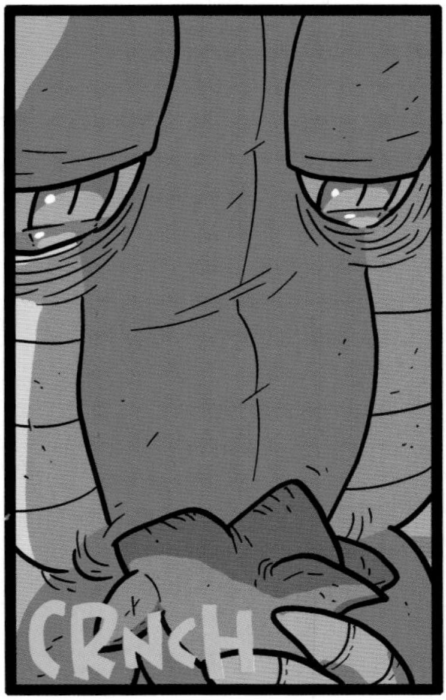
CRNCH

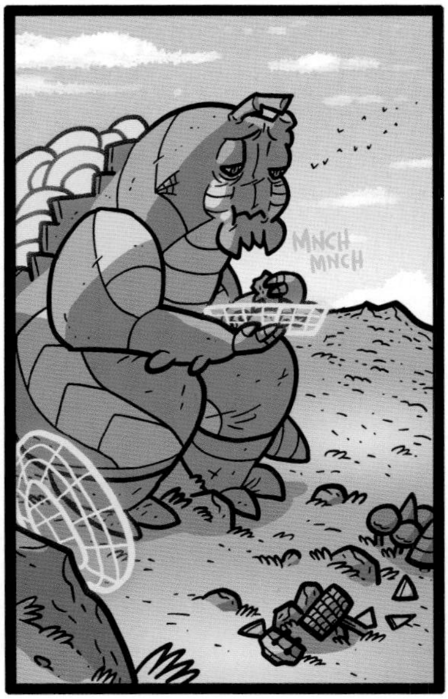
MNCH
MNCH

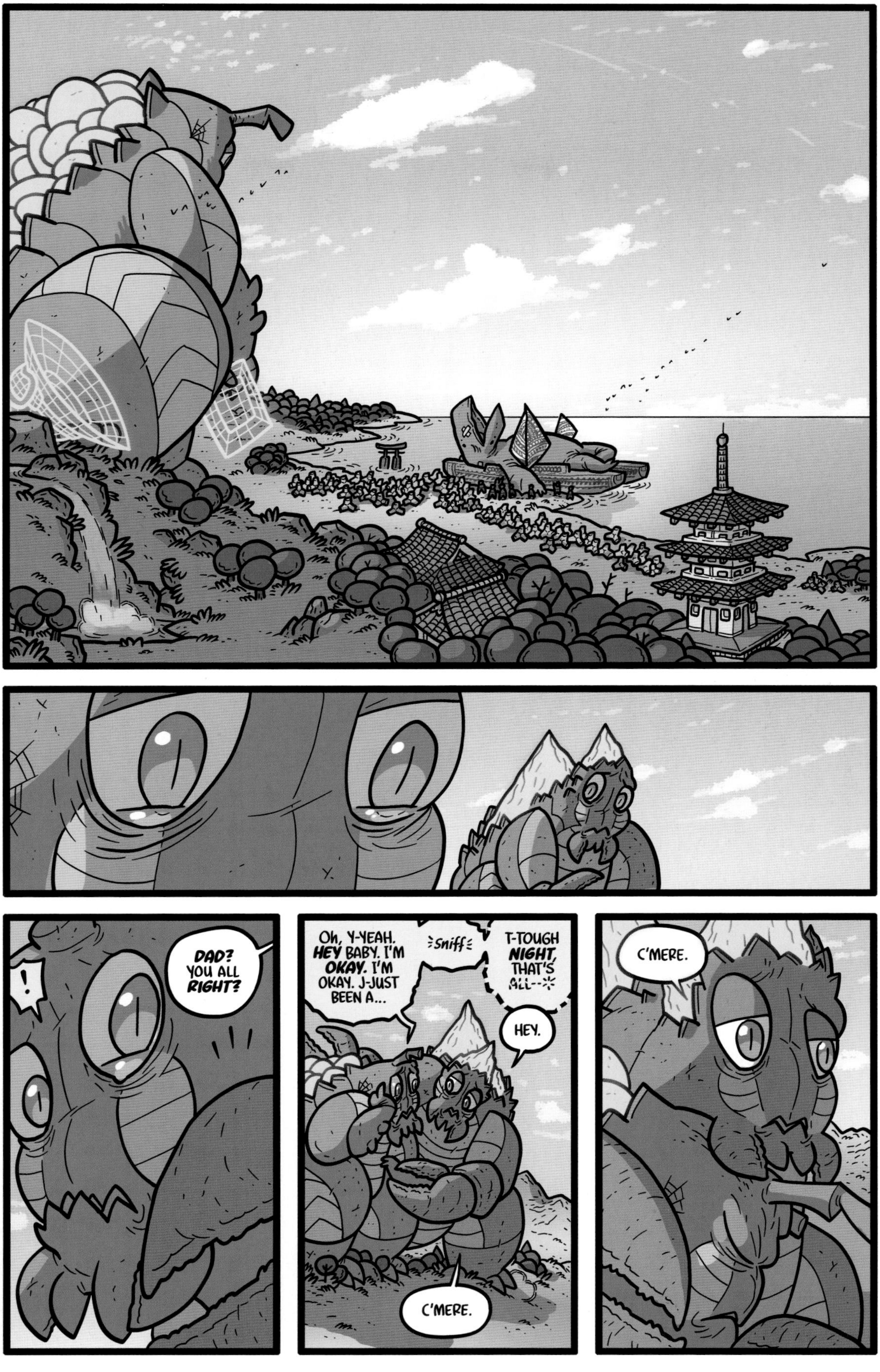
!
DAD? YOU ALL RIGHT?
Oh, Y-YEAH. HEY BABY. I'M OKAY. I'M OKAY. J-JUST BEEN A...
Sniff
T-TOUGH NIGHT, THAT'S ALL--
HEY.
C'MERE.
C'MERE.

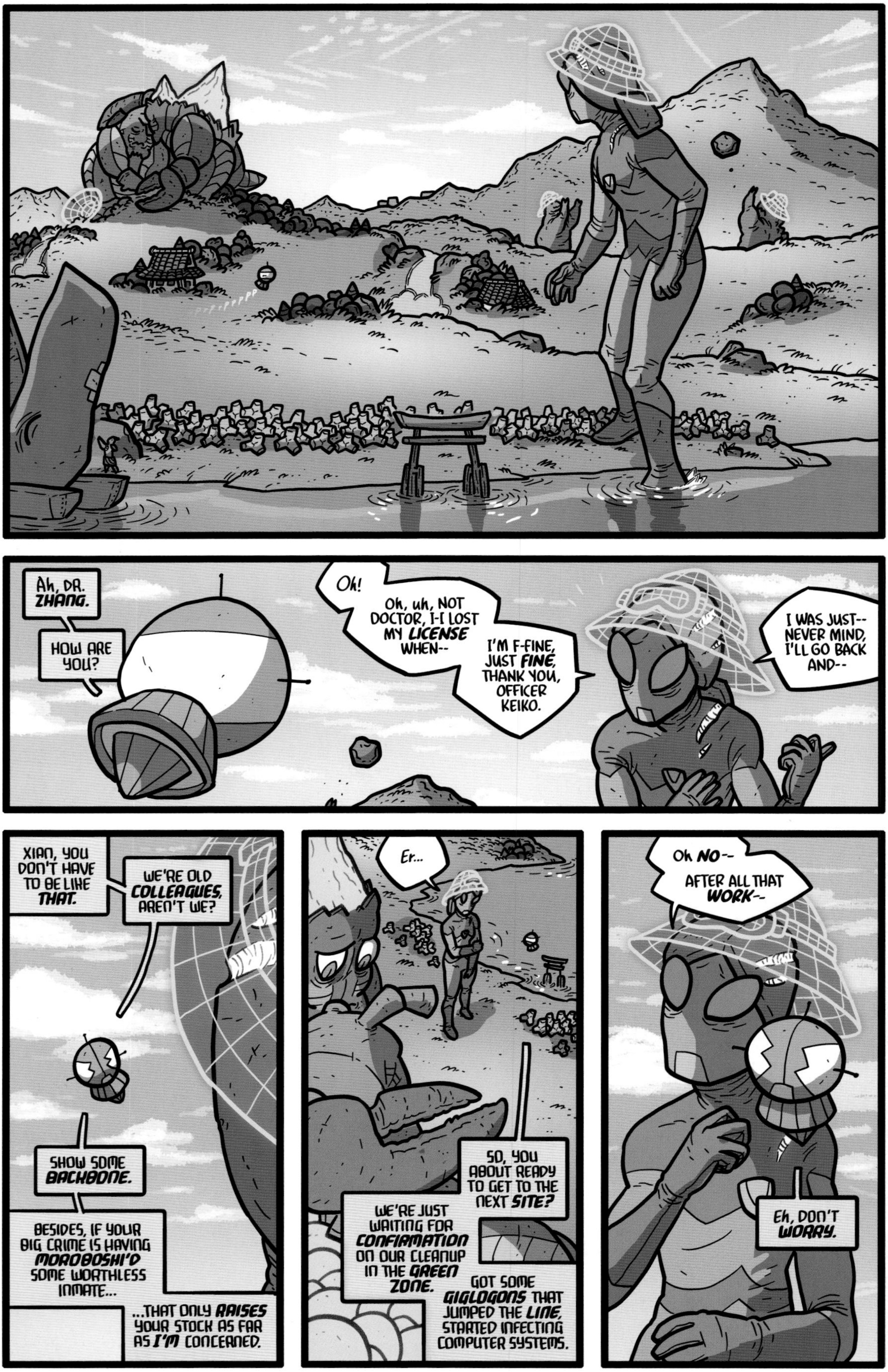
Ah, DR. ZHANG.
HOW ARE YOU?
Oh!
Oh, uh, NOT DOCTOR, I-I LOST MY LICENSE WHEN--
I'M F-FINE, JUST FINE, THANK YOU, OFFICER KEIKO.
I WAS JUST-- NEVER MIND, I'LL GO BACK AND--
XIAN, YOU DON'T HAVE TO BE LIKE THAT.
WE'RE OLD COLLEAGUES, AREN'T WE?
SHOW SOME BACKBONE.
BESIDES, IF YOUR BIG CRIME IS HAVING MOROBOSHI'D SOME WORTHLESS INMATE...
...THAT ONLY RAISES YOUR STOCK AS FAR AS I'M CONCERNED.
Er...
SO, YOU ABOUT READY TO GET TO THE NEXT SITE?
WE'RE JUST WAITING FOR CONFIRMATION ON OUR CLEANUP IN THE GREEN ZONE.
GOT SOME GIGLOGONS THAT JUMPED THE LINE, STARTED INFECTING COMPUTER SYSTEMS.
Oh NO--
AFTER ALL THAT WORK--
Eh, DON'T WORRY.

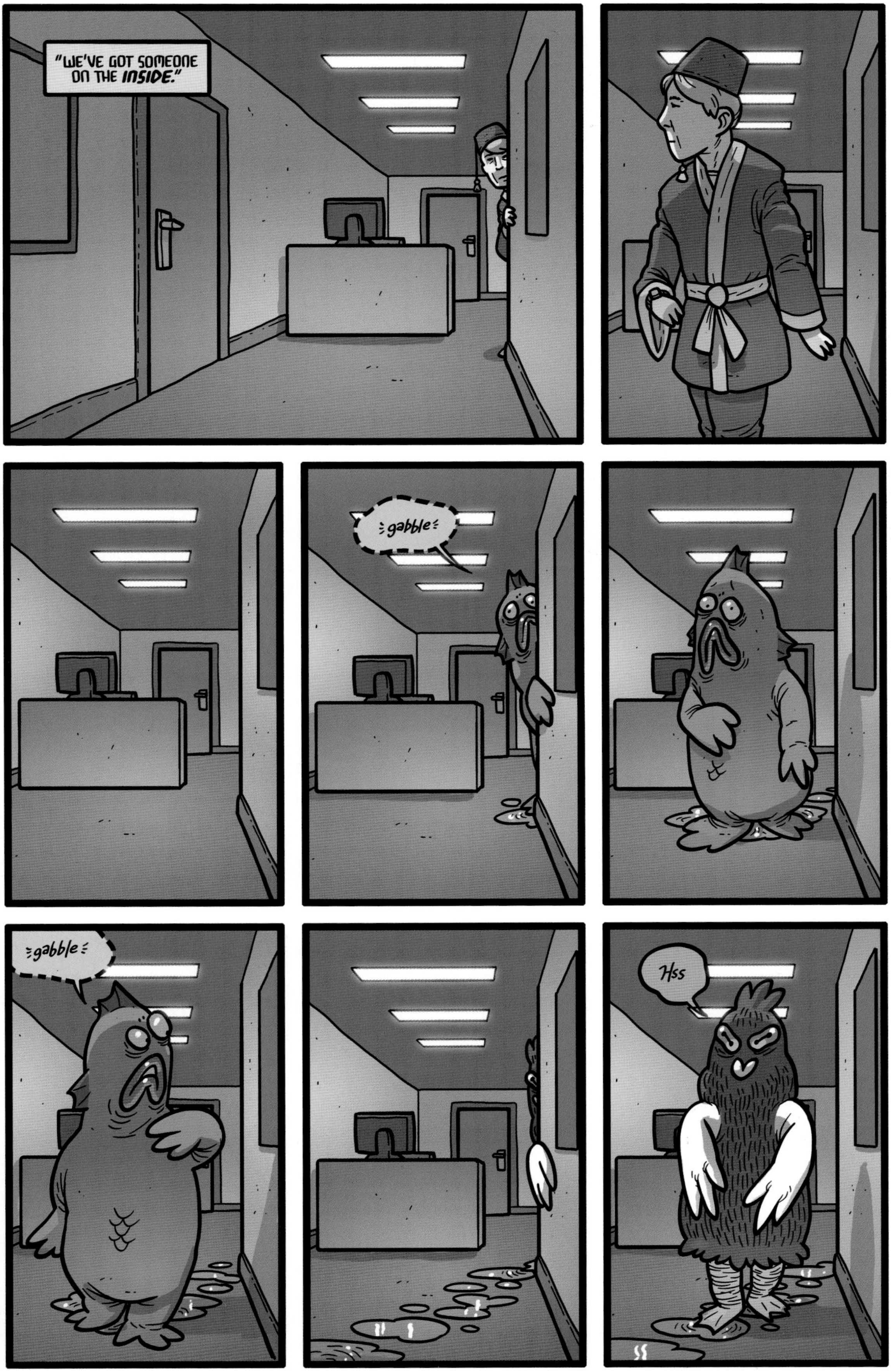
"WE'VE GOT SOMEONE ON THE INSIDE."
gabble
gabble
Hss

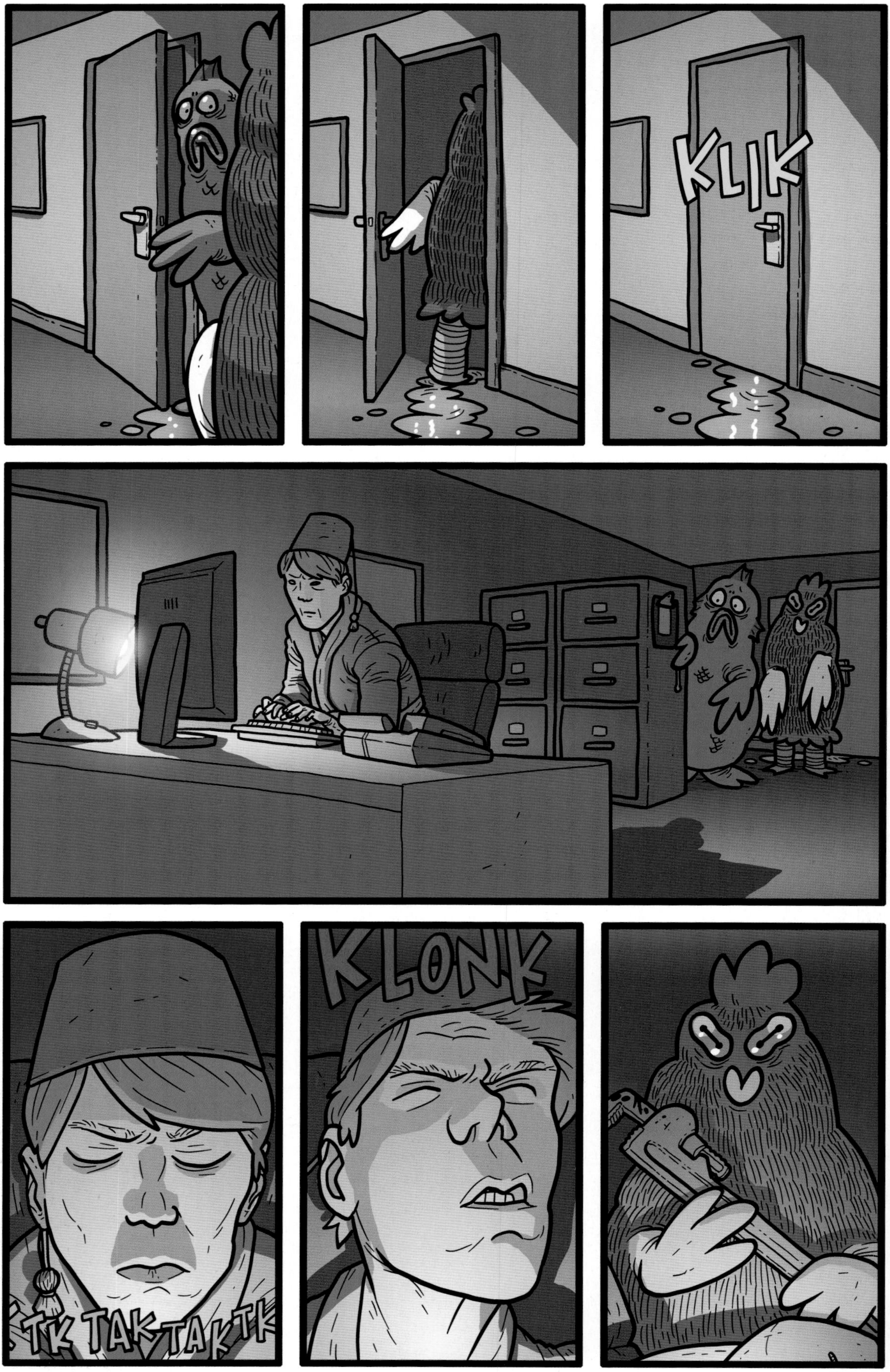
KLIK
TK TAK TAK TK
KLONK

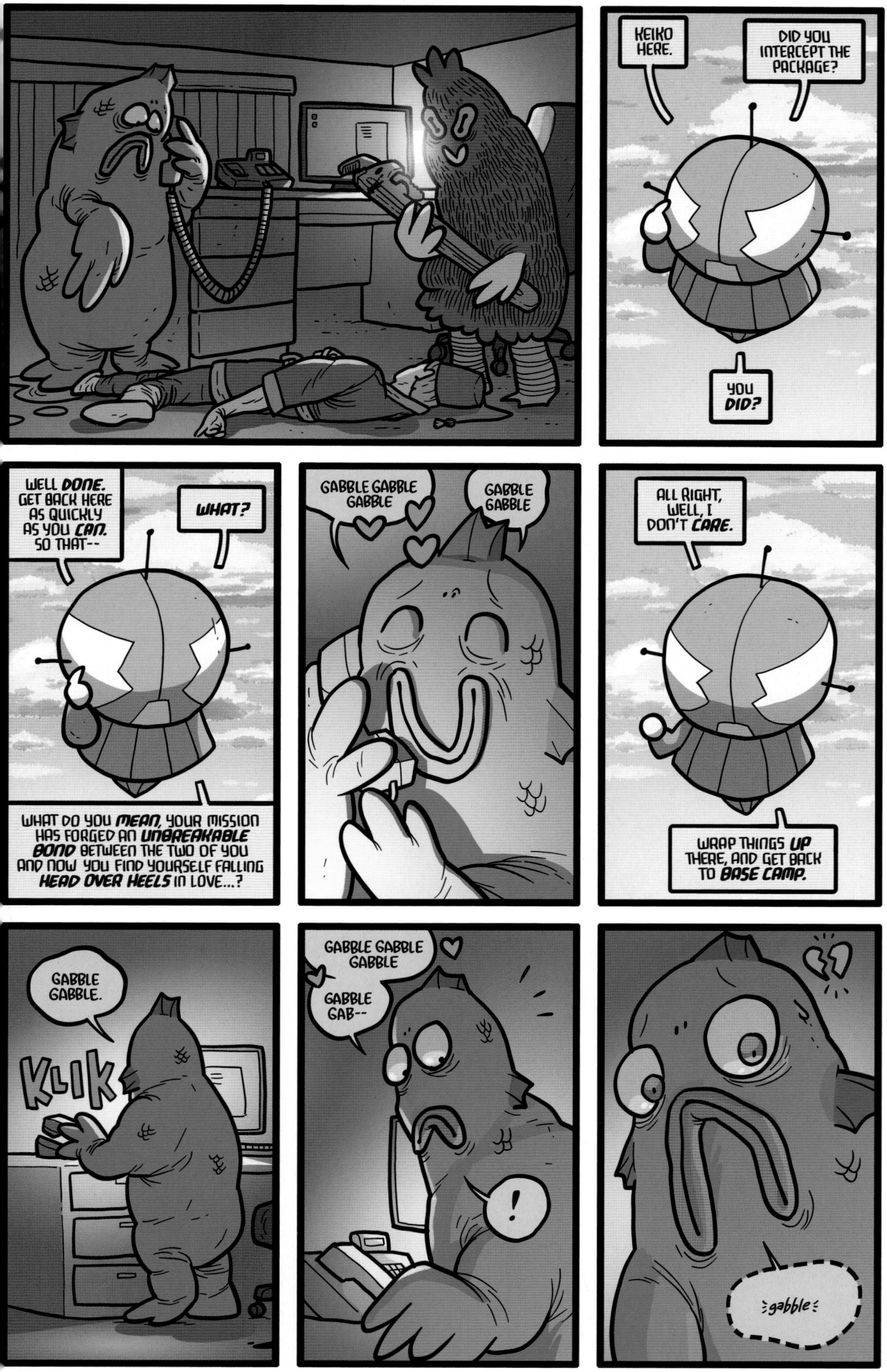

KEIKO HERE.
DID YOU INTERCEPT THE PACKAGE?
YOU DID?
WELL DONE. GET BACK HERE AS QUICKLY AS YOU CAN. SO THAT--
WHAT?
WHAT DO YOU MEAN, YOUR MISSION HAS FORGED AN UNBREAKABLE BOND BETWEEN THE TWO OF YOU AND NOW YOU FIND YOURSELF FALLING HEAD OVER HEELS IN LOVE...?
GABBLE GABBLE GABBLE
GABBLE GABBLE
ALL RIGHT, WELL, I DON'T CARE.
WRAP THINGS UP THERE, AND GET BACK TO BASE CAMP.
GABBLE GABBLE.
KLIK
GABBLE GABBLE GABBLE
GABBLE GAB--
!
gabble

"It's that creepy *SMILE*, you know?"

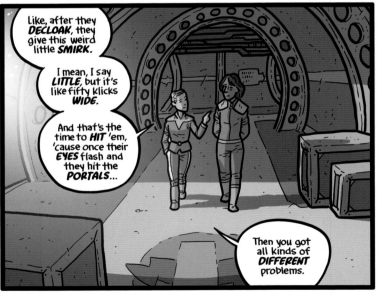

Like, after they *DECLOAK*, they give this weird little *SMIRK*.

I mean, I say *LITTLE*, but it's like fifty klicks *WIDE*.

And that's the time to *HIT* 'em, 'cause once their *EYES* flash and they hit the *PORTALS*...

Then you got all kinds of *DIFFERENT* problems.

So that's what I keep *REMINDING* myself.

The *SMILE* is *GO TIME*.

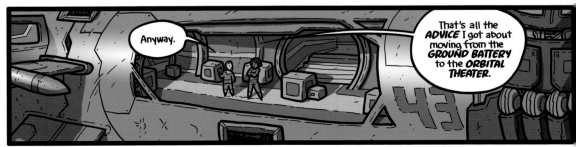

Anyway.

That's all the *ADVICE* I got about moving from the *GROUND BATTERY* to the *ORBITAL THEATER*.

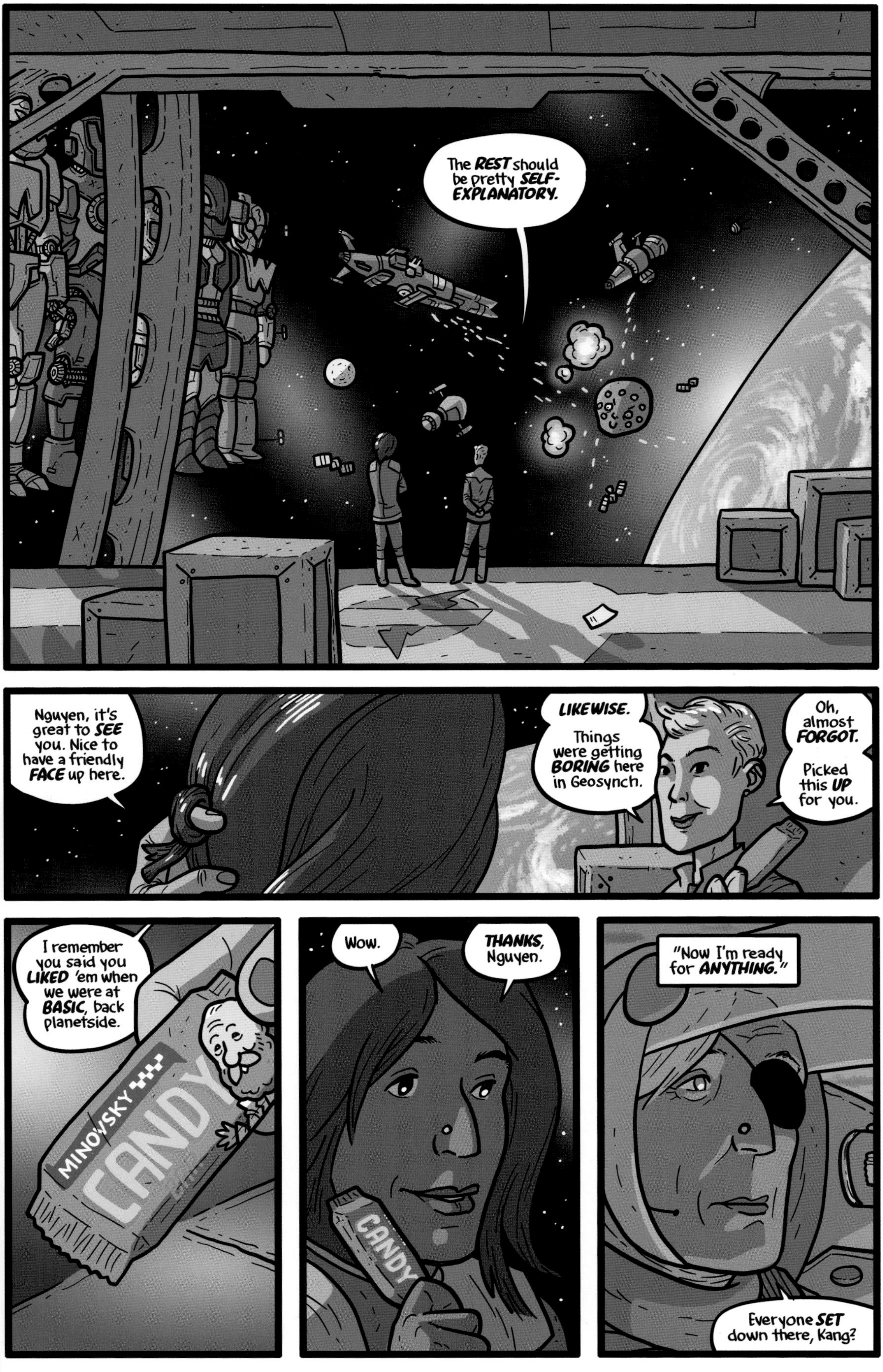
The REST should be pretty SELF-EXPLANATORY.
Nguyen, it's great to SEE you. Nice to have a friendly FACE up here.
LIKEWISE.
Things were getting BORING here in Geosynch.
Oh, almost FORGOT.
Picked this UP for you.
I remember you said you LIKED 'em when we were at BASIC, back planetside.
MINOVSKY
CANDY
Wow.
THANKS, Nguyen.
CANDY
"Now I'm ready for ANYTHING."
Everyone SET down there, Kang?

YEAH, SO FAR. THE TOKYO CREW IS TRICKLING *IN*, BUT...

OKAY, *GOOD.*

I WANT EVERYONE *FOCUSED* AND NO *SLACKING.*

THE HEADS *CANNOT* BE ALLOWED TO OPEN THAT *PORTAL.*

SINGH--

WHEN YOU *SPOT* ONE, DOUBLETIME IT *OVER* THERE, KEEP IT IN ONE *PLACE* UNTIL I GET IT IN THE *CROSSHAIRS.*

AND THEN WHEN I HIT THE *BUTTON,* GET THE HELL OUT OF THE *WAY.*

TEAM GREAT SATELLITE

SINGH, *C'MON,* THESE INMATES ARE *EXHAUSTED.*

THEY'RE NOT EXACTLY ABLE TO--

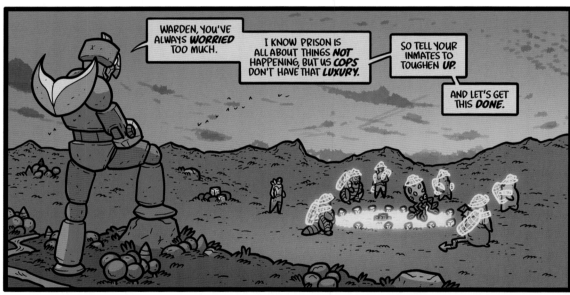

WARDEN, YOU'VE ALWAYS *WORRIED* TOO MUCH.

I KNOW PRISON IS ALL ABOUT THINGS *NOT* HAPPENING, BUT US *COPS* DON'T HAVE THAT *LUXURY.*

SO TELL YOUR INMATES TO TOUGHEN *UP.*

AND LET'S GET THIS *DONE.*

ALL RIGHT, CREW, YOU HEARD THE *COLONEL.*

I NEED YOU *ALL* TO--

OKAY!

THERE! *THERE!* YOU SEE THAT *SHIMMER?*

IT'S *DECLOAKING!* INMATES--

TAKE *AIM.*

AND **LAUNCH!**

THAT'S IT, THAT'S **IT!** WE'VE **STOPPED** IT.

OKAY, SINGH.

THE ROCKS AREN'T **DOING** ANY **DAMAGE,** BUT WE'VE GOT THE HEAD IN **POSITION.**

IT'S **TIME.**

ACTIVATE THE **SATELLITE.**

SINGH?

SINGH, DO YOU **COPY?**

SINGH!

DAMN IT, SINGH, WE **CAN'T** LET IT--

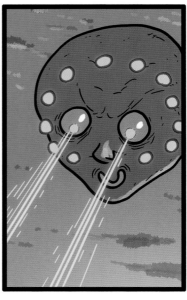

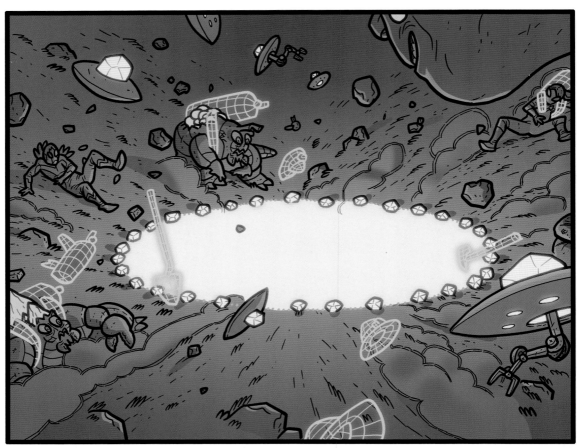

SINGH, WHERE **ARE** YOU??

SINGH!

MINOVSKY

EPISODE 4

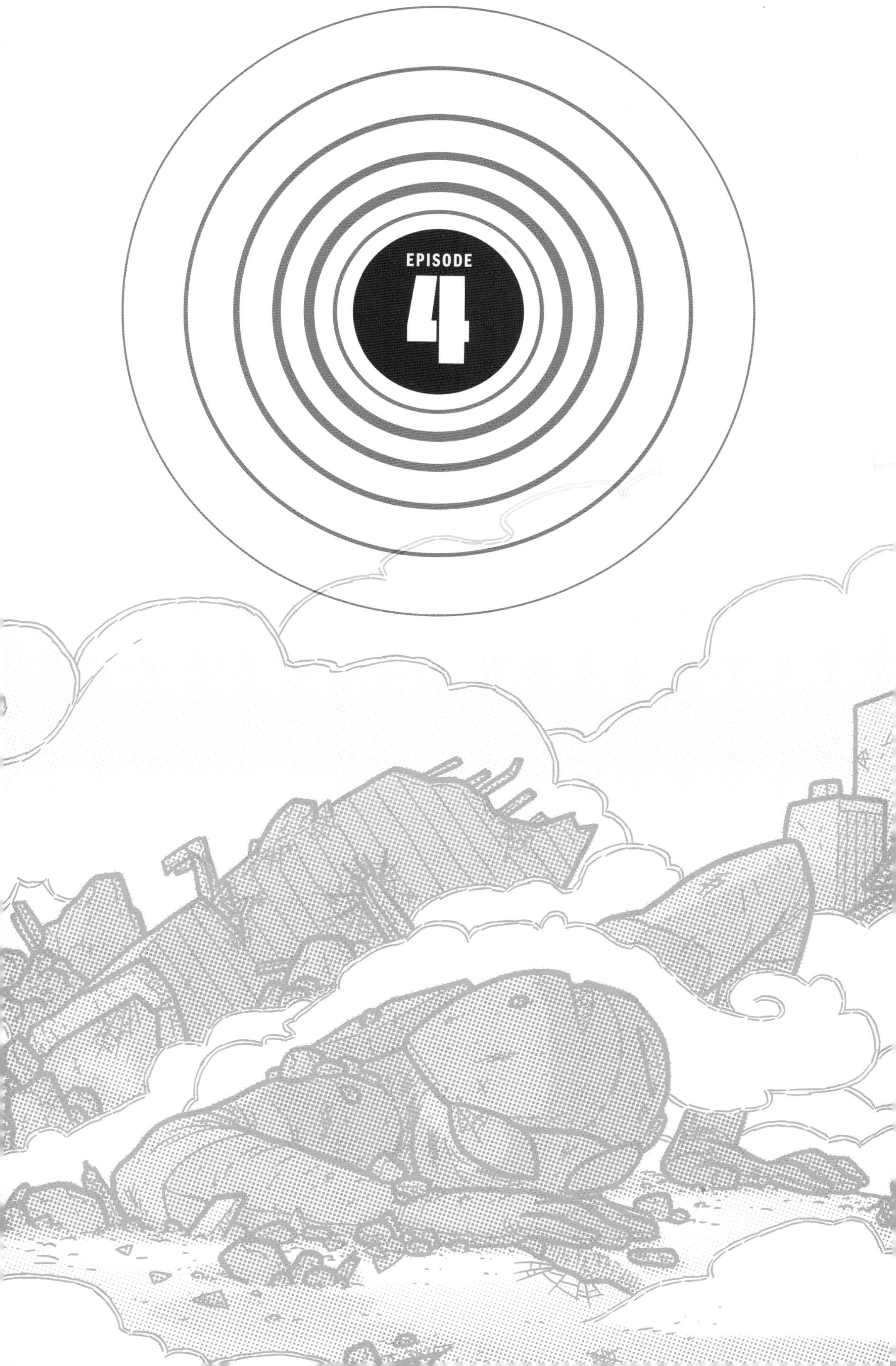

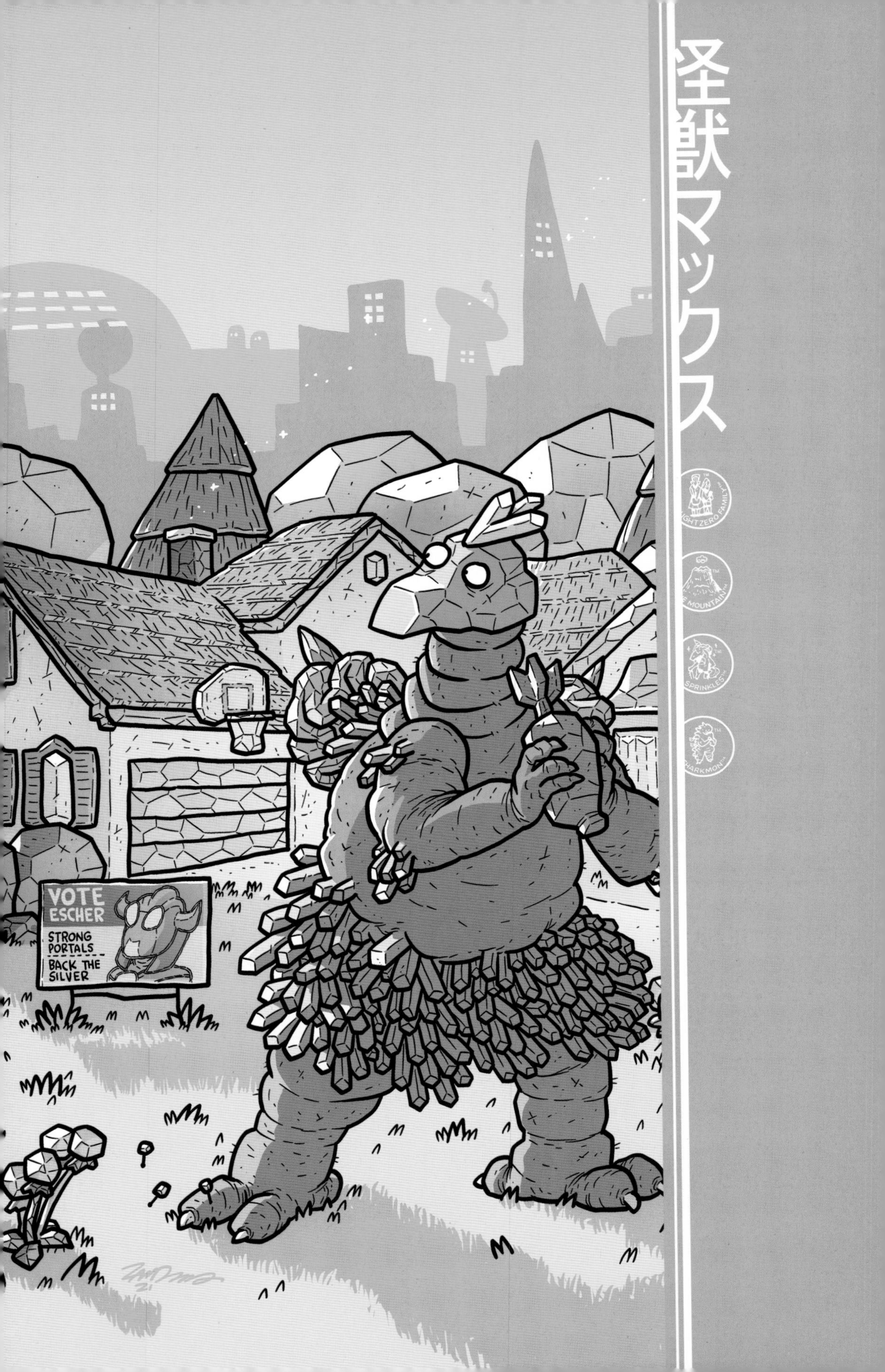
怪獣マックス
VOTE ESCHER
STRONG PORTALS
BACK THE SILVER

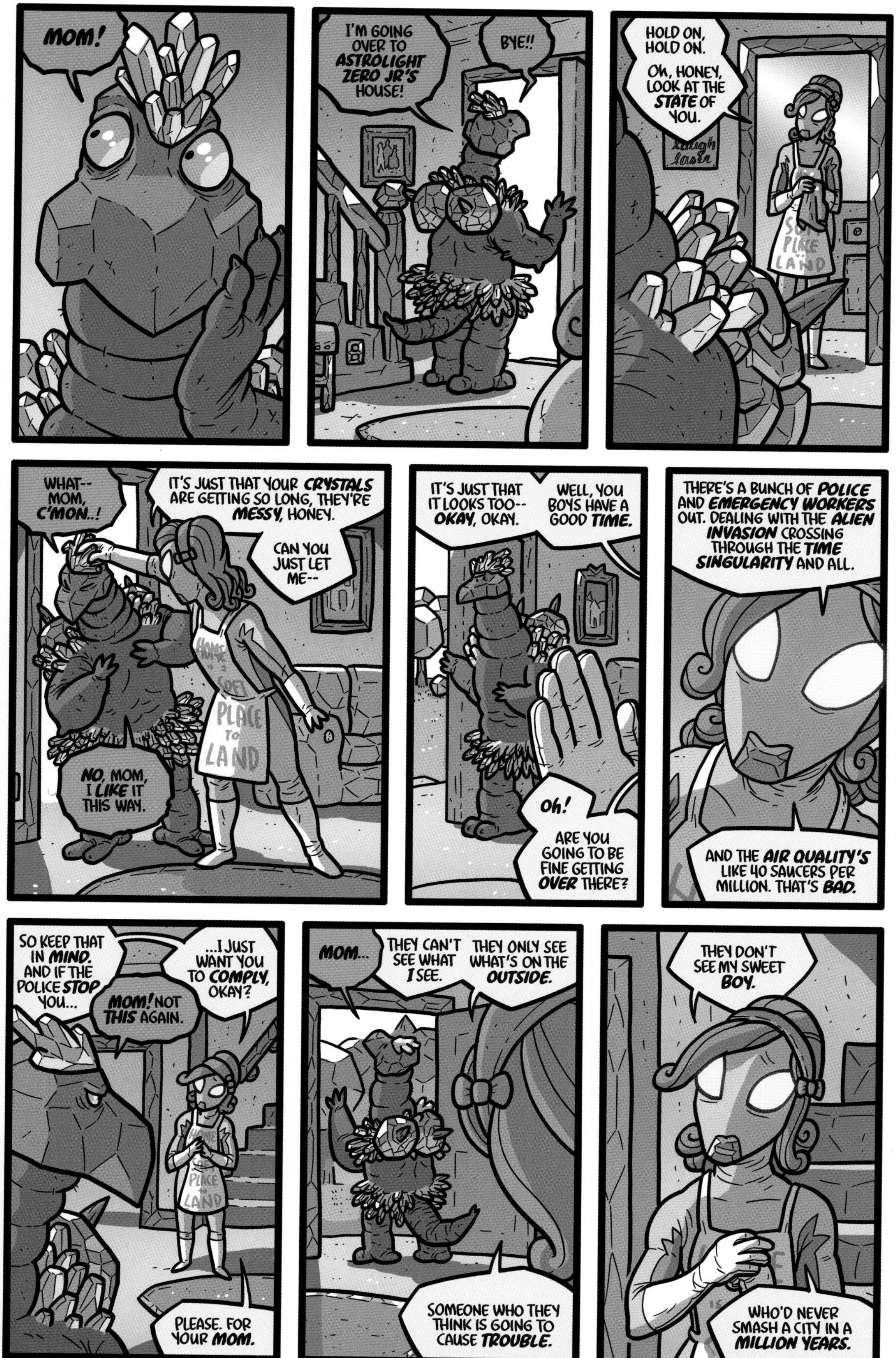
MOM!
I'M GOING OVER TO ASTROLIGHT ZERO JR'S HOUSE!
BYE!!
HOLD ON, HOLD ON.
Oh, HONEY, LOOK AT THE STATE OF YOU.
WHAT-- MOM, C'MON..!
IT'S JUST THAT YOUR CRYSTALS ARE GETTING SO LONG, THEY'RE MESSY, HONEY.
CAN YOU JUST LET ME--
NO, MOM, I LIKE IT THIS WAY.
HOME IS A SOFT PLACE TO LAND
IT'S JUST THAT IT LOOKS TOO-- OKAY, OKAY.
WELL, YOU BOYS HAVE A GOOD TIME.
Oh!
ARE YOU GOING TO BE FINE GETTING OVER THERE?
THERE'S A BUNCH OF POLICE AND EMERGENCY WORKERS OUT. DEALING WITH THE ALIEN INVASION CROSSING THROUGH THE TIME SINGULARITY AND ALL.
AND THE AIR QUALITY'S LIKE 40 SAUCERS PER MILLION. THAT'S BAD.
SO KEEP THAT IN MIND. AND IF THE POLICE STOP YOU...
MOM! NOT THIS AGAIN.
...I JUST WANT YOU TO COMPLY, OKAY?
PLEASE. FOR YOUR MOM.
MOM...
THEY CAN'T SEE WHAT I SEE.
THEY ONLY SEE WHAT'S ON THE OUTSIDE.
SOMEONE WHO THEY THINK IS GOING TO CAUSE TROUBLE.
THEY DON'T SEE MY SWEET BOY.
WHO'D NEVER SMASH A CITY IN A MILLION YEARS.

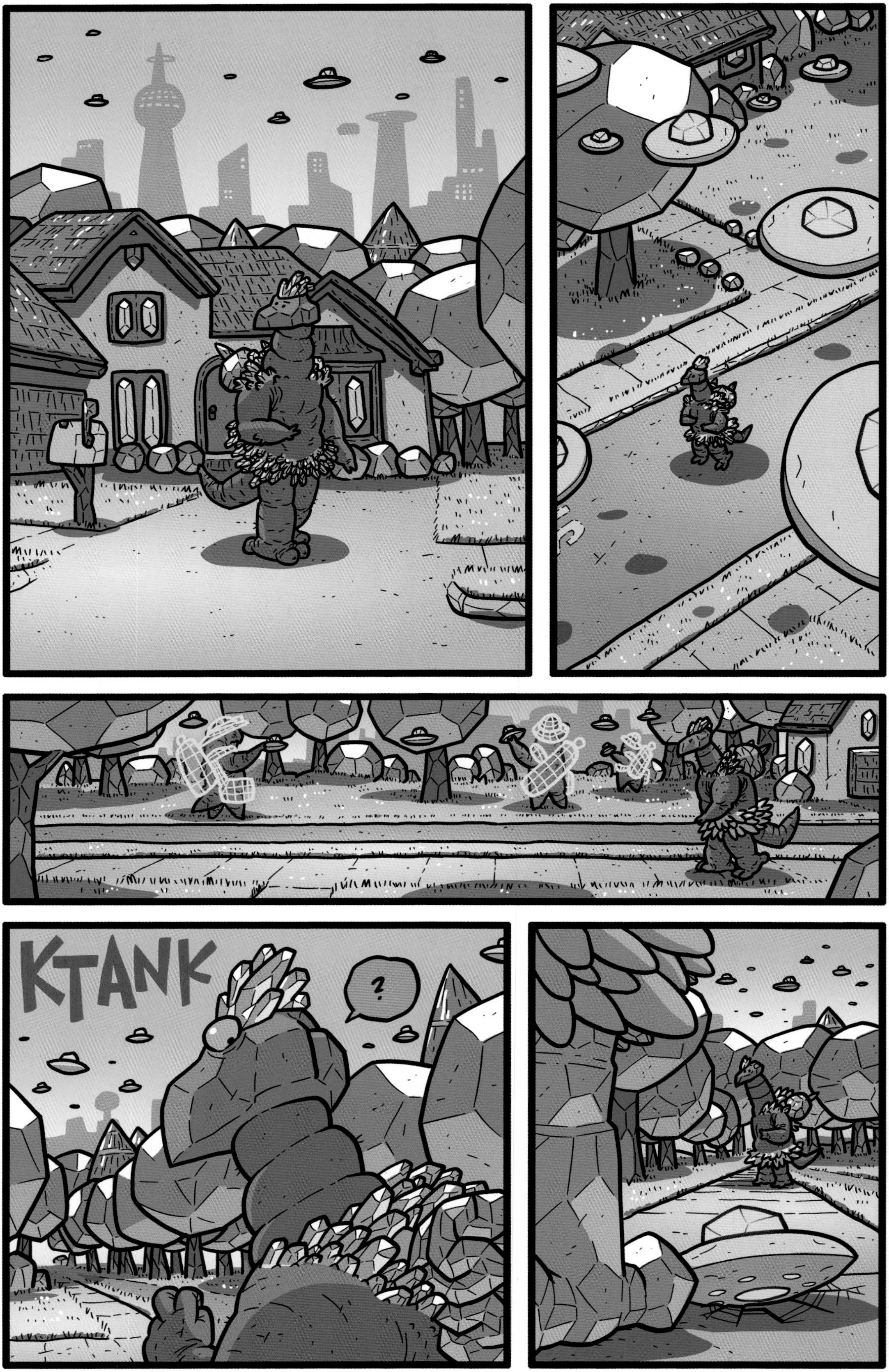
KTANK
?

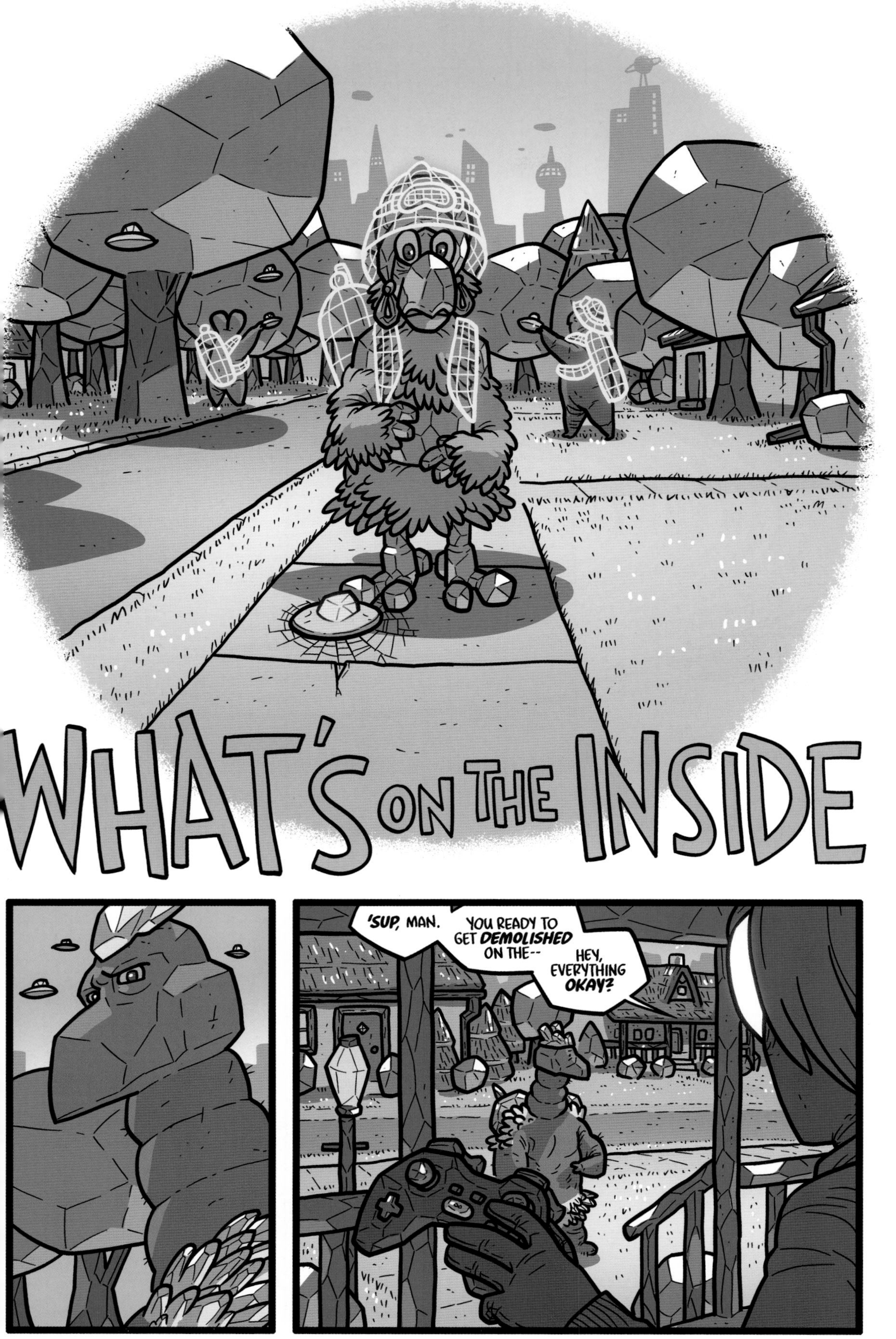
WHAT'S ON THE INSIDE
'SUP, MAN.
YOU READY TO GET DEMOLISHED ON THE--
HEY, EVERYTHING OKAY?

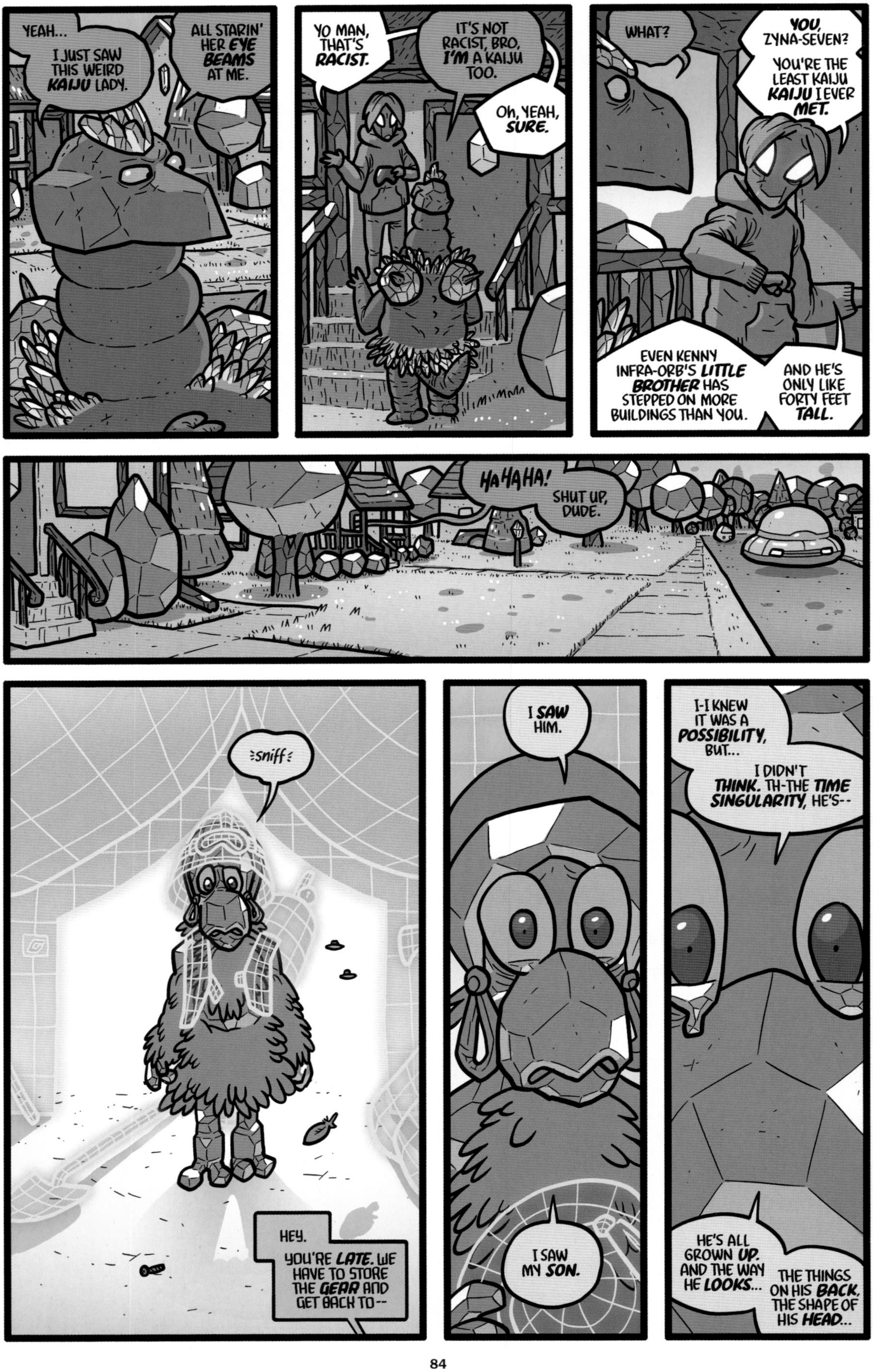
YEAH...
I JUST SAW THIS WEIRD KAIJU LADY.
ALL STARIN' HER EYE BEAMS AT ME.
YO MAN, THAT'S RACIST.
IT'S NOT RACIST, BRO, I'M A KAIJU TOO.
Oh, YEAH, SURE.
WHAT?
YOU, ZYNA-SEVEN?
YOU'RE THE LEAST KAIJU KAIJU I EVER MET.
EVEN KENNY INFRA-ORB'S LITTLE BROTHER HAS STEPPED ON MORE BUILDINGS THAN YOU.
AND HE'S ONLY LIKE FORTY FEET TALL.
HAHAHA!
SHUT UP, DUDE.
sniff
HEY.
YOU'RE LATE. WE HAVE TO STORE THE GEAR AND GET BACK TO--
I SAW HIM.
I SAW MY SON.
I-I KNEW IT WAS A POSSIBILITY, BUT...
I DIDN'T THINK. TH-THE TIME SINGULARITY, HE'S--
HE'S ALL GROWN UP. AND THE WAY HE LOOKS...
THE THINGS ON HIS BACK, THE SHAPE OF HIS HEAD...

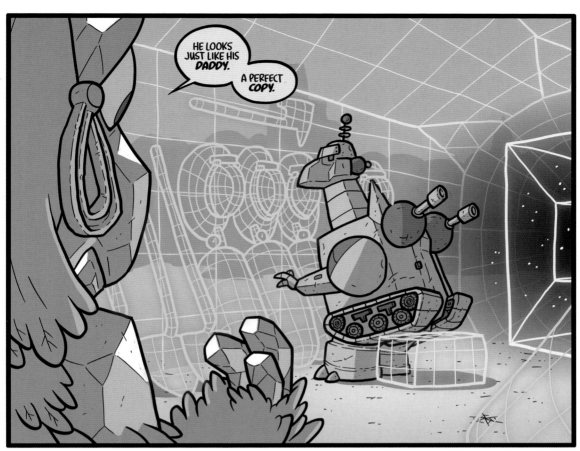

HE LOOKS JUST LIKE HIS *DADDY*.

A PERFECT *COPY*.

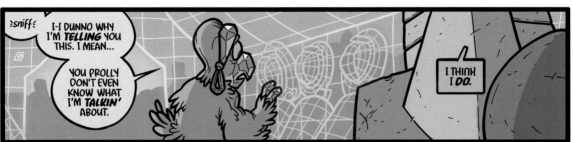

≈sniff≈

I-I DUNNO WHY I'M *TELLING* YOU THIS. I MEAN...

YOU PROLLY DON'T EVEN KNOW WHAT I'M *TALKIN'* ABOUT.

I THINK I *DO*.

IT'S A PAINFUL *ARTIFACT* OF YOUR OLD LIFE. FRAGMENTS LIKE THAT CAN HIT PRETTY *HARD*.

≈sniff≈

BUT *BELIEVE* ME, IT'S GOING TO BE *OKAY*.

WE'RE ALMOST *DONE* WITH THE SAUCERS.

THEN THE *PORTAL* WILL AUTOMATICALLY CLOSE UP AND WE CAN... YOU KNOW.

GO ON WITH OUR *LIVES*.

≈Sniff≈ YEAH.

I GUESS.

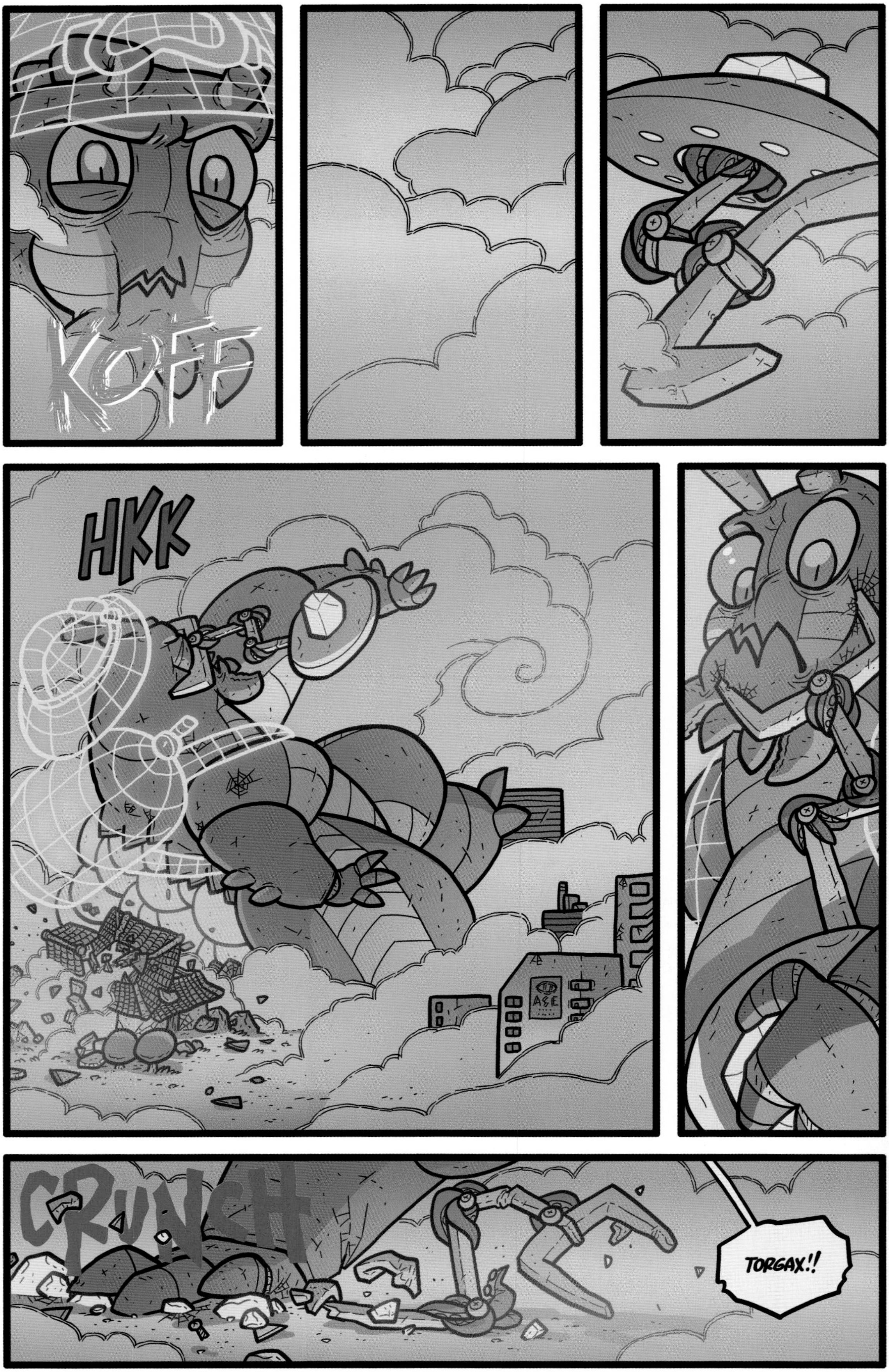
KOFF
HKK
CRUNCH
TORGAX!!

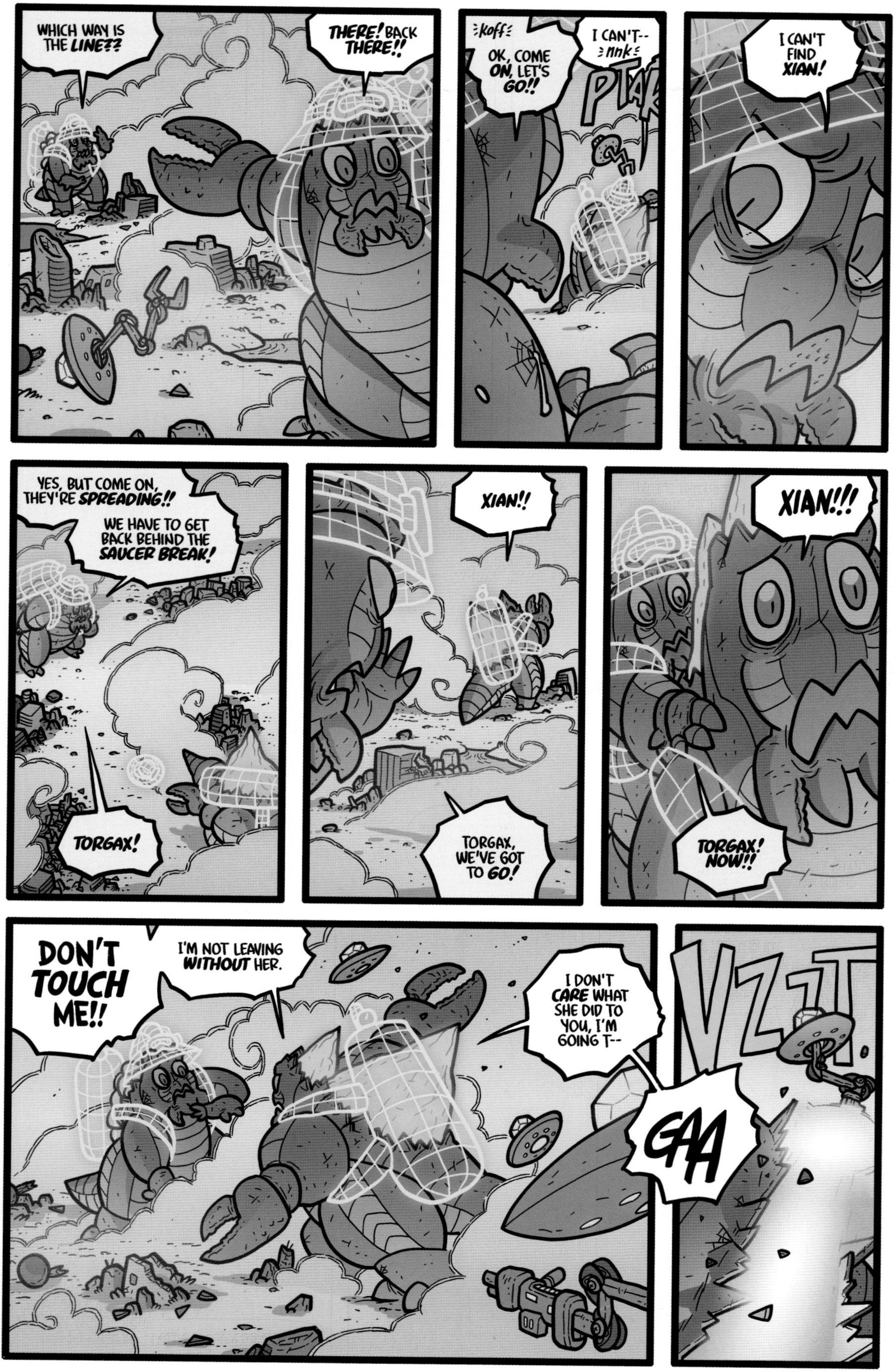
WHICH WAY IS THE LINE??
THERE! BACK THERE!!
koff
OK, COME ON, LET'S GO!!
I CAN'T-- nnk
PTAK
I CAN'T FIND XIAN!
YES, BUT COME ON, THEY'RE SPREADING!!
WE HAVE TO GET BACK BEHIND THE SAUCER BREAK!
TORGAX!
XIAN!!
TORGAX, WE'VE GOT TO GO!
XIAN!!!
TORGAX! NOW!!
DON'T TOUCH ME!!
I'M NOT LEAVING WITHOUT HER.
I DON'T CARE WHAT SHE DID TO YOU, I'M GOING T--
GAA
VZZT

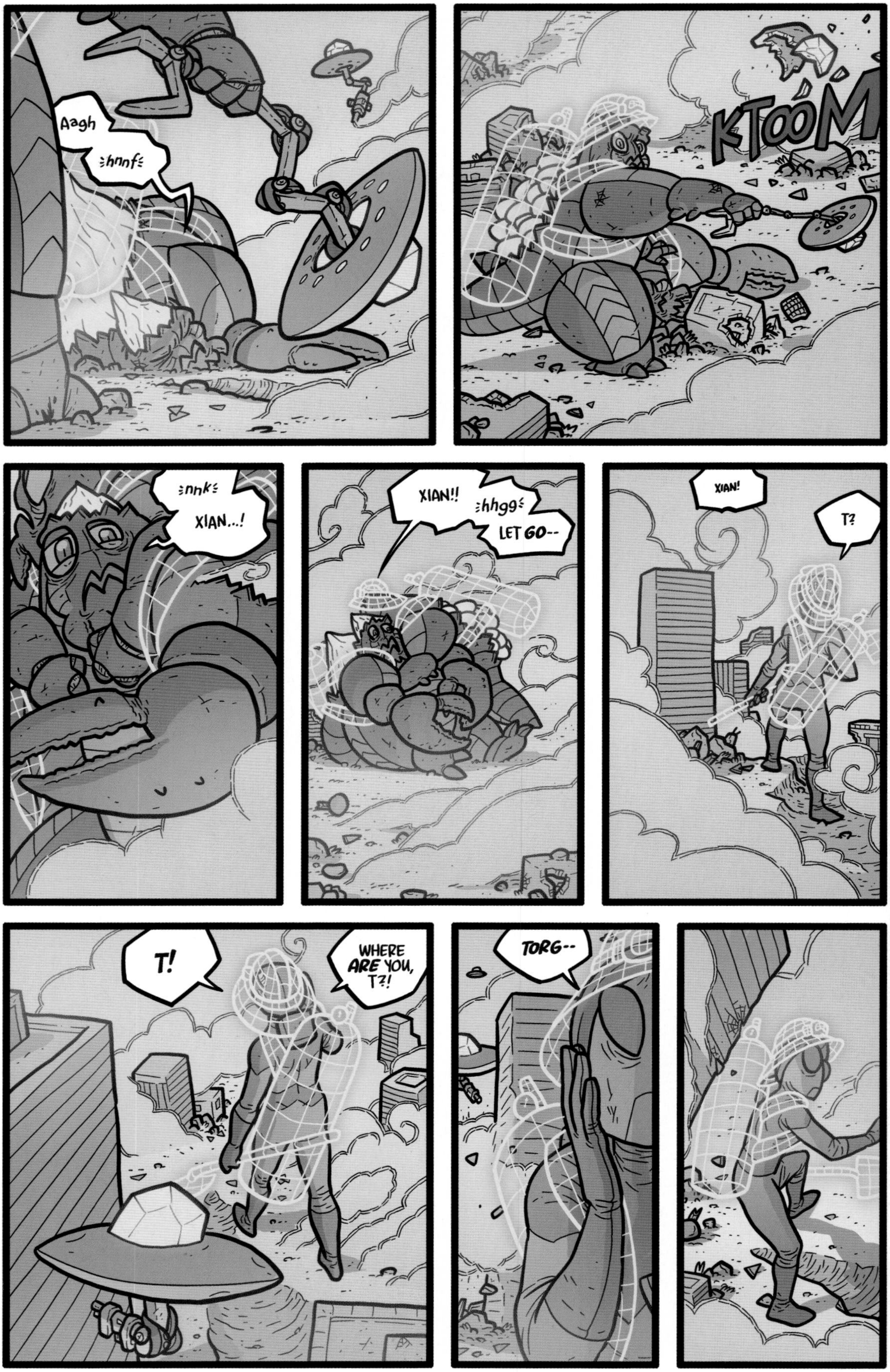
Aagh
hnnf
KTOOM
nnk
XIAN...!
XIAN!!
hhgg
LET GO--
XIAN!
T?
T!
WHERE ARE YOU, T?!
TORG--

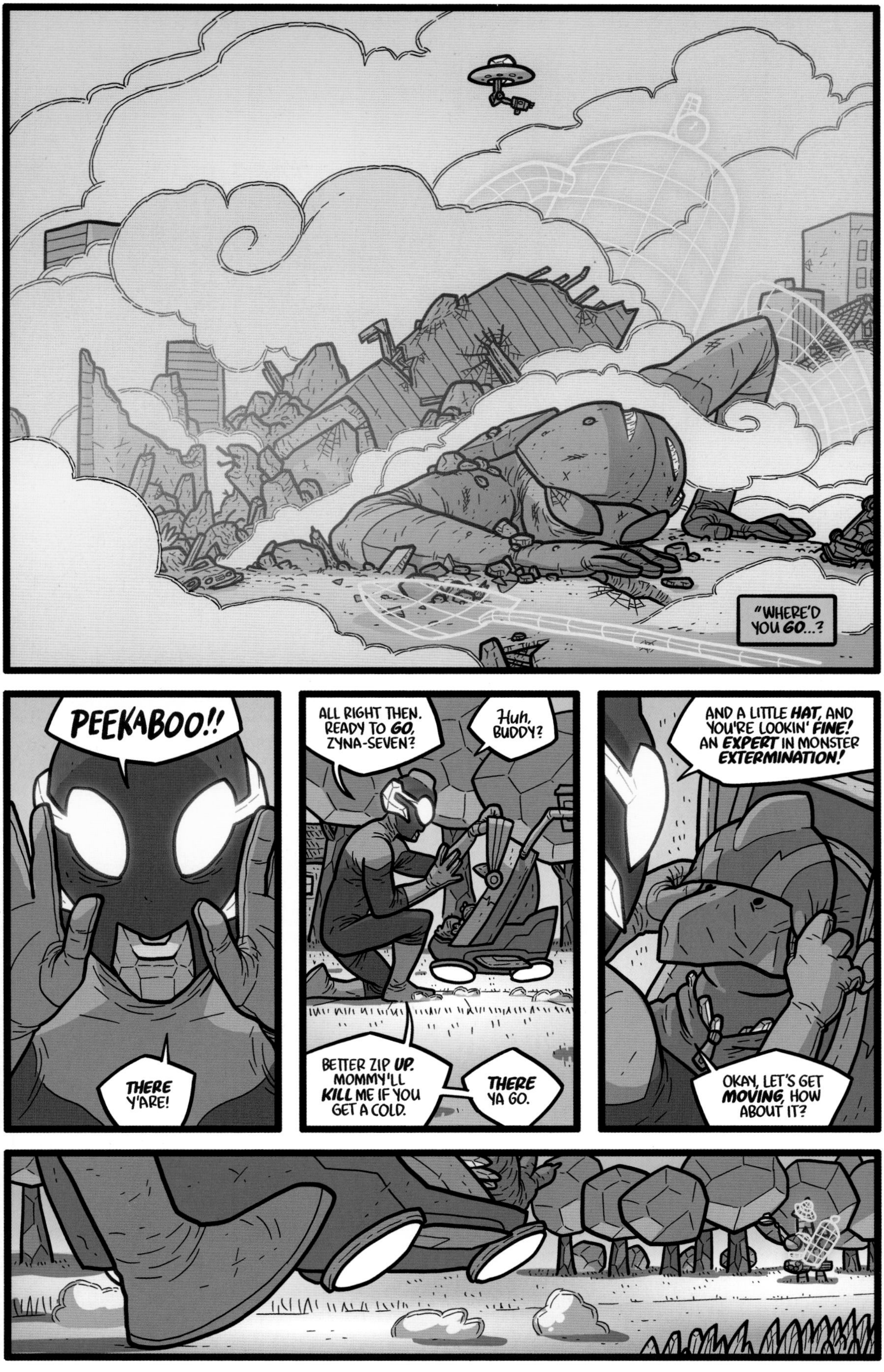
"WHERE'D YOU GO...?
PEEKABOO!!
THERE Y'ARE!
ALL RIGHT THEN. READY TO GO, ZYNA-SEVEN?
Huh, BUDDY?
BETTER ZIP UP. MOMMY'LL KILL ME IF YOU GET A COLD.
THERE YA GO.
AND A LITTLE HAT, AND YOU'RE LOOKIN' FINE! AN EXPERT IN MONSTER EXTERMINATION!
OKAY, LET'S GET MOVING, HOW ABOUT IT?

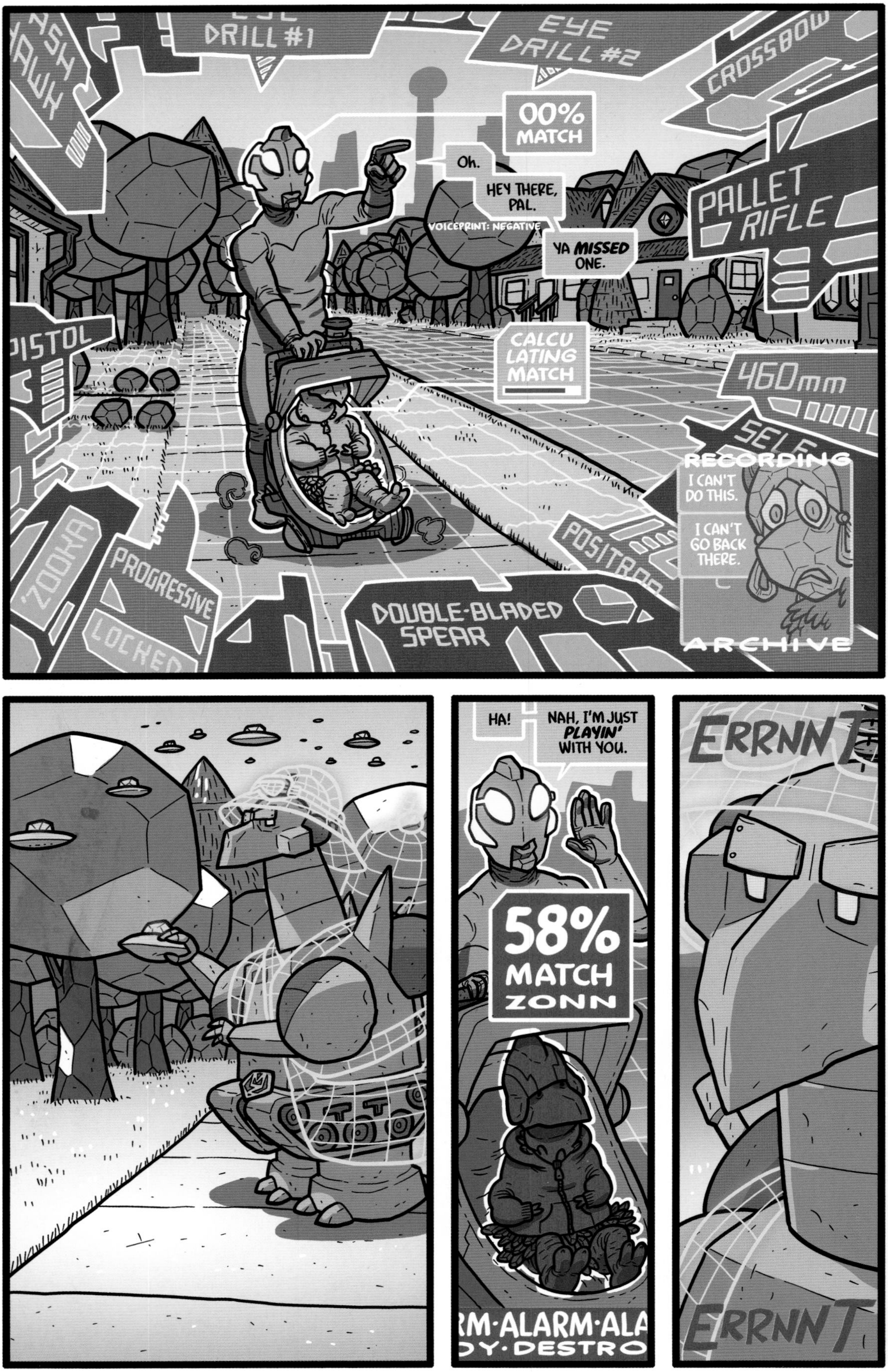

EYE DRILL #1
EYE DRILL #2
CROSSBOW
00% MATCH
Oh.
HEY THERE, PAL.
VOICEPRINT: NEGATIVE
YA MISSED ONE.
PALLET RIFLE
PISTOL
CALCU LATING MATCH
460mm
RECORDING
I CAN'T DO THIS.
I CAN'T GO BACK THERE.
ARCHIVE
'ZOOKA
PROGRESSIVE
DOUBLE-BLADED SPEAR
HA!
NAH, I'M JUST PLAYIN' WITH YOU.
58% MATCH ZONN
ERRNNT
RM·ALARM·ALA
ERRNNT

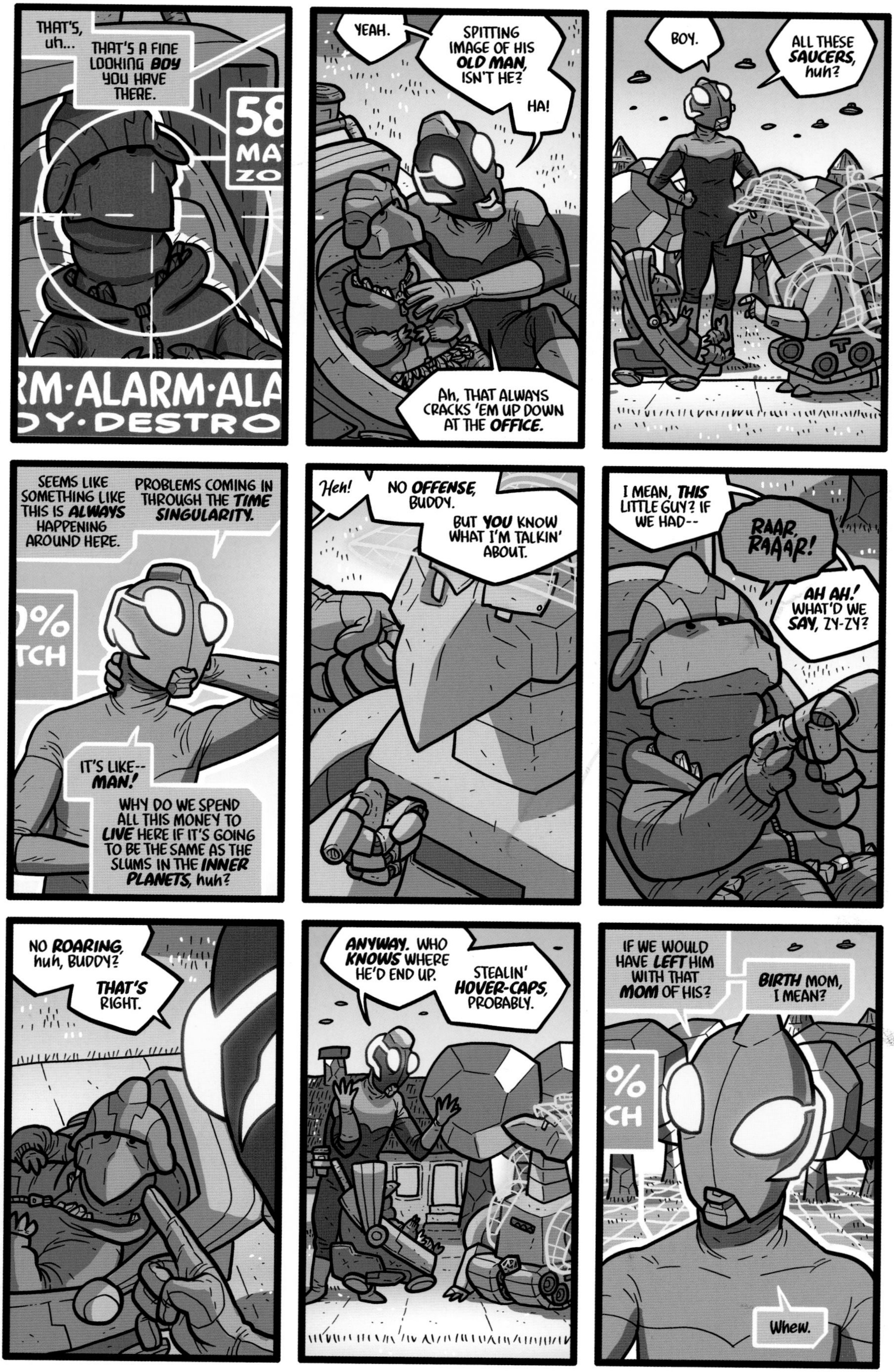
THAT'S, uh...
THAT'S A FINE LOOKING BOY YOU HAVE THERE.
58 MA ZO
RM·ALARM·ALA
DY·DESTRO
YEAH.
SPITTING IMAGE OF HIS OLD MAN, ISN'T HE?
HA!
Ah, THAT ALWAYS CRACKS 'EM UP DOWN AT THE OFFICE.
BOY.
ALL THESE SAUCERS, huh?
SEEMS LIKE SOMETHING LIKE THIS IS ALWAYS HAPPENING AROUND HERE.
PROBLEMS COMING IN THROUGH THE TIME SINGULARITY.
IT'S LIKE-- MAN!
WHY DO WE SPEND ALL THIS MONEY TO LIVE HERE IF IT'S GOING TO BE THE SAME AS THE SLUMS IN THE INNER PLANETS, huh?
Heh!
NO OFFENSE, BUDDY.
BUT YOU KNOW WHAT I'M TALKIN' ABOUT.
I MEAN, THIS LITTLE GUY? IF WE HAD--
RAAR, RAAAR!
AH AH! WHAT'D WE SAY, ZY-ZY?
NO ROARING, huh, BUDDY?
THAT'S RIGHT.
ANYWAY. WHO KNOWS WHERE HE'D END UP.
STEALIN' HOVER-CAPS, PROBABLY.
IF WE WOULD HAVE LEFT HIM WITH THAT MOM OF HIS?
BIRTH MOM, I MEAN?
Whew.

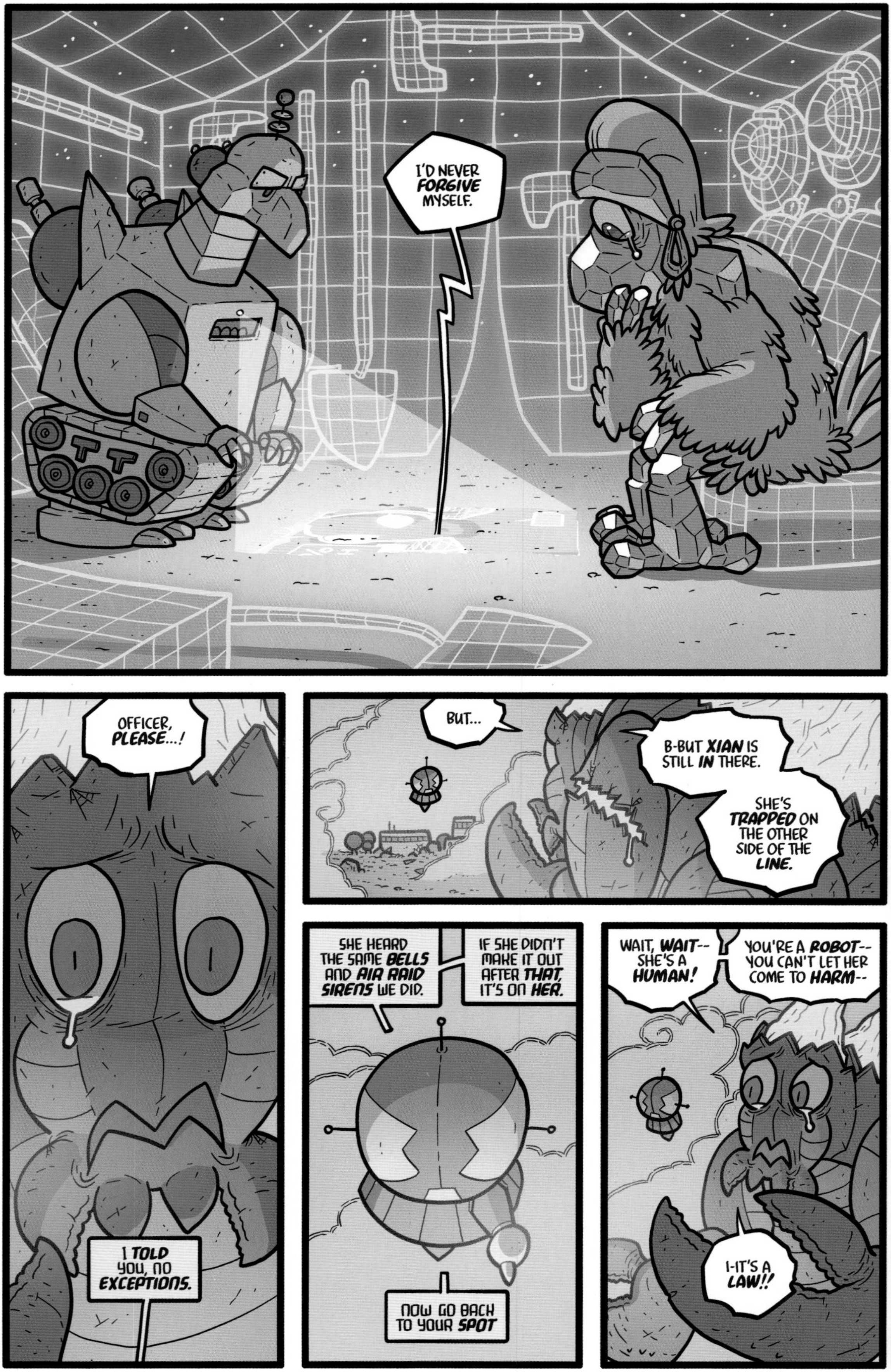
I'D NEVER FORGIVE MYSELF.
OFFICER, PLEASE...!
I TOLD YOU, NO EXCEPTIONS.
BUT...
B-BUT XIAN IS STILL IN THERE.
SHE'S TRAPPED ON THE OTHER SIDE OF THE LINE.
SHE HEARD THE SAME BELLS AND AIR RAID SIRENS WE DID.
IF SHE DIDN'T MAKE IT OUT AFTER THAT, IT'S ON HER.
NOW GO BACK TO YOUR SPOT
WAIT, WAIT-- SHE'S A HUMAN!
YOU'RE A ROBOT-- YOU CAN'T LET HER COME TO HARM--
I-IT'S A LAW!!

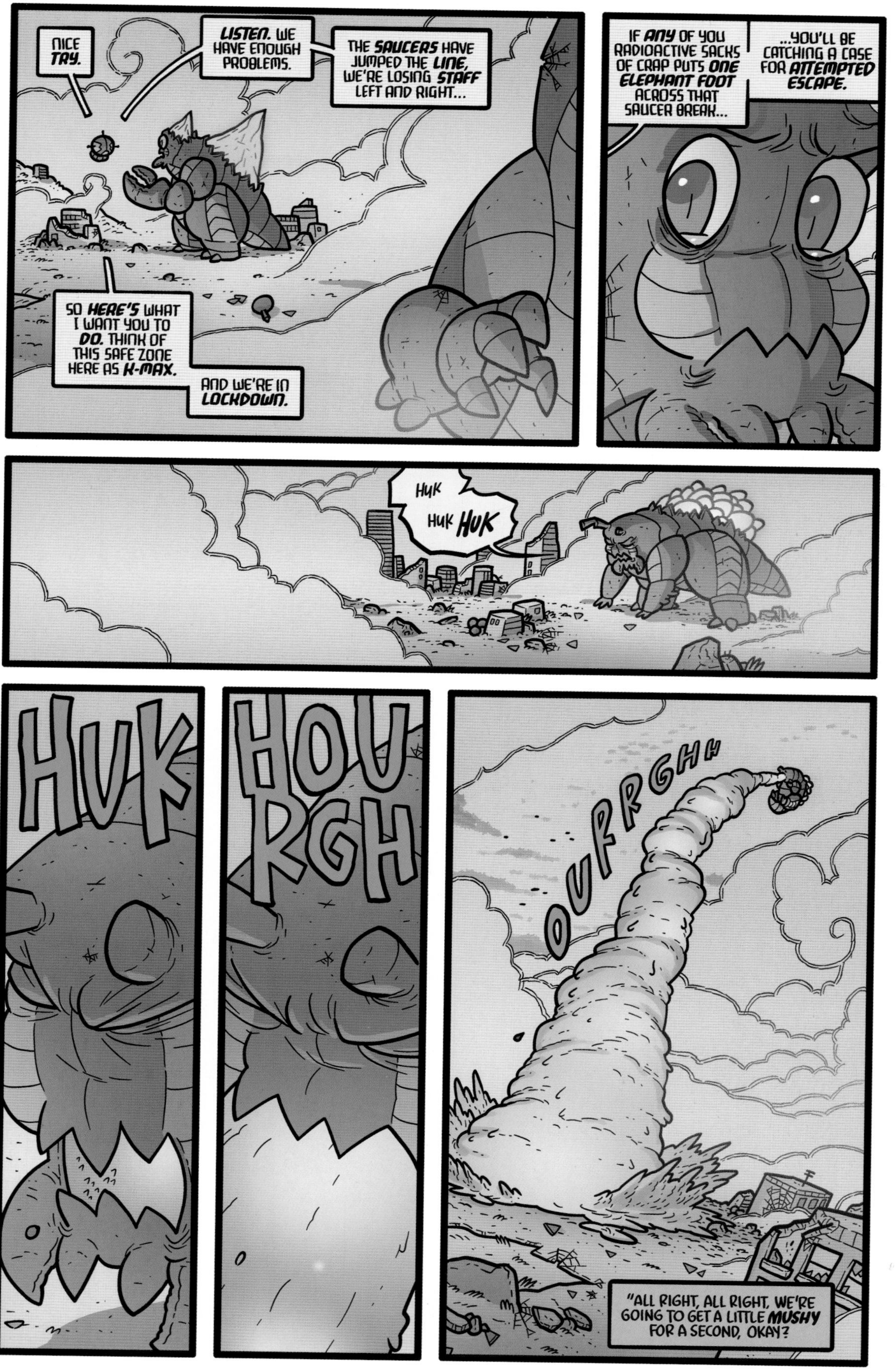
NICE TRY.
LISTEN. WE HAVE ENOUGH PROBLEMS.
THE SAUCERS HAVE JUMPED THE LINE, WE'RE LOSING STAFF LEFT AND RIGHT...
SO HERE'S WHAT I WANT YOU TO DO. THINK OF THIS SAFE ZONE HERE AS K-MAX.
AND WE'RE IN LOCKDOWN.
IF ANY OF YOU RADIOACTIVE SACKS OF CRAP PUTS ONE ELEPHANT FOOT ACROSS THAT SAUCER BREAK...
...YOU'LL BE CATCHING A CASE FOR ATTEMPTED ESCAPE.
HUK HUK HUK
HUK
HOU RGH
OUFRGHH
"ALL RIGHT, ALL RIGHT, WE'RE GOING TO GET A LITTLE MUSHY FOR A SECOND, OKAY?

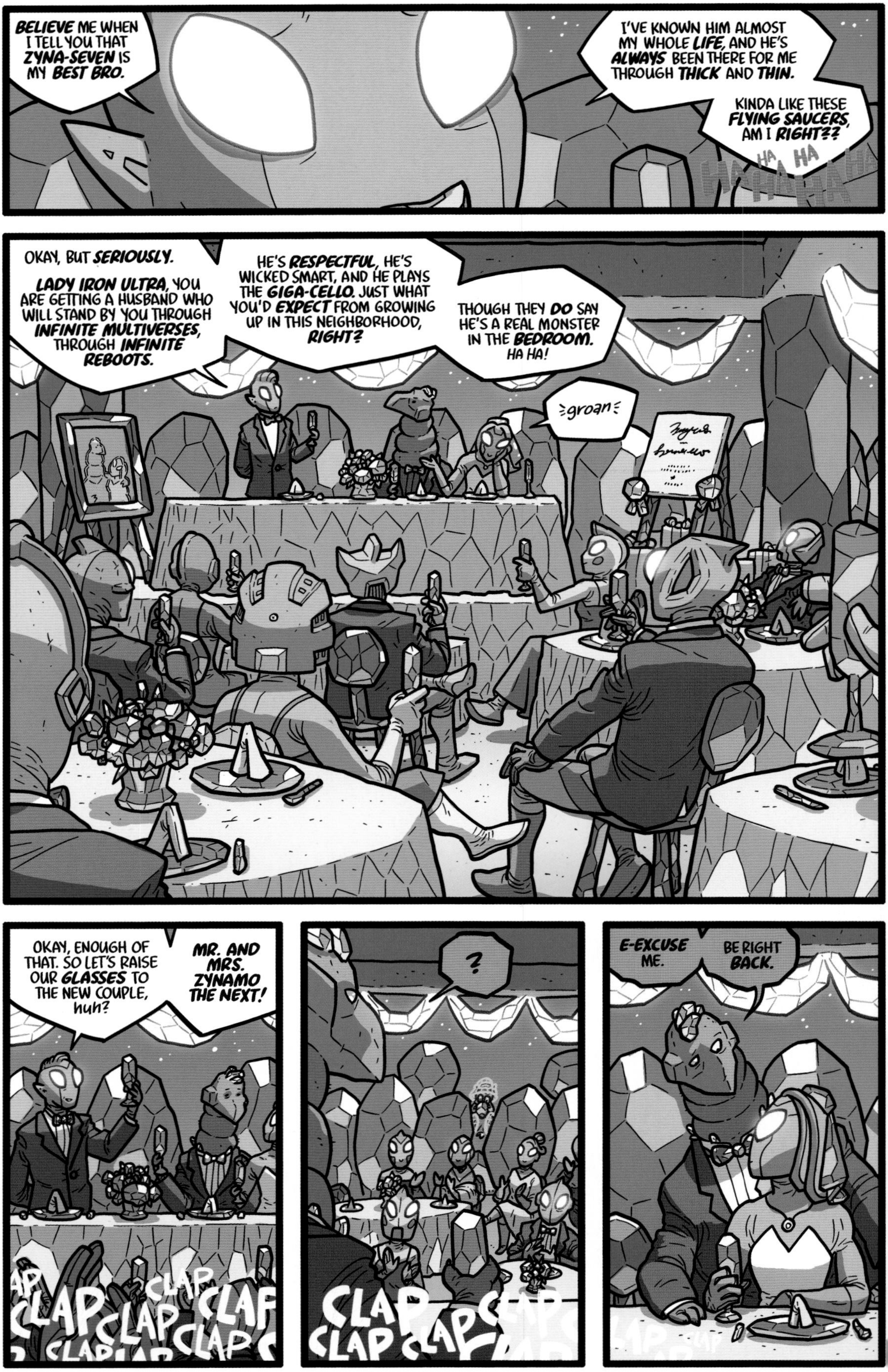

BELIEVE ME WHEN I TELL YOU THAT ZYNA-SEVEN IS MY BEST BRO.
I'VE KNOWN HIM ALMOST MY WHOLE LIFE, AND HE'S ALWAYS BEEN THERE FOR ME THROUGH THICK AND THIN.
KINDA LIKE THESE FLYING SAUCERS, AM I RIGHT??
HA HA HA HA HA HA
OKAY, BUT SERIOUSLY.
LADY IRON ULTRA, YOU ARE GETTING A HUSBAND WHO WILL STAND BY YOU THROUGH INFINITE MULTIVERSES, THROUGH INFINITE REBOOTS.
HE'S RESPECTFUL, HE'S WICKED SMART, AND HE PLAYS THE GIGA-CELLO. JUST WHAT YOU'D EXPECT FROM GROWING UP IN THIS NEIGHBORHOOD, RIGHT?
THOUGH THEY DO SAY HE'S A REAL MONSTER IN THE BEDROOM. HA HA!
groan
OKAY, ENOUGH OF THAT. SO LET'S RAISE OUR GLASSES TO THE NEW COUPLE, huh?
MR. AND MRS. ZYNAMO THE NEXT!
CLAP CLAP CLAP CLAP CLAP
?
CLAP CLAP CLAP CLAP
E-EXCUSE ME.
BE RIGHT BACK.

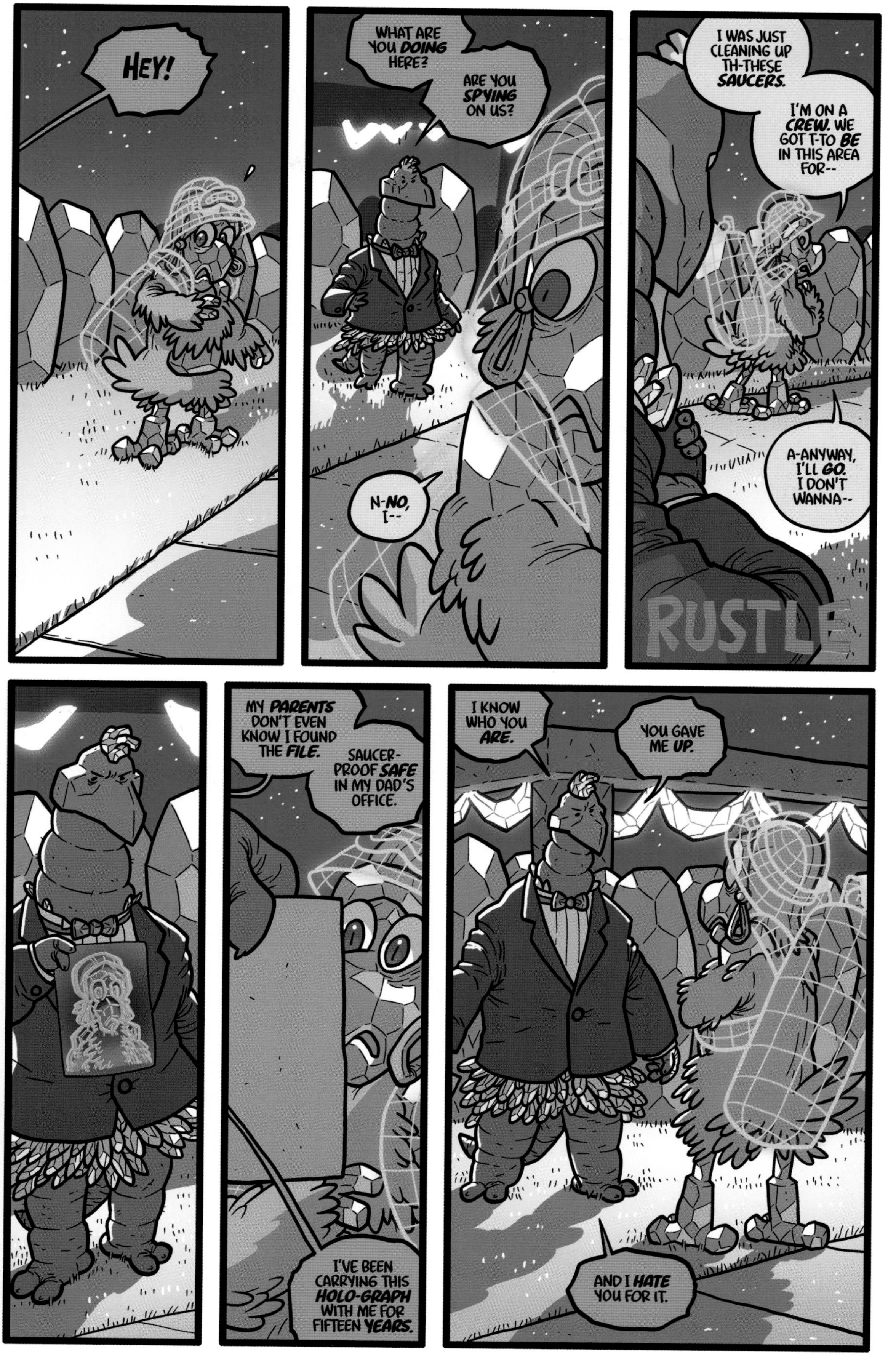
HEY!
WHAT ARE YOU *DOING* HERE?
ARE YOU *SPYING* ON US?
N-*NO*, I--
I WAS JUST CLEANING UP TH-THESE *SAUCERS*.
I'M ON A *CREW*. WE GOT T-TO *BE* IN THIS AREA FOR--
A-ANYWAY, I'LL *GO*. I DON'T WANNA--
RUSTLE
MY *PARENTS* DON'T EVEN KNOW I FOUND THE *FILE*.
SAUCER-PROOF *SAFE* IN MY DAD'S OFFICE.
I'VE BEEN CARRYING THIS *HOLO-GRAPH* WITH ME FOR FIFTEEN *YEARS*.
I KNOW WHO YOU *ARE*.
YOU GAVE ME *UP*.
AND I *HATE* YOU FOR IT.

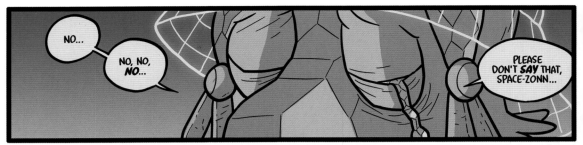

NO...

NO, NO, *NO*...

PLEASE DON'T *SAY* THAT, SPACE-ZONN...

THAT'S NOT MY *NAME!* WHAT KIND OF NAME *IS* THAT??

THIS IS WHAT I'M *TALKING* ABOUT.

THIS IS WHAT *YOU* PUT IN ME.

THIS *COLOR.* THIS *BODY.* *RADIATION BREATH.*

THIS COLLECTION OF REASONS THAT GIRLS *LAUGHED* WHEN I ASKED THEM ON A DATE. WHY IT TOOK ME *YEARS* TO GET A DECENT JOB.

"ARE YOU SURE YOU WANT TO *WORK* HERE? YOU MIGHT KNOCK THE *BUILDING* DOWN."

HA HA.

OH MY GOJ, TH-THEY *SAID* THAT..?

OF *COURSE* THEY DID!! THEY SAID IT ALL THE GOD DAMNED *TIME!!*

B-BUT...

H-HOW *CAN* THEY?

LOOK AT YOU.

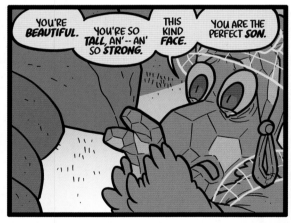

YOU'RE *BEAUTIFUL.*

YOU'RE SO *TALL,* AN'-- AN' SO *STRONG.*

THIS KIND *FACE.*

YOU ARE THE PERFECT *SON.*

JUST HOW YOU *ARE.*

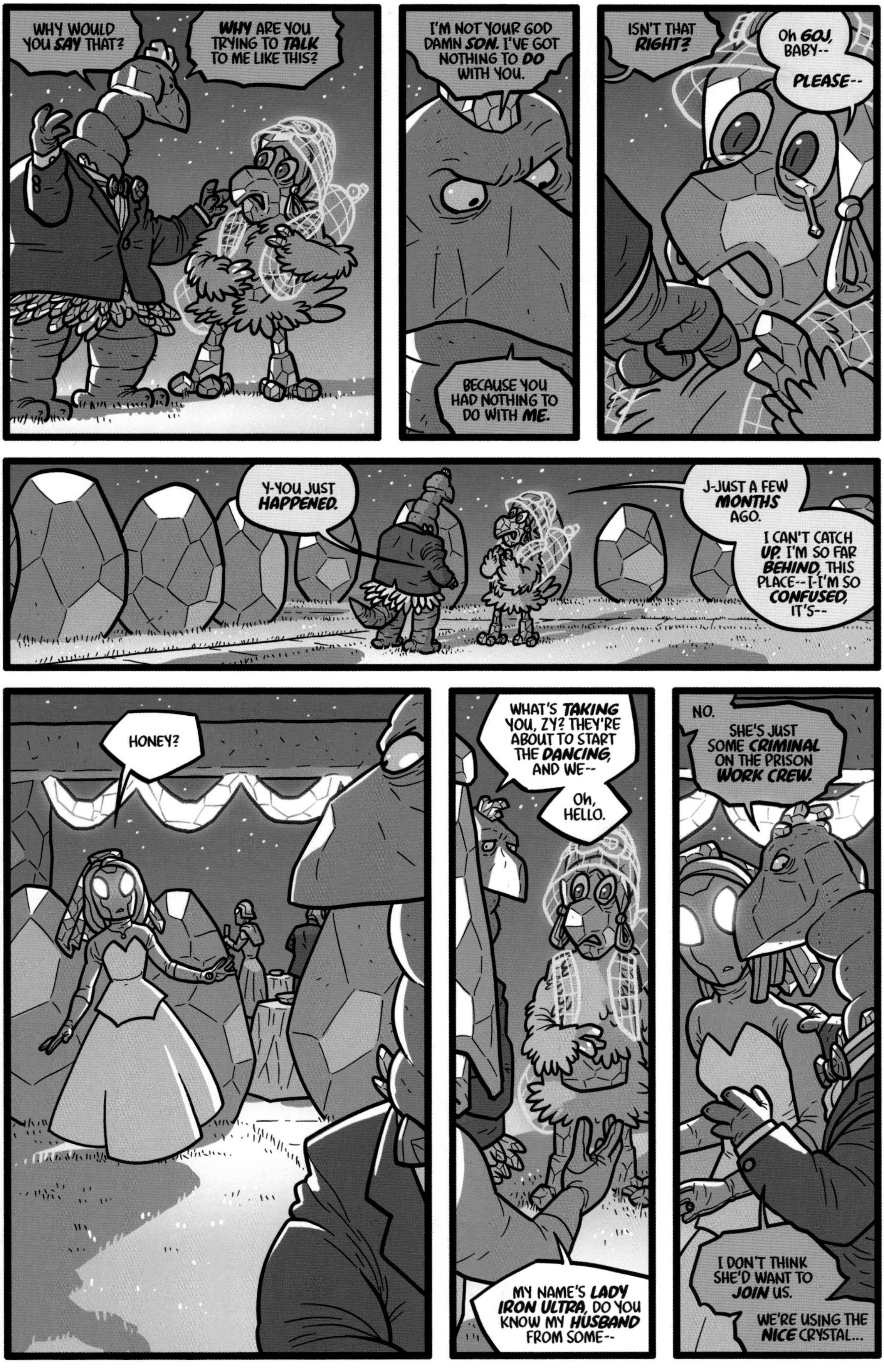
WHY WOULD YOU SAY THAT?
WHY ARE YOU TRYING TO TALK TO ME LIKE THIS?
I'M NOT YOUR GOD DAMN SON. I'VE GOT NOTHING TO DO WITH YOU.
BECAUSE YOU HAD NOTHING TO DO WITH ME.
ISN'T THAT RIGHT?
Oh GOJ, BABY--
PLEASE--
Y-YOU JUST HAPPENED.
J-JUST A FEW MONTHS AGO.
I CAN'T CATCH UP. I'M SO FAR BEHIND, THIS PLACE--I-I'M SO CONFUSED, IT'S--
HONEY?
WHAT'S TAKING YOU, ZY? THEY'RE ABOUT TO START THE DANCING, AND WE--
Oh, HELLO.
MY NAME'S LADY IRON ULTRA, DO YOU KNOW MY HUSBAND FROM SOME--
NO.
SHE'S JUST SOME CRIMINAL ON THE PRISON WORK CREW.
I DON'T THINK SHE'D WANT TO JOIN US.
WE'RE USING THE NICE CRYSTAL...

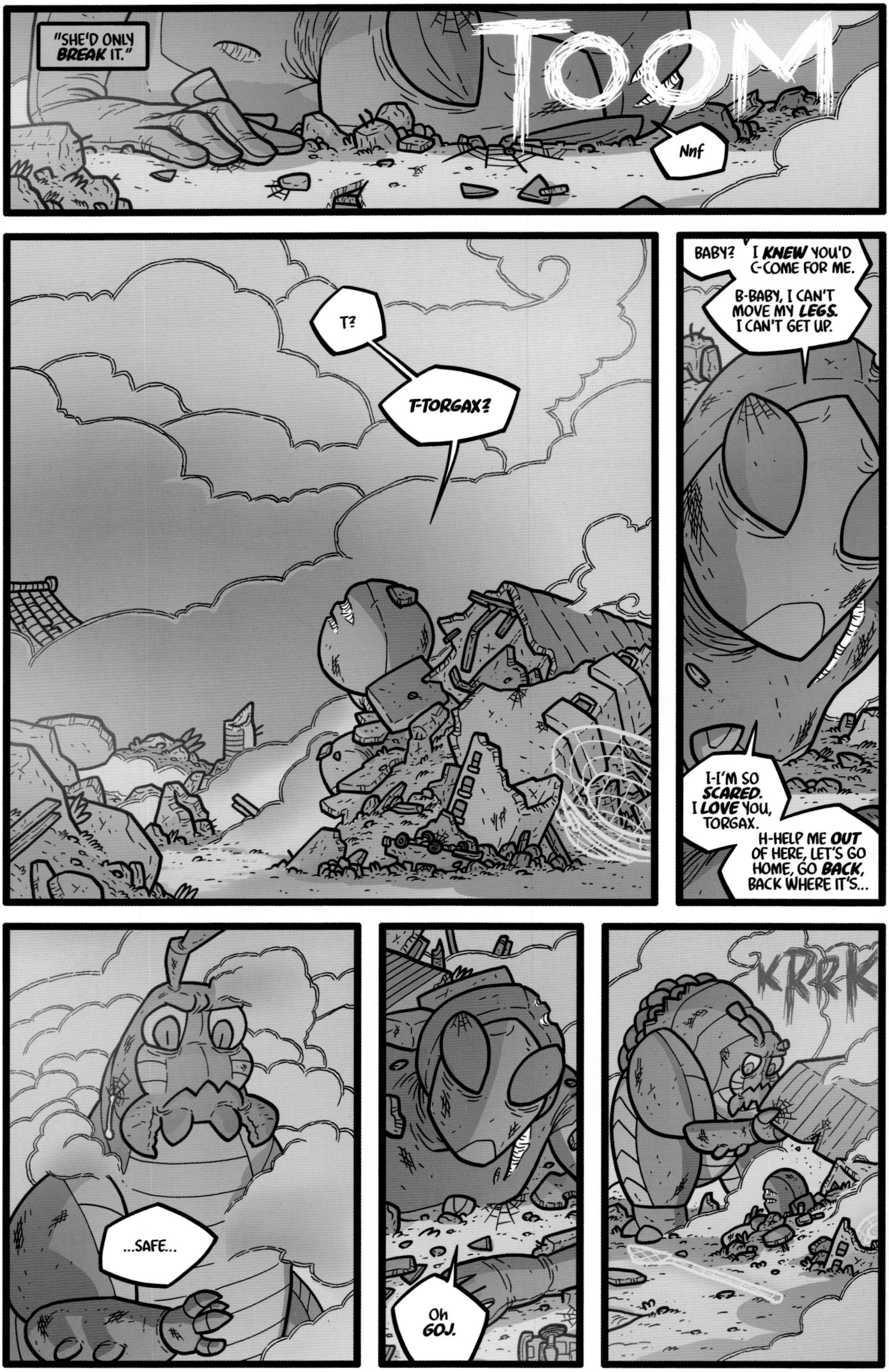
"SHE'D ONLY BREAK IT."
TOOM
Nnf
T?
T-TORGAX?
BABY?
I KNEW YOU'D C-COME FOR ME.
B-BABY, I CAN'T MOVE MY LEGS. I CAN'T GET UP.
I-I'M SO SCARED. I LOVE YOU, TORGAX.
H-HELP ME OUT OF HERE, LET'S GO HOME, GO BACK, BACK WHERE IT'S...
...SAFE...
Oh GOJ.
KRRK

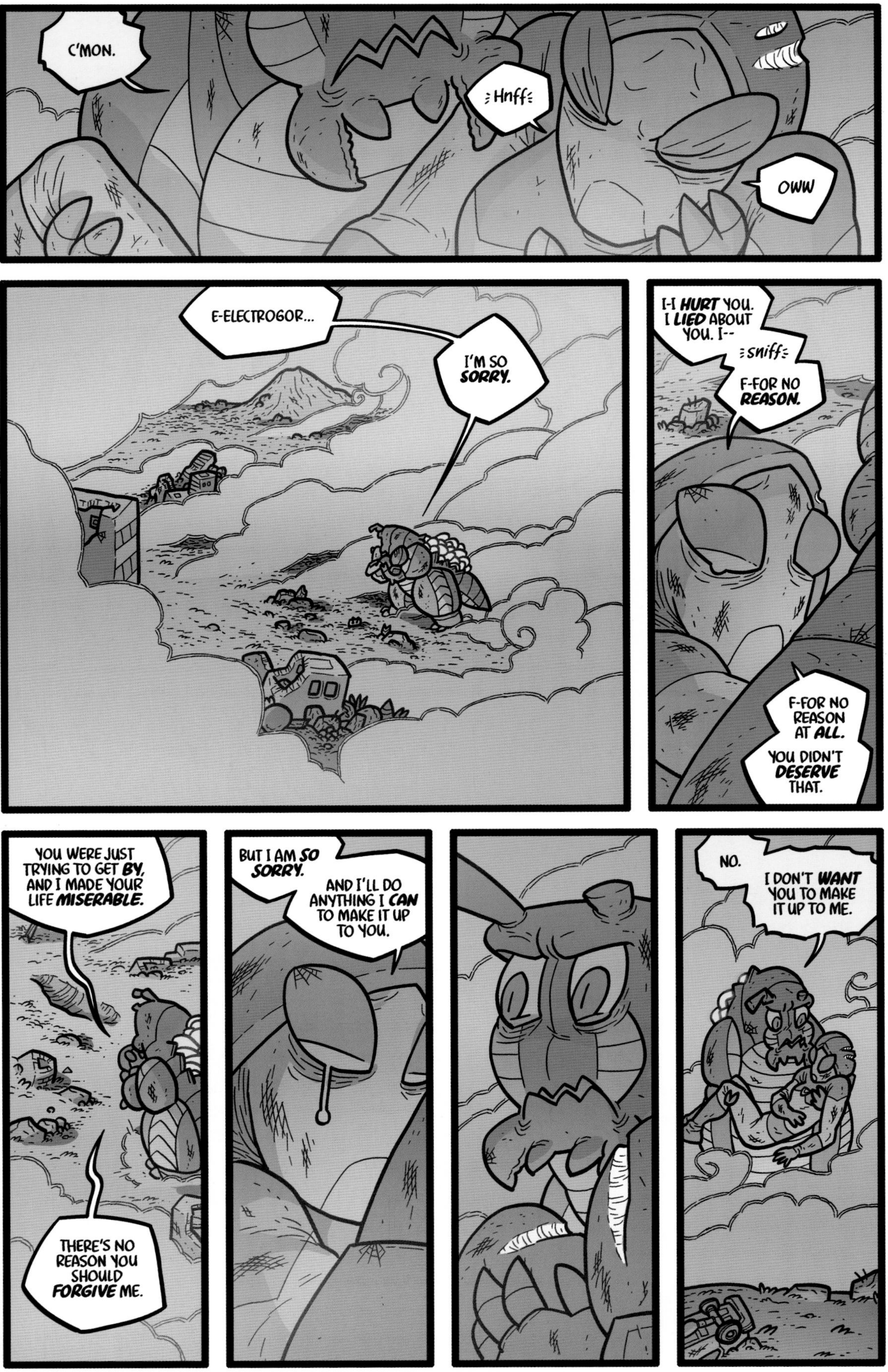
C'MON.
Hnff
OWW
E-ELECTROGOR...
I'M SO SORRY.
I-I HURT YOU. I LIED ABOUT YOU. I--
sniff
F-FOR NO REASON.
F-FOR NO REASON AT ALL.
YOU DIDN'T DESERVE THAT.
YOU WERE JUST TRYING TO GET BY, AND I MADE YOUR LIFE MISERABLE.
THERE'S NO REASON YOU SHOULD FORGIVE ME.
BUT I AM SO SORRY.
AND I'LL DO ANYTHING I CAN TO MAKE IT UP TO YOU.
NO.
I DON'T WANT YOU TO MAKE IT UP TO ME.

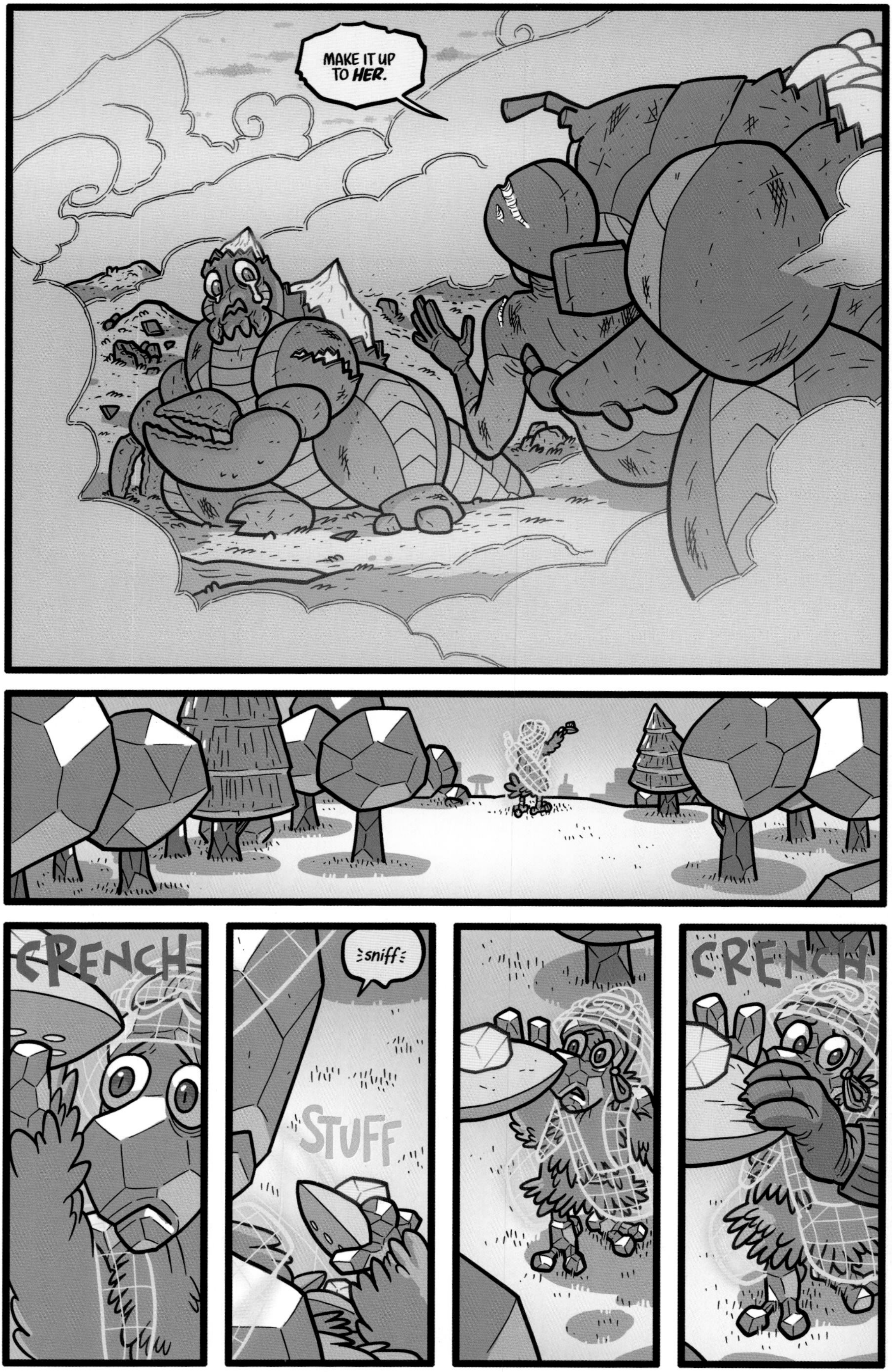
MAKE IT UP TO HER.
CRENCH
sniff
STUFF
CRENCH

LOOKS LIKE YOU'RE ALMOST *DONE*.

B-BABY? *SPACE-ZONN*--?

SORRY, I-I MEAN, *ZYNA-SEVEN?*

HI.

YOU CAN CALL ME *SPACE-ZONN* IF YOU LIKE.

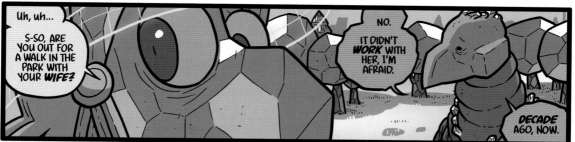

Uh, uh...

S-SO, ARE YOU OUT FOR A WALK IN THE PARK WITH YOUR *WIFE?*

NO.

IT DIDN'T *WORK* WITH HER, I'M AFRAID.

DECADE AGO, NOW.

D-DECADE?

I WORKED FOR HER DAD'S *COMPANY* STARTING THE MOMENT WE GOT *MARRIED*.

AND I *NEVER* MOVED UP, NOT *ONE* PROMOTION.

NOT A GOOD FIT, *CULTURE-WISE*, HE SAID.

GOOD *WORKER*, THOUGH. "PERFECT IN MY *ROLE*."

SHE SAID IT DIDN'T *MATTER*.

SHE SAID SHE *LOVED* ME, SAID WE DIDN'T *NEED* ANY MORE MONEY.

BUT AT THE END OF THE *DAY*, I DIDN'T FEEL *LOVED* AT *ALL*.

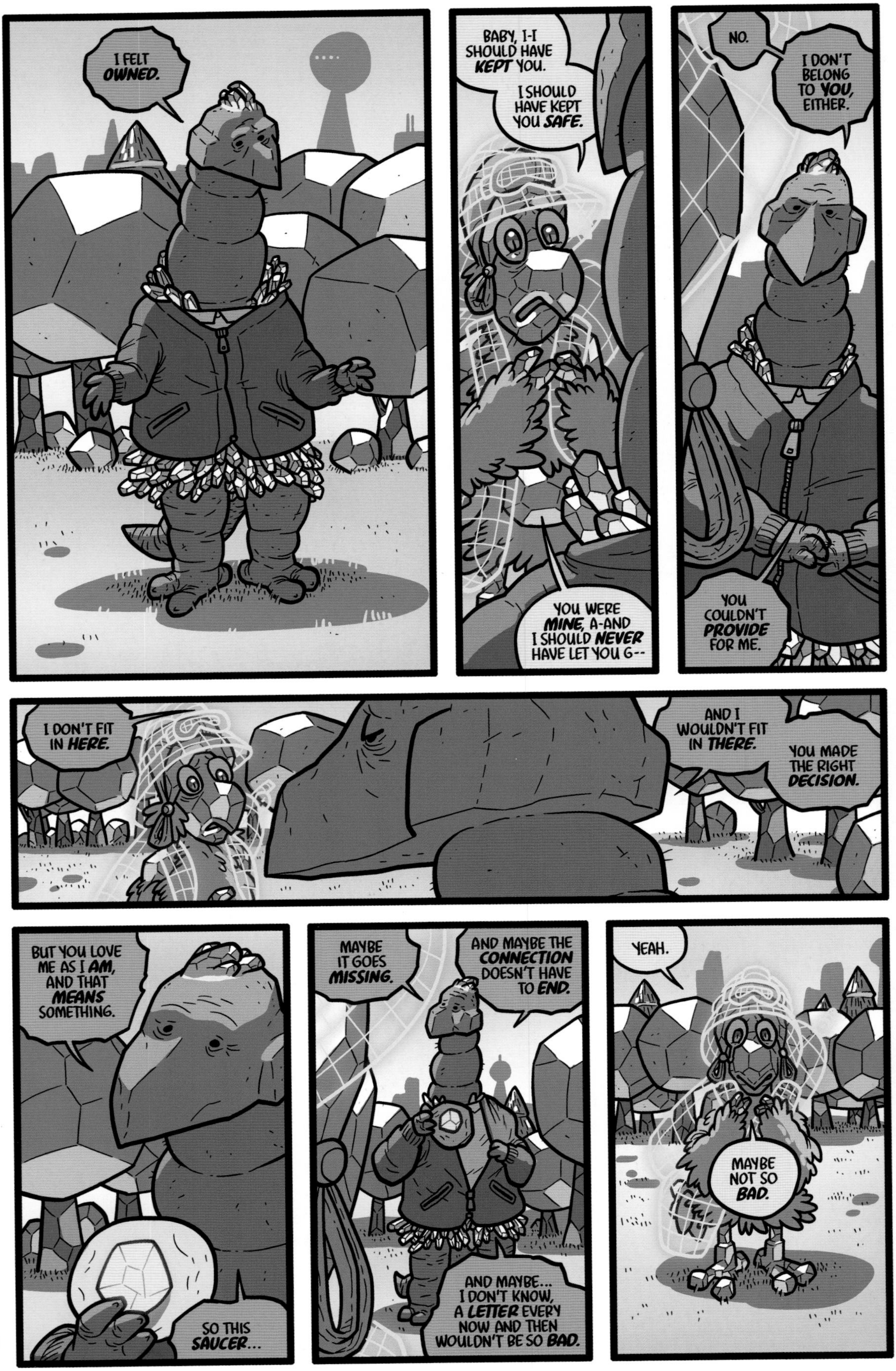

I FELT **OWNED.**
...
BABY, I-I SHOULD HAVE **KEPT** YOU.
I SHOULD HAVE KEPT YOU **SAFE.**
YOU WERE **MINE,** A-AND I SHOULD **NEVER** HAVE LET YOU G--
NO.
I DON'T BELONG TO **YOU,** EITHER.
YOU COULDN'T **PROVIDE** FOR ME.
I DON'T FIT IN **HERE.**
AND I WOULDN'T FIT IN **THERE.**
YOU MADE THE RIGHT **DECISION.**
BUT YOU LOVE ME AS I **AM,** AND THAT **MEANS** SOMETHING.
SO THIS **SAUCER...**
MAYBE IT GOES **MISSING.**
AND MAYBE THE **CONNECTION** DOESN'T HAVE TO **END.**
AND MAYBE... I DON'T KNOW, A **LETTER** EVERY NOW AND THEN WOULDN'T BE SO **BAD.**
YEAH.
MAYBE NOT SO **BAD.**

EPISODE 5

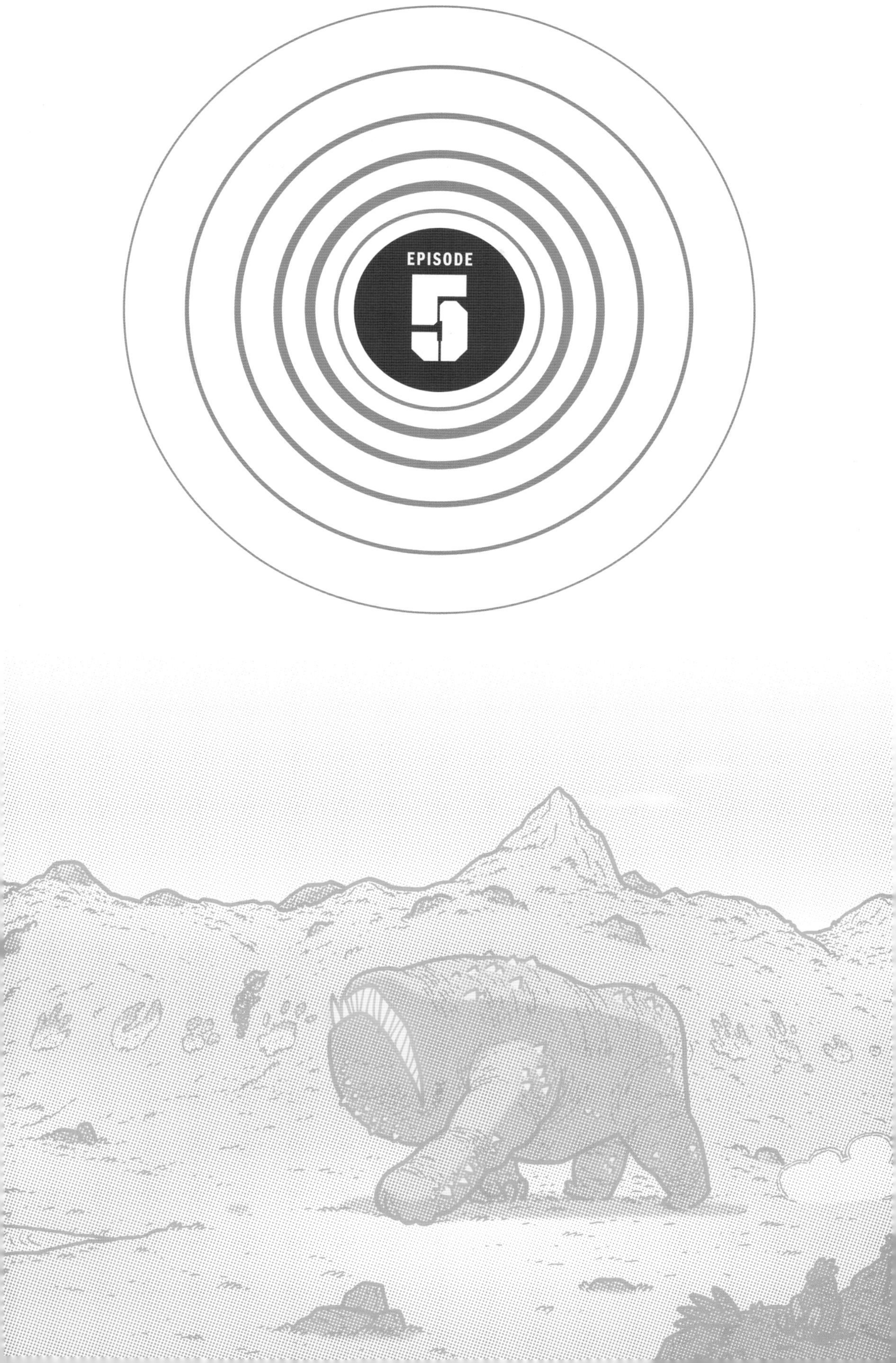

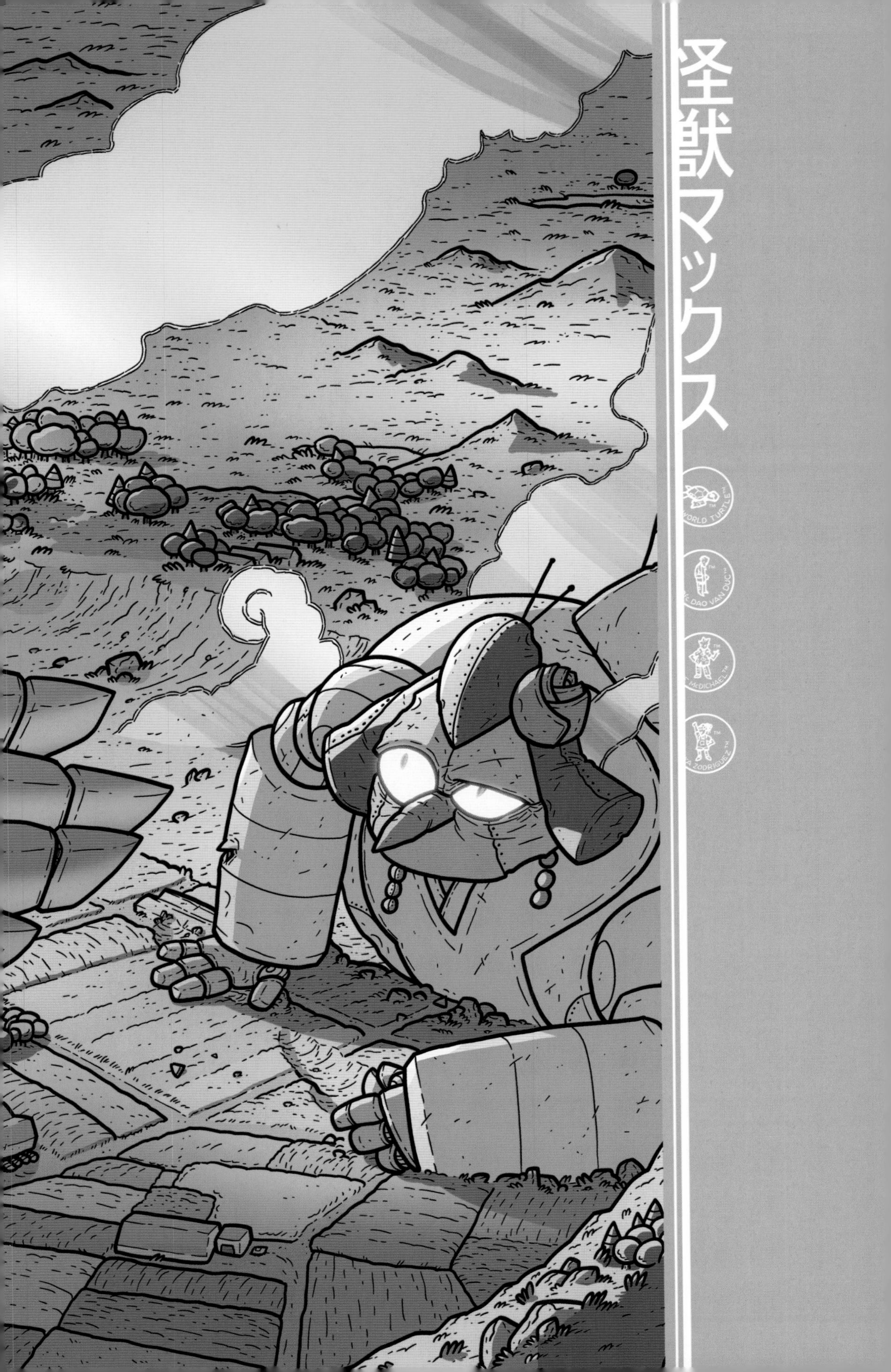

圣獣マックス
WORLD TURTLE™
DAO VAN DUC™
McDICHAEL™
ZODRIGUEZ™

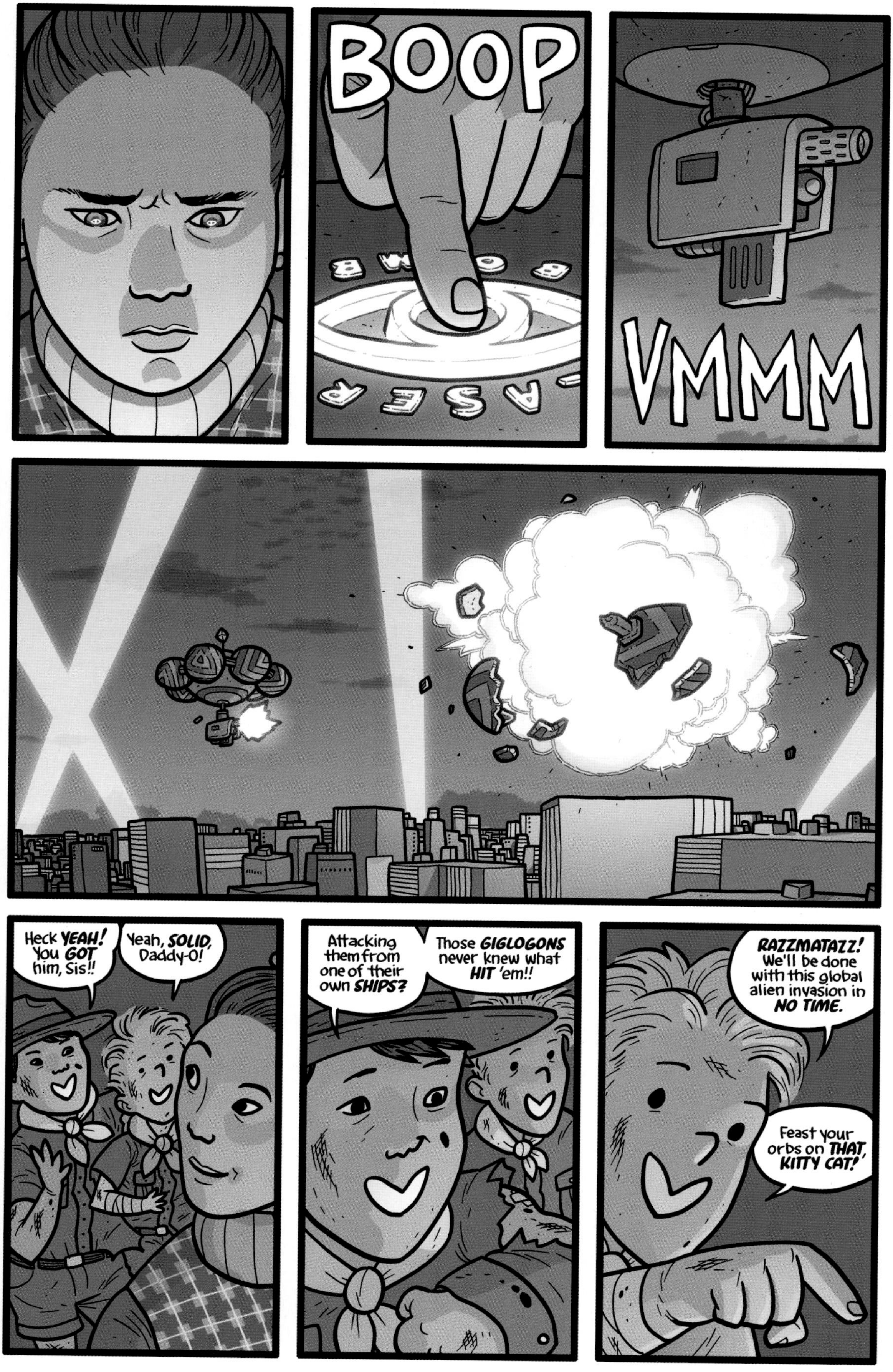

BOOP
VMMM
Heck **YEAH!** You **GOT** him, Sis!!
Yeah, **SOLID,** Daddy-O!
Attacking them from one of their own **SHIPS?**
Those **GIGLOGONS** never knew what **HIT** 'em!!
RAZZMATAZZ! We'll be done with this global alien invasion in **NO TIME.**
Feast your orbs on **THAT, KITTY CAT!**

With the *GHOST OF ZUGAIGO* on our side...

...we can't *LOSE!*

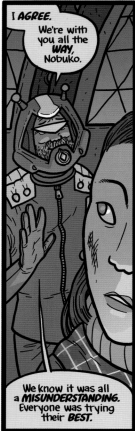

I AGREE. We're with you all the *WAY,* Nobuko.

We know it was all a *MISUNDERSTANDING.* Everyone was trying their *BEST.*

We *KNEW* it was going to come out all right in the *END.*

YEAH!

Isn't it *SIMPLE* once we decide to work *TOGETHER?*

Oh, *NOBU-CHAN.*

You can't know how *GOOD* it feels to hear you *SAY* that.

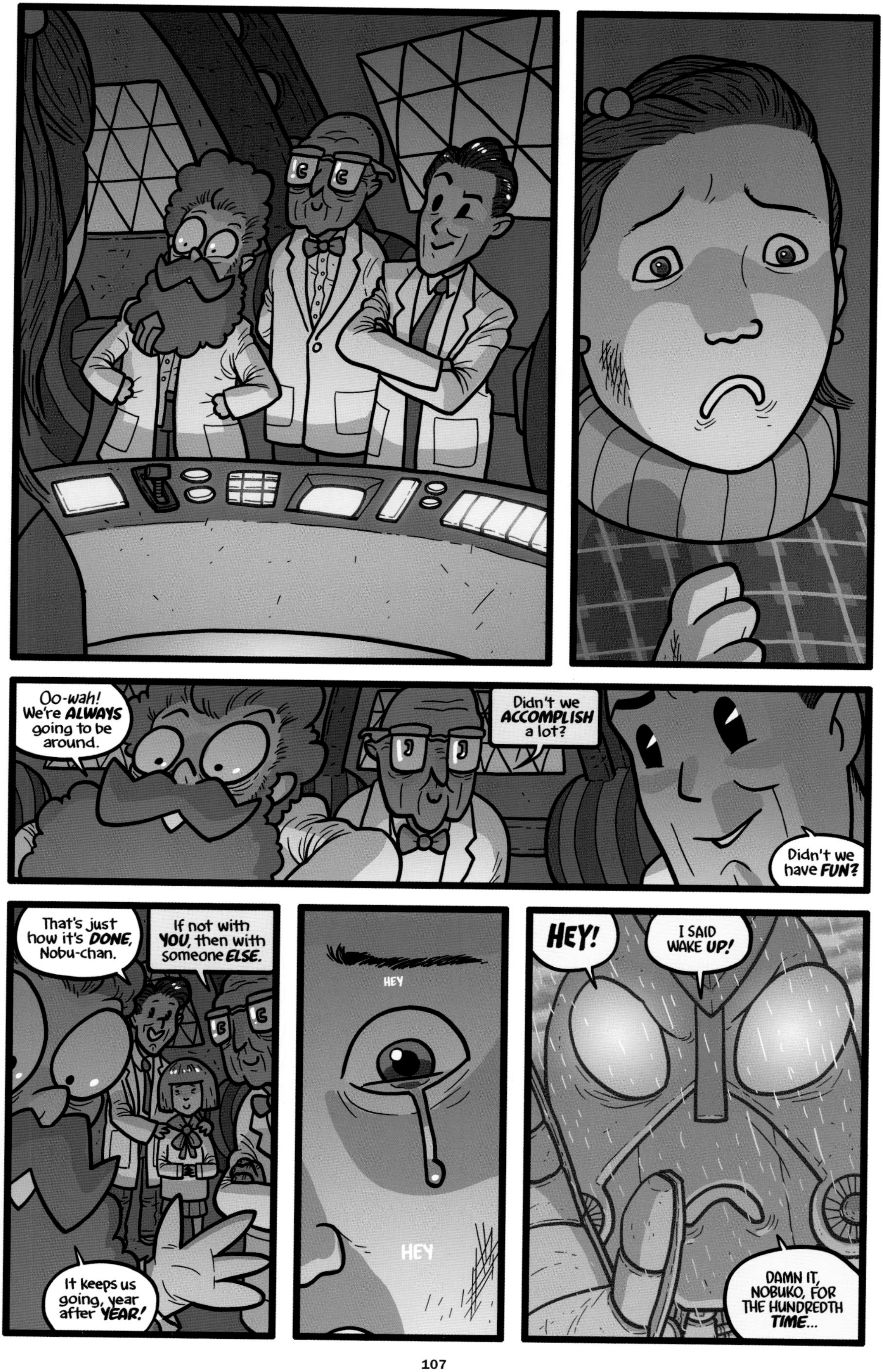
Oo-wah! We're **ALWAYS** going to be around.
Didn't we **ACCOMPLISH** a lot?
Didn't we have **FUN**?
That's just how it's **DONE**, Nobu-chan.
If not with **YOU**, then with someone **ELSE**.
It keeps us going, year after **YEAR!**
HEY
HEY
HEY!
I SAID WAKE **UP!**
DAMN IT, NOBUKO, FOR THE HUNDREDTH **TIME**...

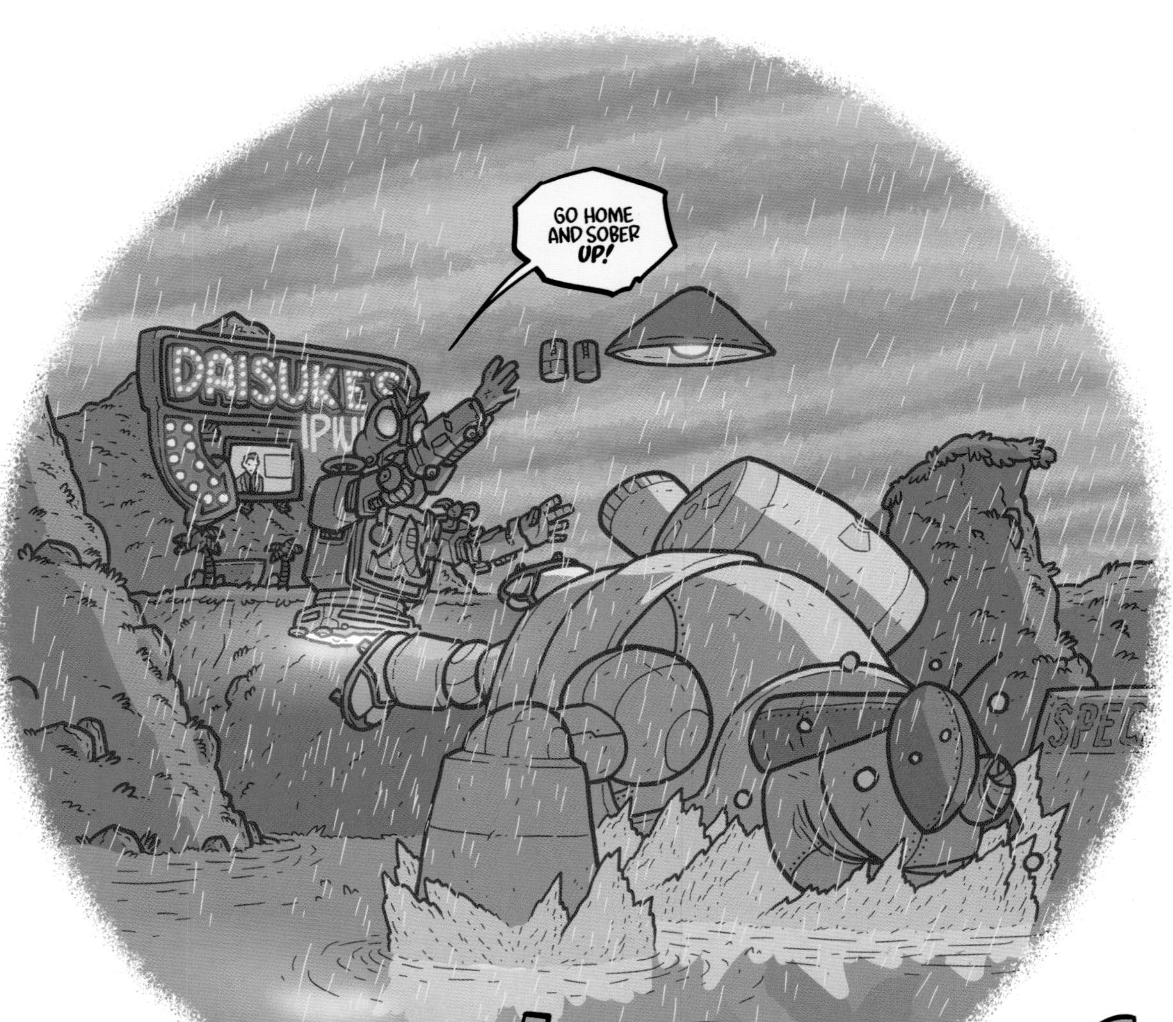
GO HOME AND SOBER UP!
DAISUKE'S
IPW
SPEC

IT NEVER ENDS

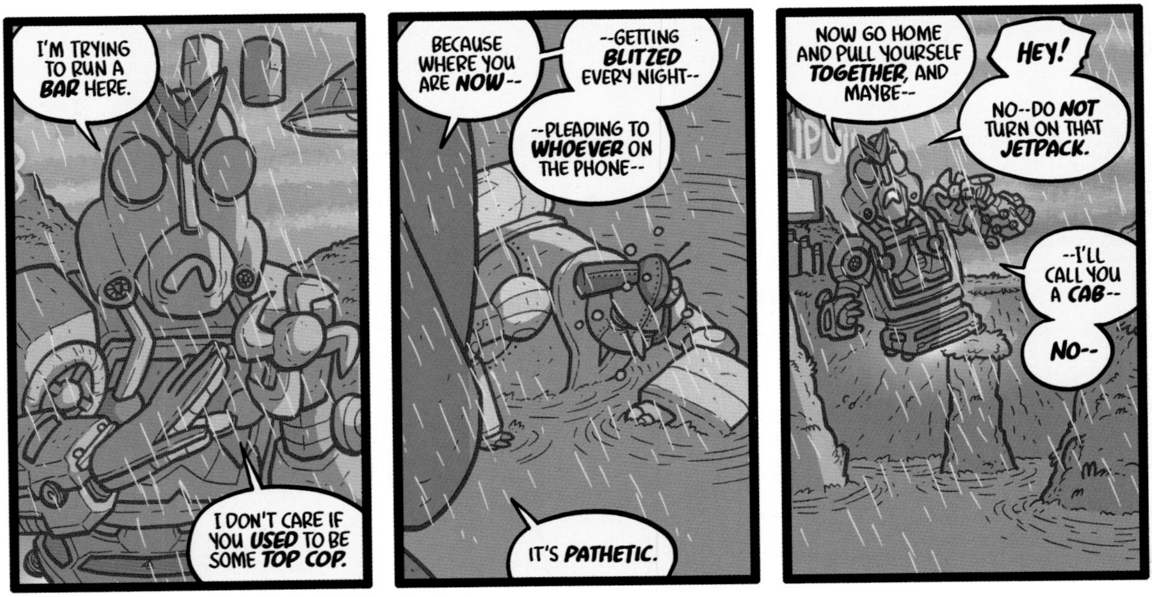
I'M TRYING TO RUN A BAR HERE.
I DON'T CARE IF YOU USED TO BE SOME TOP COP.
BECAUSE WHERE YOU ARE NOW--
--GETTING BLITZED EVERY NIGHT--
--PLEADING TO WHOEVER ON THE PHONE--
IT'S PATHETIC.
NOW GO HOME AND PULL YOURSELF TOGETHER, AND MAYBE--
HEY!
NO--DO NOT TURN ON THAT JETPACK.
--I'LL CALL YOU A CAB--
NO--

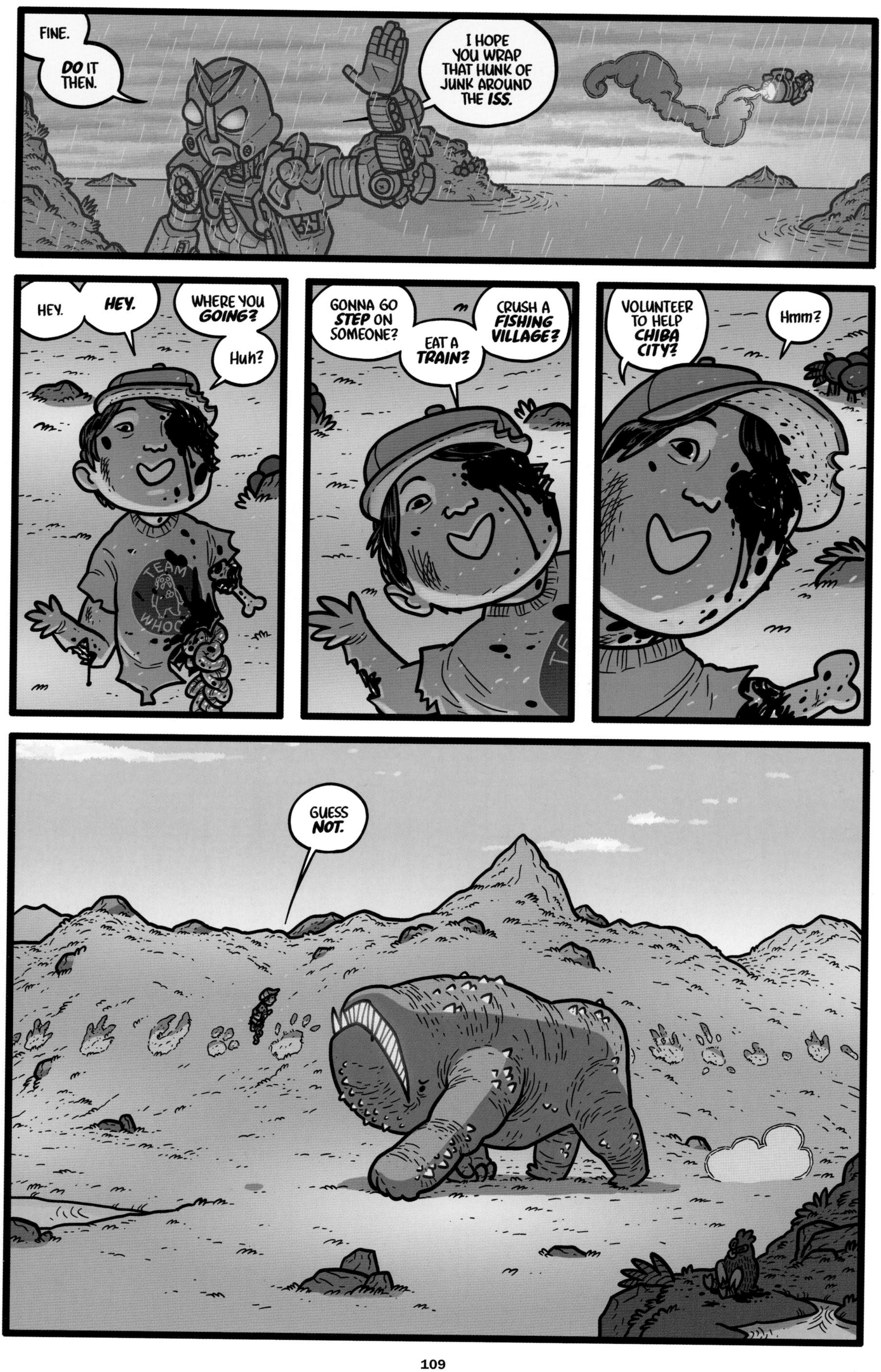
FINE. DO IT THEN.
I HOPE YOU WRAP THAT HUNK OF JUNK AROUND THE ISS.
HEY.
HEY.
WHERE YOU GOING?
Huh?
GONNA GO STEP ON SOMEONE?
EAT A TRAIN?
CRUSH A FISHING VILLAGE?
VOLUNTEER TO HELP CHIBA CITY?
Hmm?
GUESS NOT.
TEAM WHOO

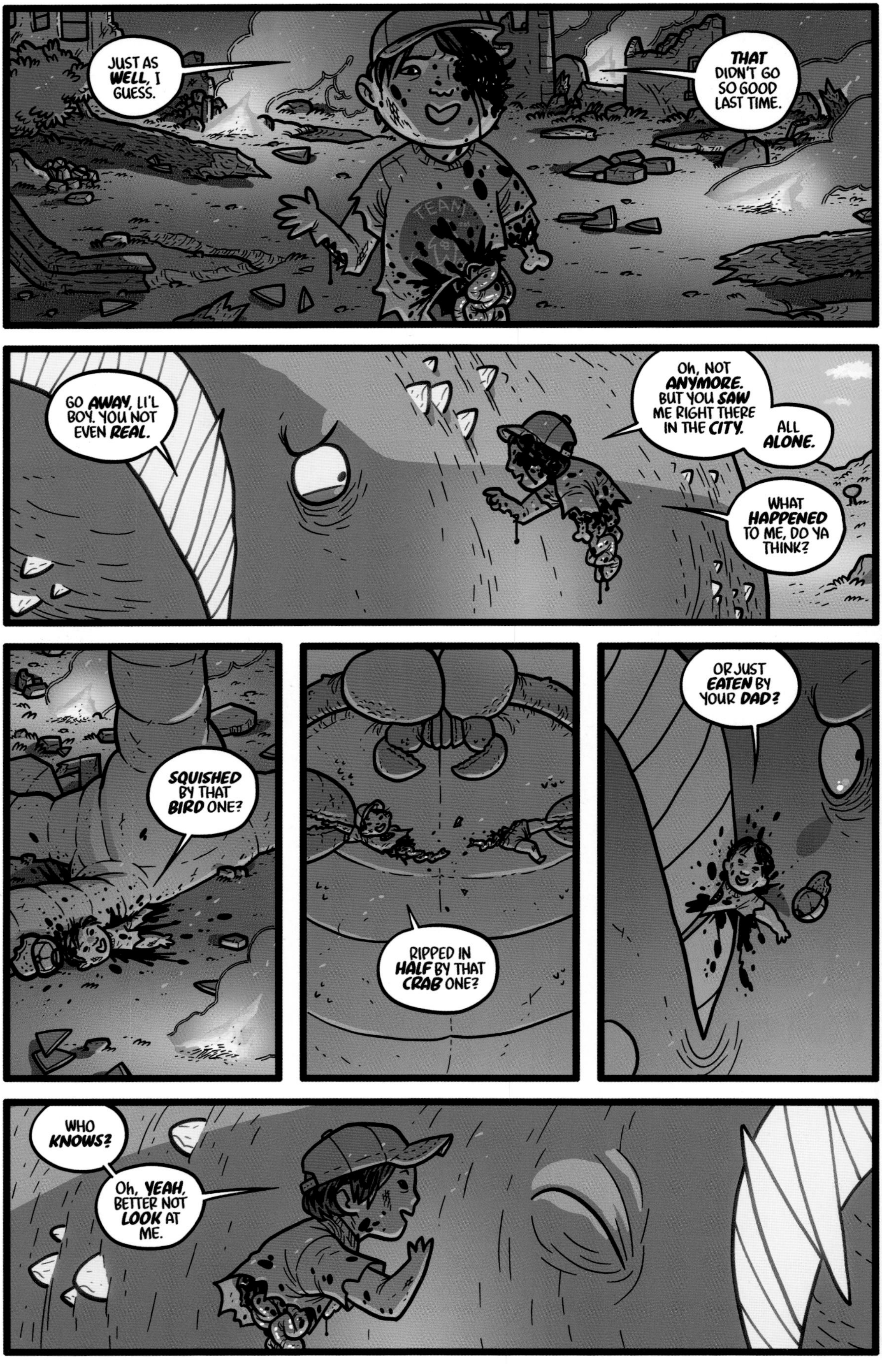
JUST AS WELL, I GUESS.
THAT DIDN'T GO SO GOOD LAST TIME.
GO AWAY, LI'L BOY. YOU NOT EVEN REAL.
Oh, NOT ANYMORE. BUT YOU SAW ME RIGHT THERE IN THE CITY.
ALL ALONE.
WHAT HAPPENED TO ME, DO YA THINK?
SQUISHED BY THAT BIRD ONE?
RIPPED IN HALF BY THAT CRAB ONE?
OR JUST EATEN BY YOUR DAD?
WHO KNOWS?
Oh, YEAH, BETTER NOT LOOK AT ME.

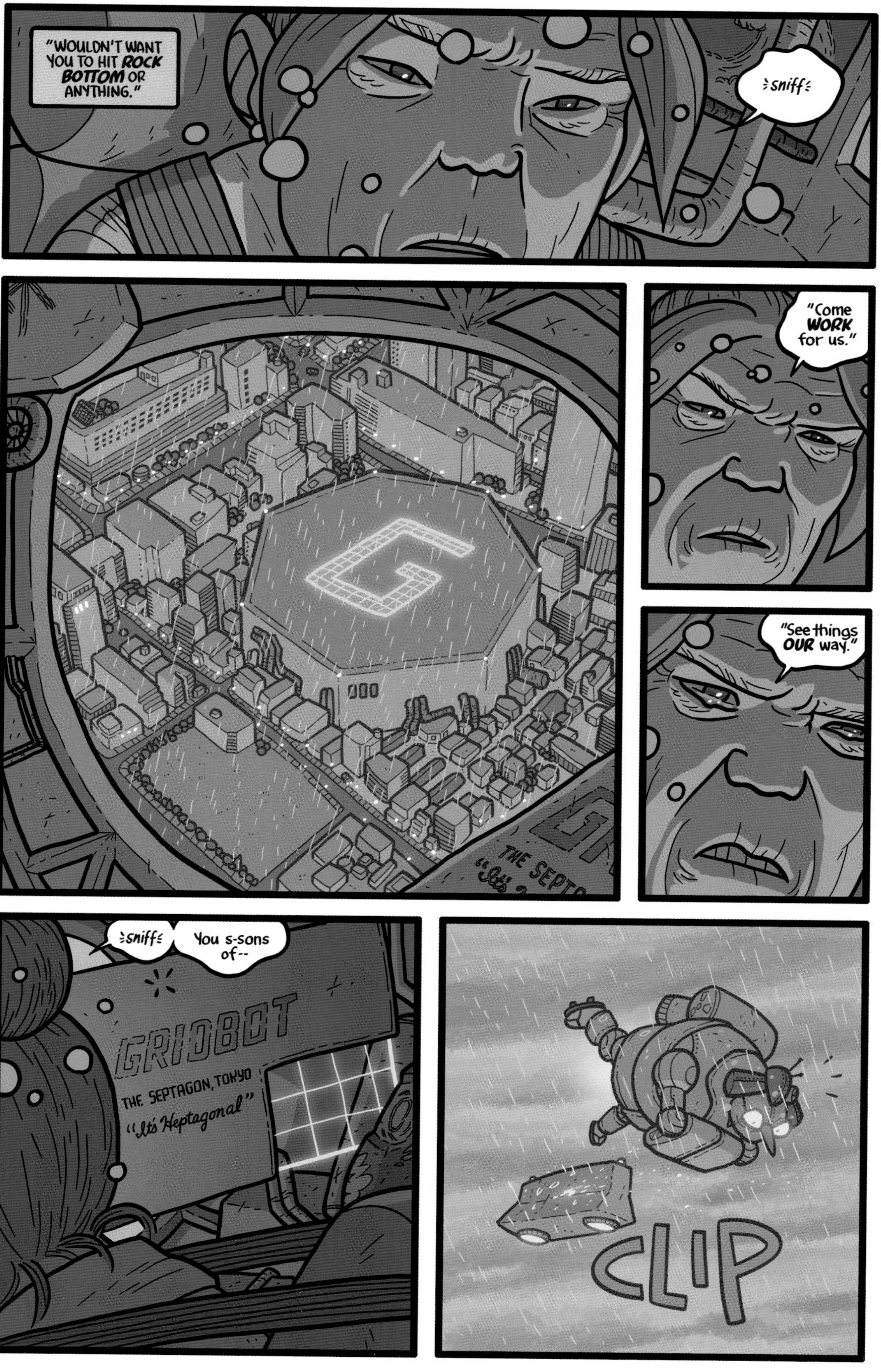
"WOULDN'T WANT YOU TO HIT ROCK BOTTOM OR ANYTHING."
sniff
"Come WORK for us."
"See things OUR way."
sniff
You s-sons of--
GRIDBOT
THE SEPTAGON, TOKYO
"It's Heptagonal"
CLIP

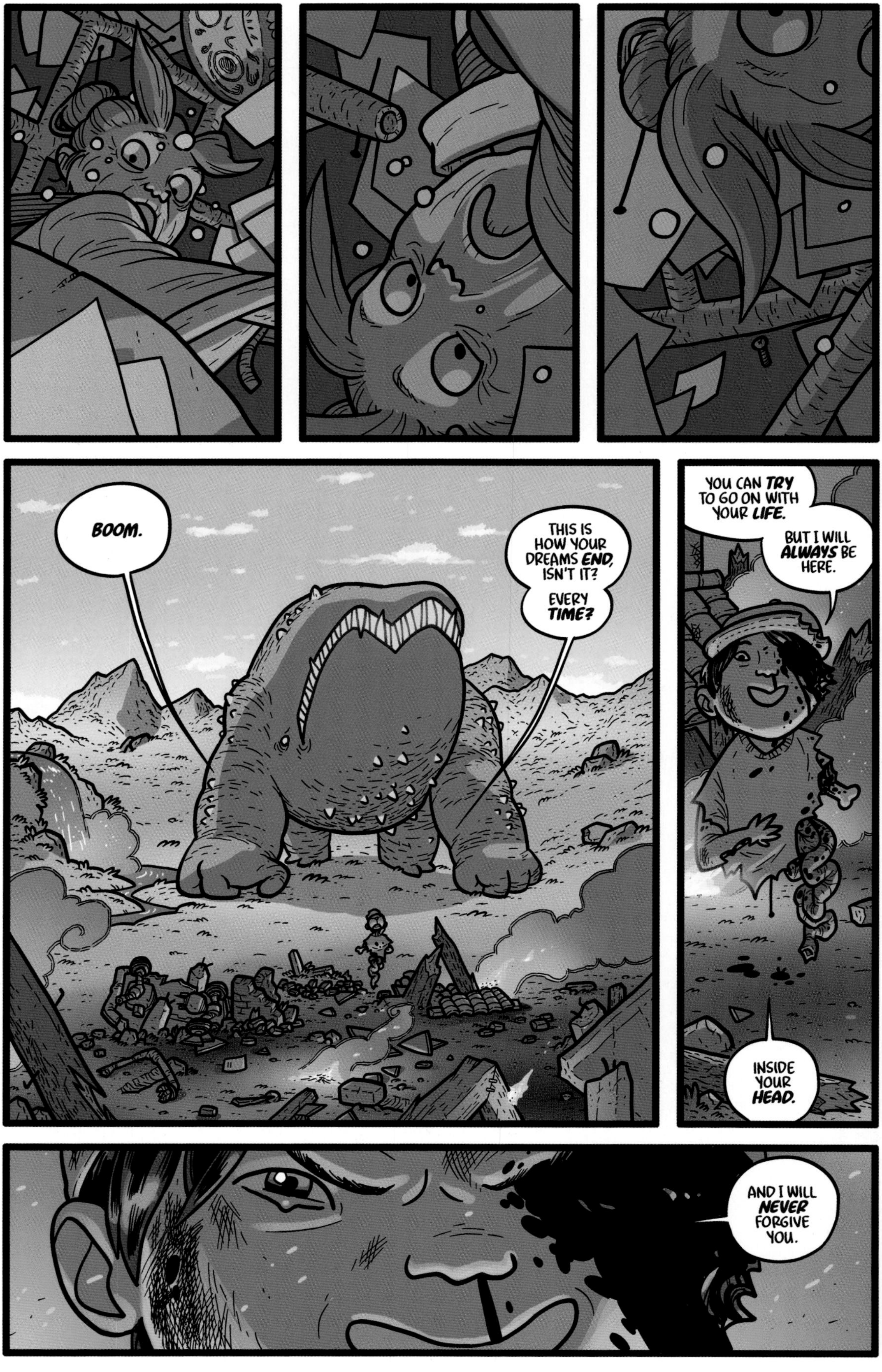
BOOM.
THIS IS HOW YOUR DREAMS END, ISN'T IT?
EVERY TIME?
YOU CAN TRY TO GO ON WITH YOUR LIFE.
BUT I WILL ALWAYS BE HERE.
INSIDE YOUR HEAD.
AND I WILL NEVER FORGIVE YOU.

Ohh, I KNOW WHO YOU'RE GOING TO SEE.
IT'S CUTE THAT YOU THINK YOU CAN RECONCILE WITH THEM.
THEY HATE YOUR GUTS.
VISITING
BESIDES...
WHO COULD EVER THINK THAT YOU HAD ANY GOOD IN YOU?
Hmm?
WELL, ANYWAY...
I'D BETTER GO.
"LET YOU HAVE YOUR STUPID LITTLE MEETING."

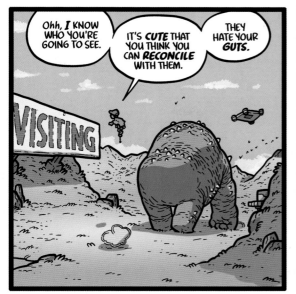

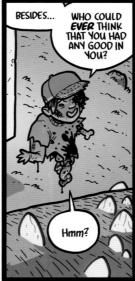

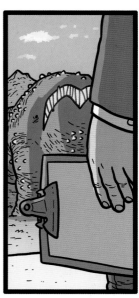

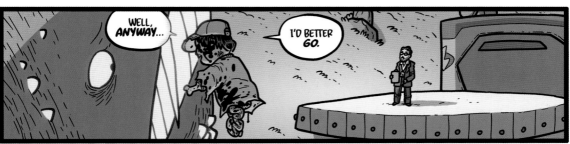

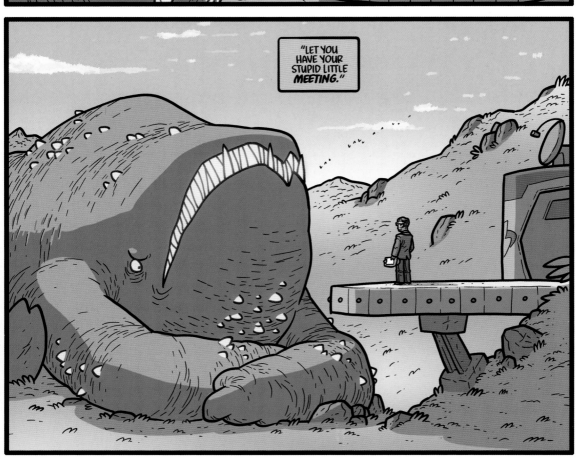

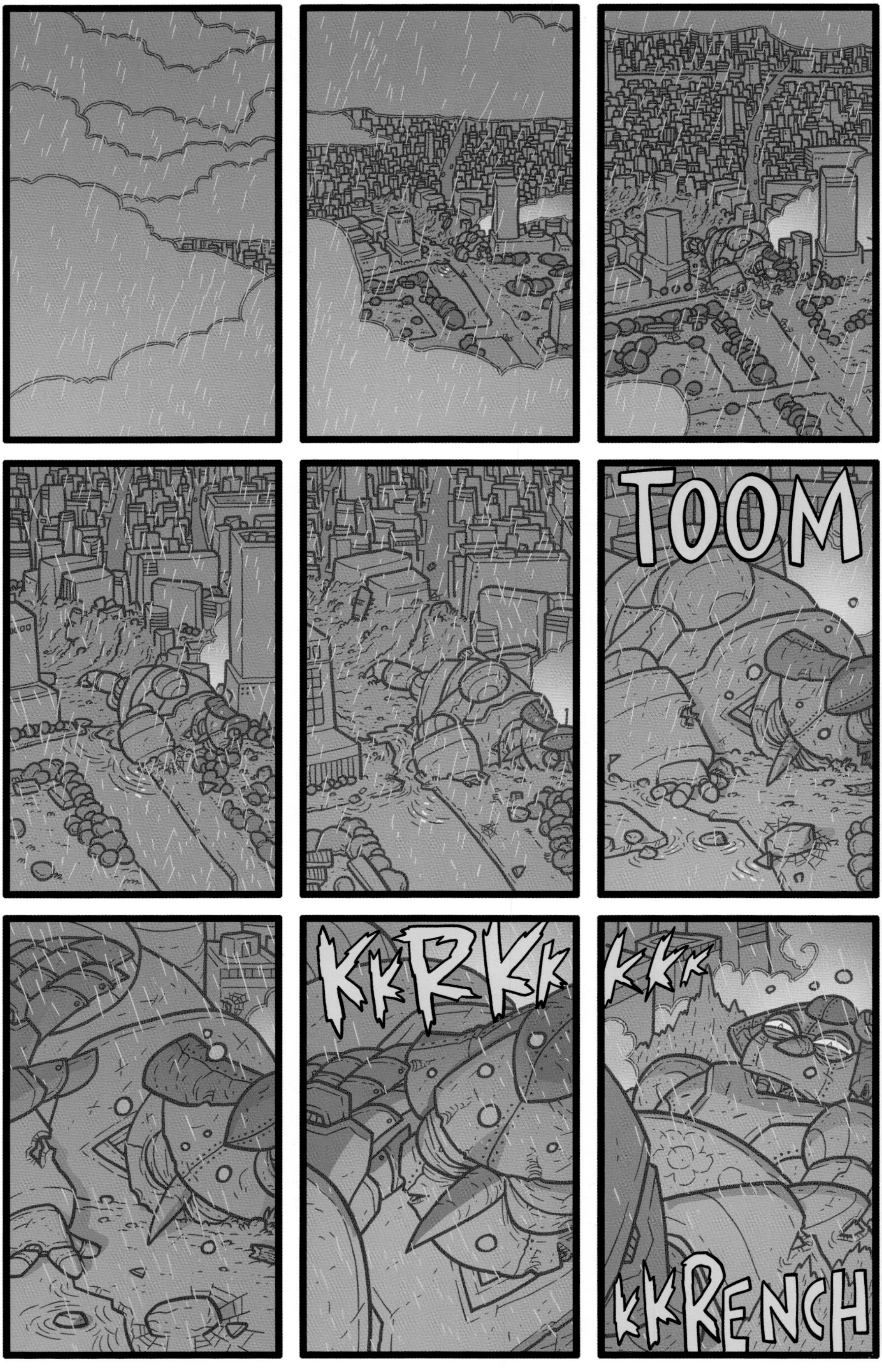
TOOM
KKRKK KKK
KKRENCH

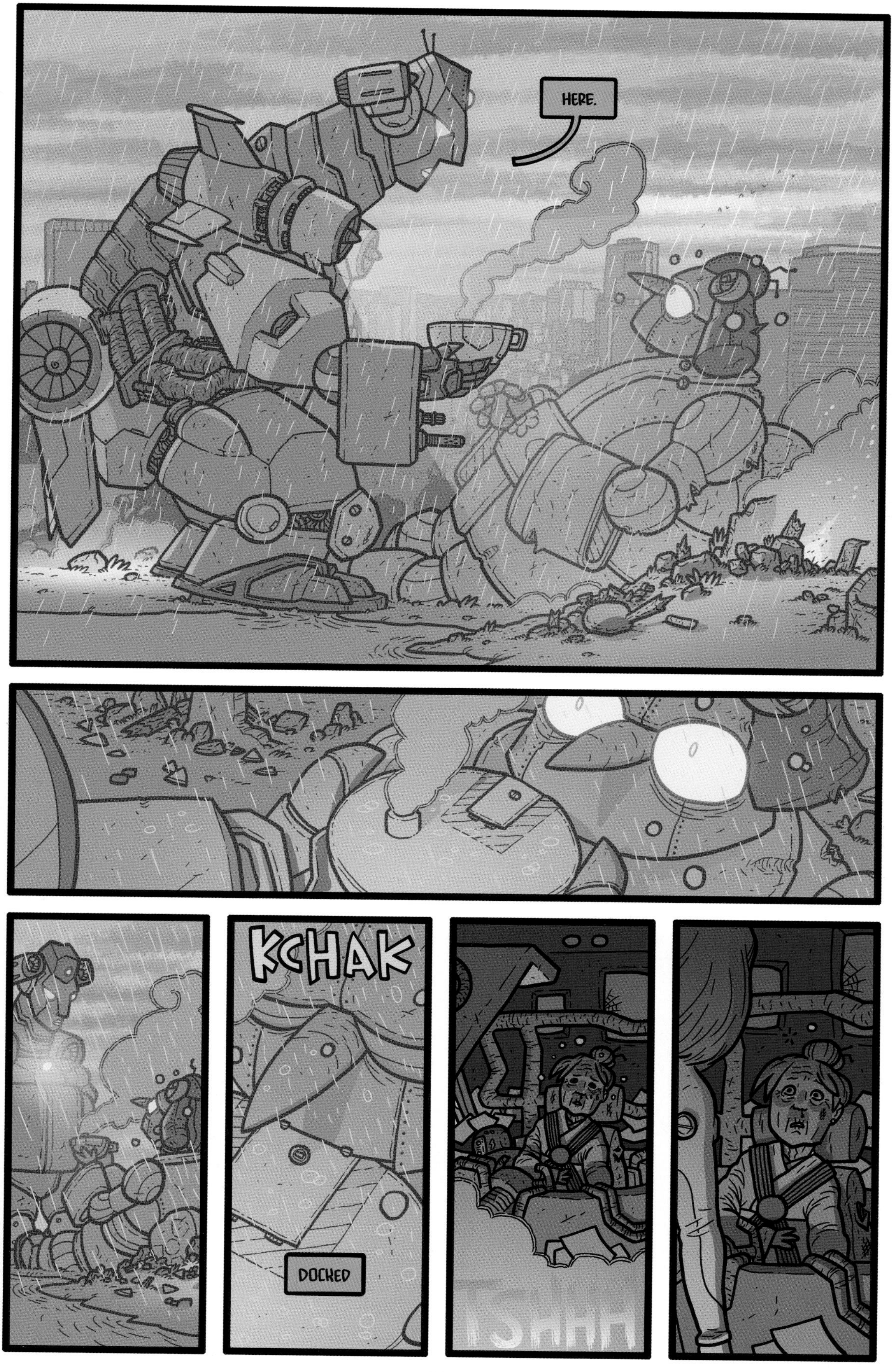
HERE.
KCHAK
DOCKED
TSHHH

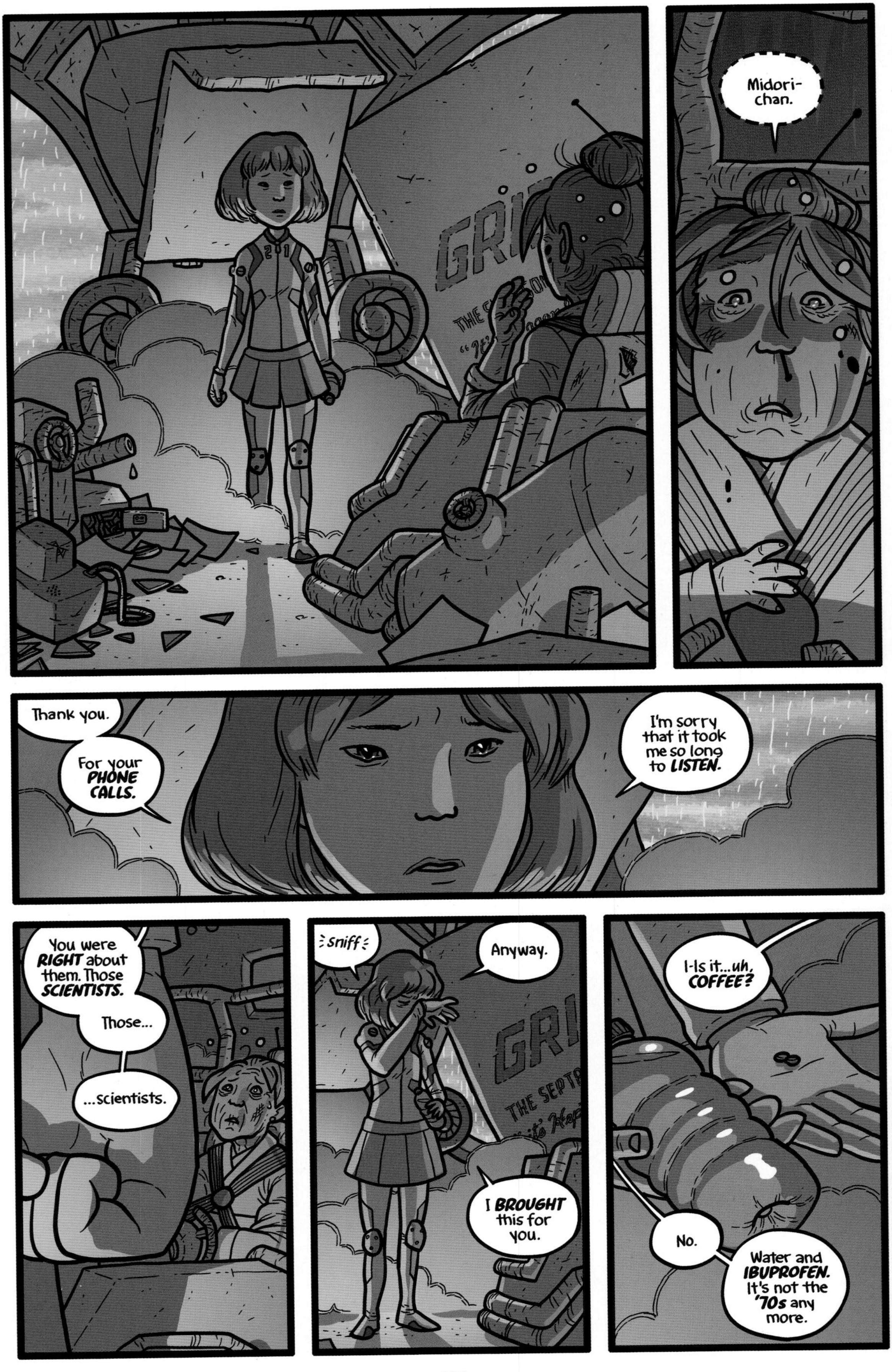
Midori-chan.
Thank you.
For your PHONE CALLS.
I'm sorry that it took me so long to LISTEN.
You were RIGHT about them. Those SCIENTISTS.
Those...
...scientists.
Sniff
Anyway.
I BROUGHT this for you.
I-Is it...uh, COFFEE?
No.
Water and IBUPROFEN. It's not the '70s any more.

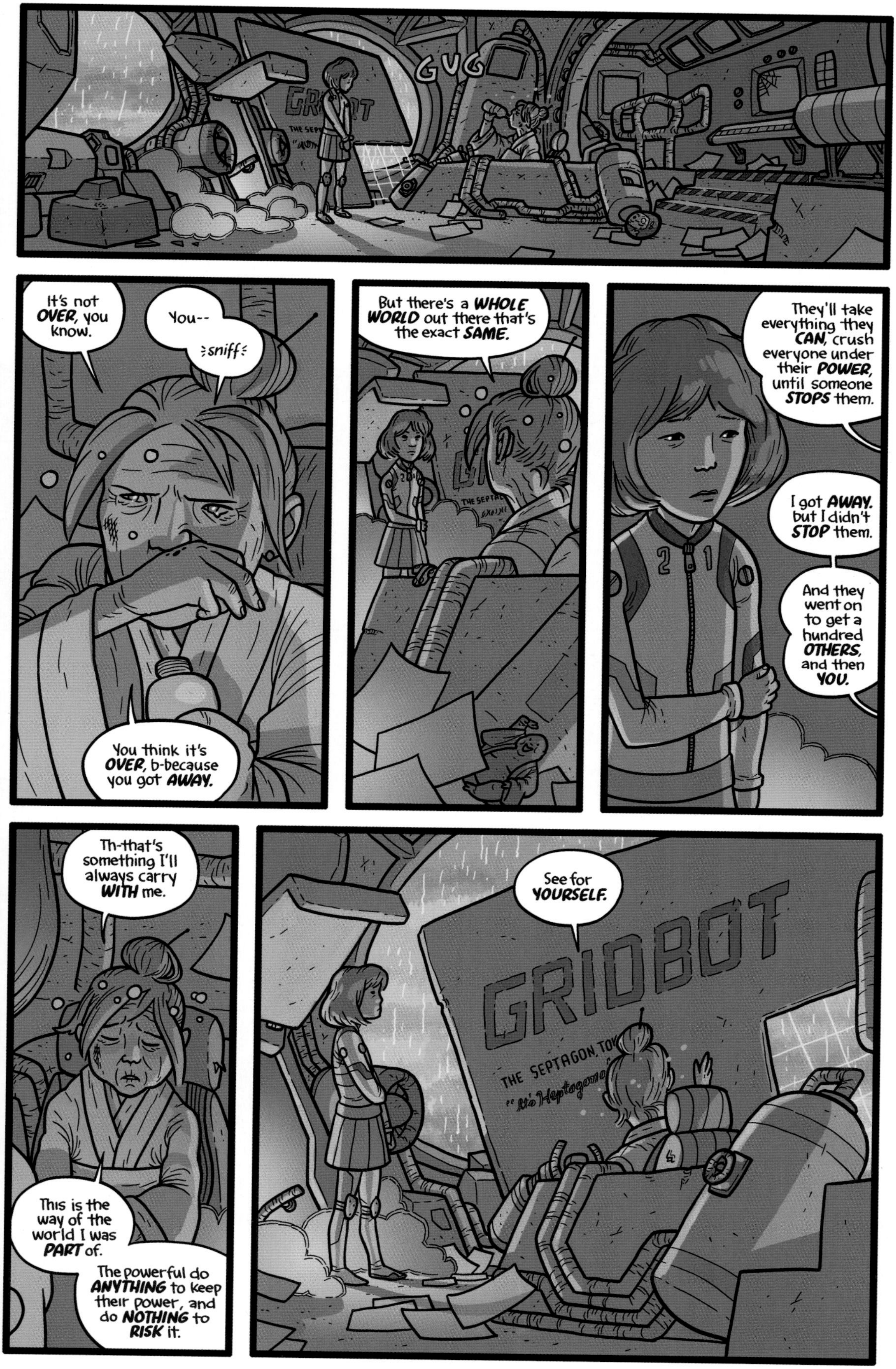
GUG
GRIDBOT
It's not OVER, you know.
You--
sniff
You think it's OVER, b-because you got AWAY.
But there's a WHOLE WORLD out there that's the exact SAME.
They'll take everything they CAN, crush everyone under their POWER, until someone STOPS them.
I got AWAY. but I didn't STOP them.
And they went on to get a hundred OTHERS, and then YOU.
Th-that's something I'll always carry WITH me.
This is the way of the world I was PART of.
The powerful do ANYTHING to keep their power, and do NOTHING to RISK it.
See for YOURSELF.
GRIDBOT
THE SEPTAGON, TOY
"It's Heptagonal"

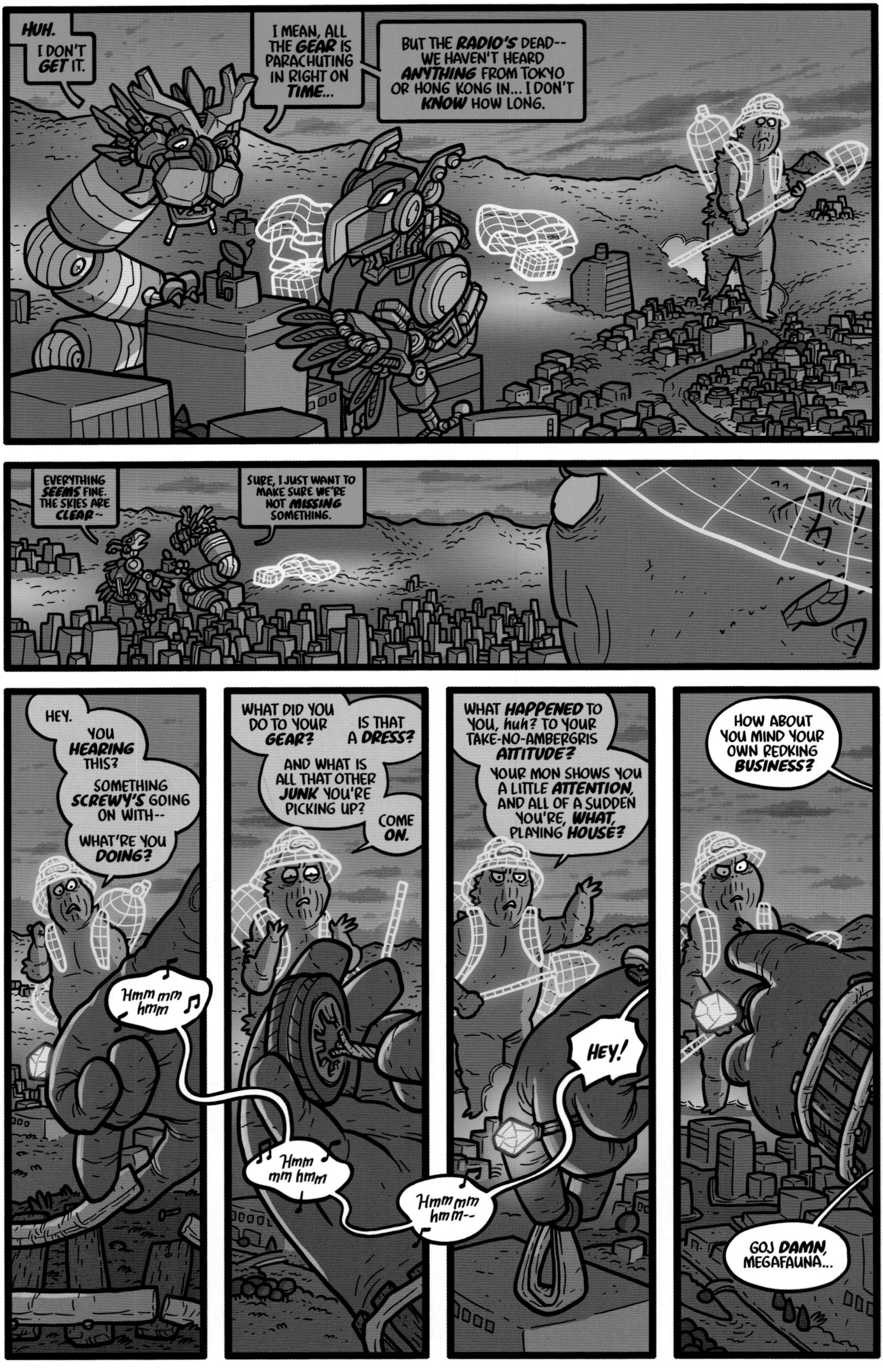
HUH.
I DON'T GET IT.
I MEAN, ALL THE GEAR IS PARACHUTING IN RIGHT ON TIME...
BUT THE RADIO'S DEAD-- WE HAVEN'T HEARD ANYTHING FROM TOKYO OR HONG KONG IN... I DON'T KNOW HOW LONG.
EVERYTHING SEEMS FINE. THE SKIES ARE CLEAR--
SURE, I JUST WANT TO MAKE SURE WE'RE NOT MISSING SOMETHING.
HEY.
YOU HEARING THIS?
SOMETHING SCREWY'S GOING ON WITH--
WHAT'RE YOU DOING?
Hmm mm hmm
WHAT DID YOU DO TO YOUR GEAR?
IS THAT A DRESS?
AND WHAT IS ALL THAT OTHER JUNK YOU'RE PICKING UP?
COME ON.
Hmm mm hmm
WHAT HAPPENED TO YOU, huh? TO YOUR TAKE-NO-AMBERGRIS ATTITUDE?
YOUR MON SHOWS YOU A LITTLE ATTENTION, AND ALL OF A SUDDEN YOU'RE, WHAT, PLAYING HOUSE?
HEY!
Hmm mm hmm--
HOW ABOUT YOU MIND YOUR OWN REDKING BUSINESS?
GOJ DAMN, MEGAFAUNA...

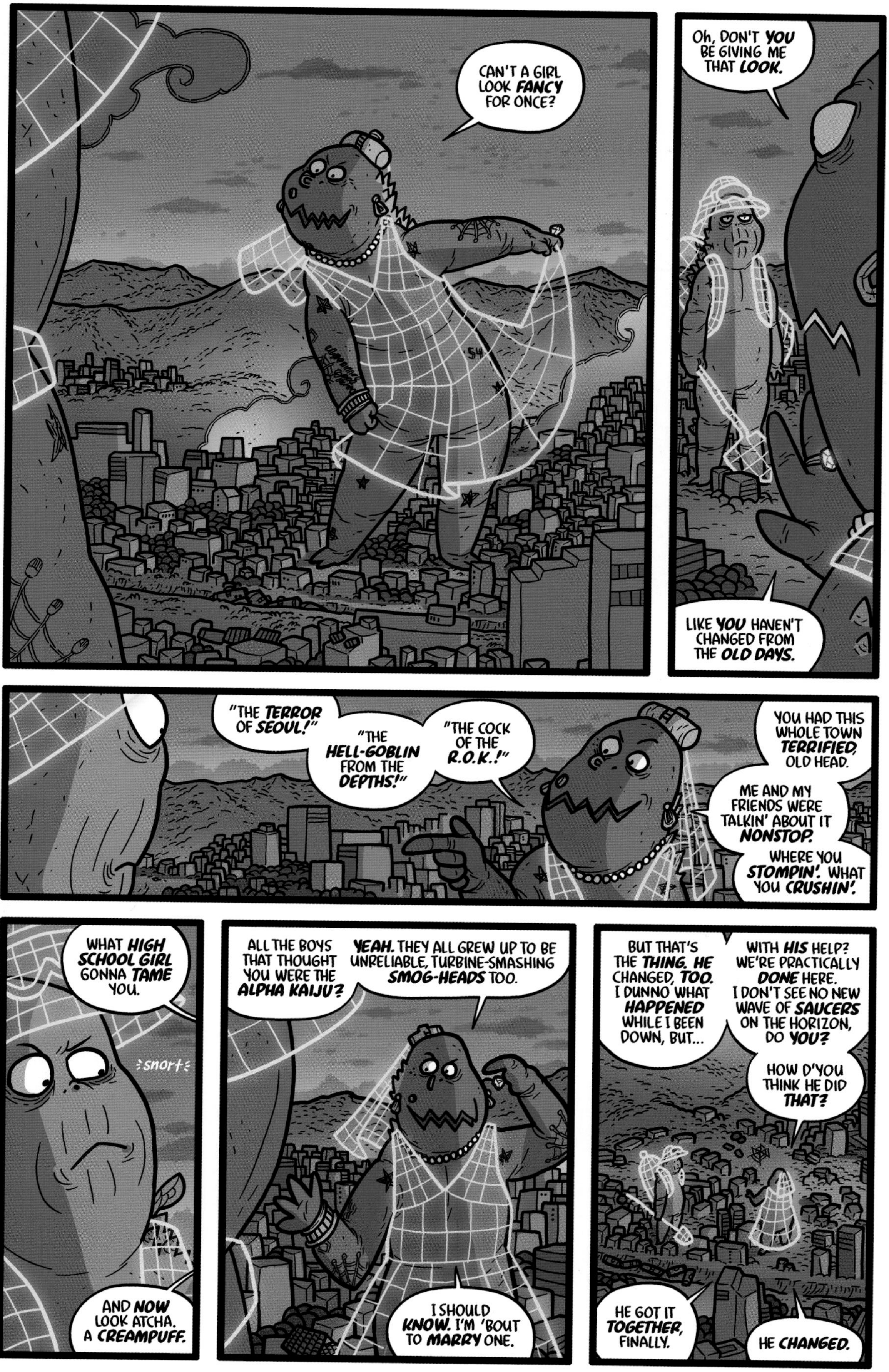

CAN'T A GIRL LOOK FANCY FOR ONCE?
Oh, DON'T YOU BE GIVING ME THAT LOOK.
LIKE YOU HAVEN'T CHANGED FROM THE OLD DAYS.
"THE TERROR OF SEOUL!"
"THE HELL-GOBLIN FROM THE DEPTHS!"
"THE COCK OF THE R.O.K.!"
YOU HAD THIS WHOLE TOWN TERRIFIED, OLD HEAD.
ME AND MY FRIENDS WERE TALKIN' ABOUT IT NONSTOP.
WHERE YOU STOMPIN'. WHAT YOU CRUSHIN'.
WHAT HIGH SCHOOL GIRL GONNA TAME YOU.
snort
AND NOW LOOK ATCHA. A CREAMPUFF.
ALL THE BOYS THAT THOUGHT YOU WERE THE ALPHA KAIJU?
YEAH. THEY ALL GREW UP TO BE UNRELIABLE, TURBINE-SMASHING SMOG-HEADS TOO.
I SHOULD KNOW. I'M 'BOUT TO MARRY ONE.
BUT THAT'S THE THING. HE CHANGED, TOO. I DUNNO WHAT HAPPENED WHILE I BEEN DOWN, BUT...
WITH HIS HELP? WE'RE PRACTICALLY DONE HERE. I DON'T SEE NO NEW WAVE OF SAUCERS ON THE HORIZON, DO YOU?
HOW D'YOU THINK HE DID THAT?
HE GOT IT TOGETHER, FINALLY.
HE CHANGED.

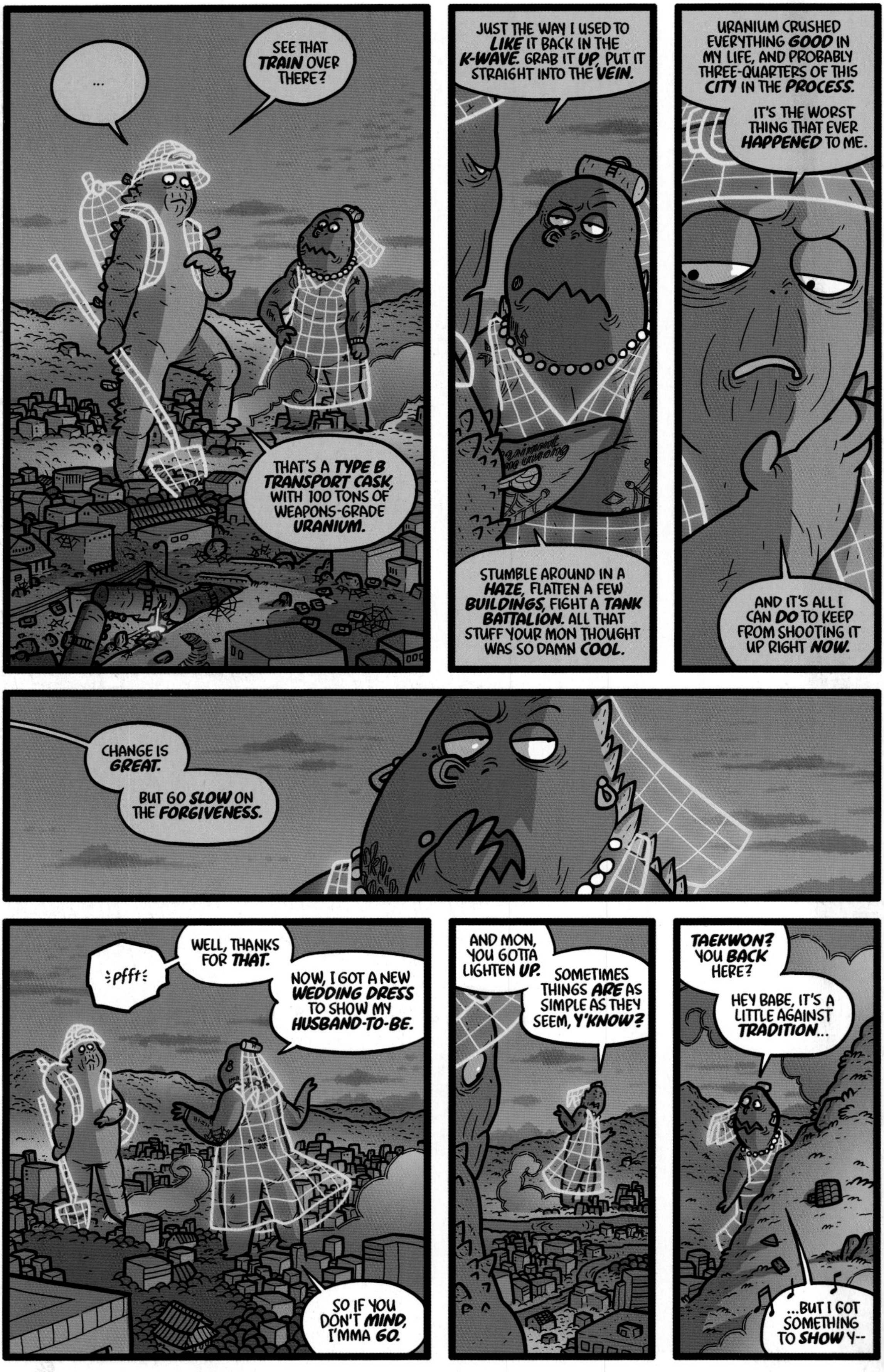
...
SEE THAT TRAIN OVER THERE?
THAT'S A TYPE B TRANSPORT CASK, WITH 100 TONS OF WEAPONS-GRADE URANIUM.
JUST THE WAY I USED TO LIKE IT BACK IN THE K-WAVE. GRAB IT UP, PUT IT STRAIGHT INTO THE VEIN.
STUMBLE AROUND IN A HAZE, FLATTEN A FEW BUILDINGS, FIGHT A TANK BATTALION. ALL THAT STUFF YOUR MON THOUGHT WAS SO DAMN COOL.
URANIUM CRUSHED EVERYTHING GOOD IN MY LIFE, AND PROBABLY THREE-QUARTERS OF THIS CITY IN THE PROCESS.
IT'S THE WORST THING THAT EVER HAPPENED TO ME.
AND IT'S ALL I CAN DO TO KEEP FROM SHOOTING IT UP RIGHT NOW.
CHANGE IS GREAT.
BUT GO SLOW ON THE FORGIVENESS.
pfft
WELL, THANKS FOR THAT.
NOW, I GOT A NEW WEDDING DRESS TO SHOW MY HUSBAND-TO-BE.
SO IF YOU DON'T MIND, I'MMA GO.
AND MON, YOU GOTTA LIGHTEN UP.
SOMETIMES THINGS ARE AS SIMPLE AS THEY SEEM, Y'KNOW?
TAEKWON? YOU BACK HERE?
HEY BABE, IT'S A LITTLE AGAINST TRADITION...
...BUT I GOT SOMETHING TO SHOW Y--

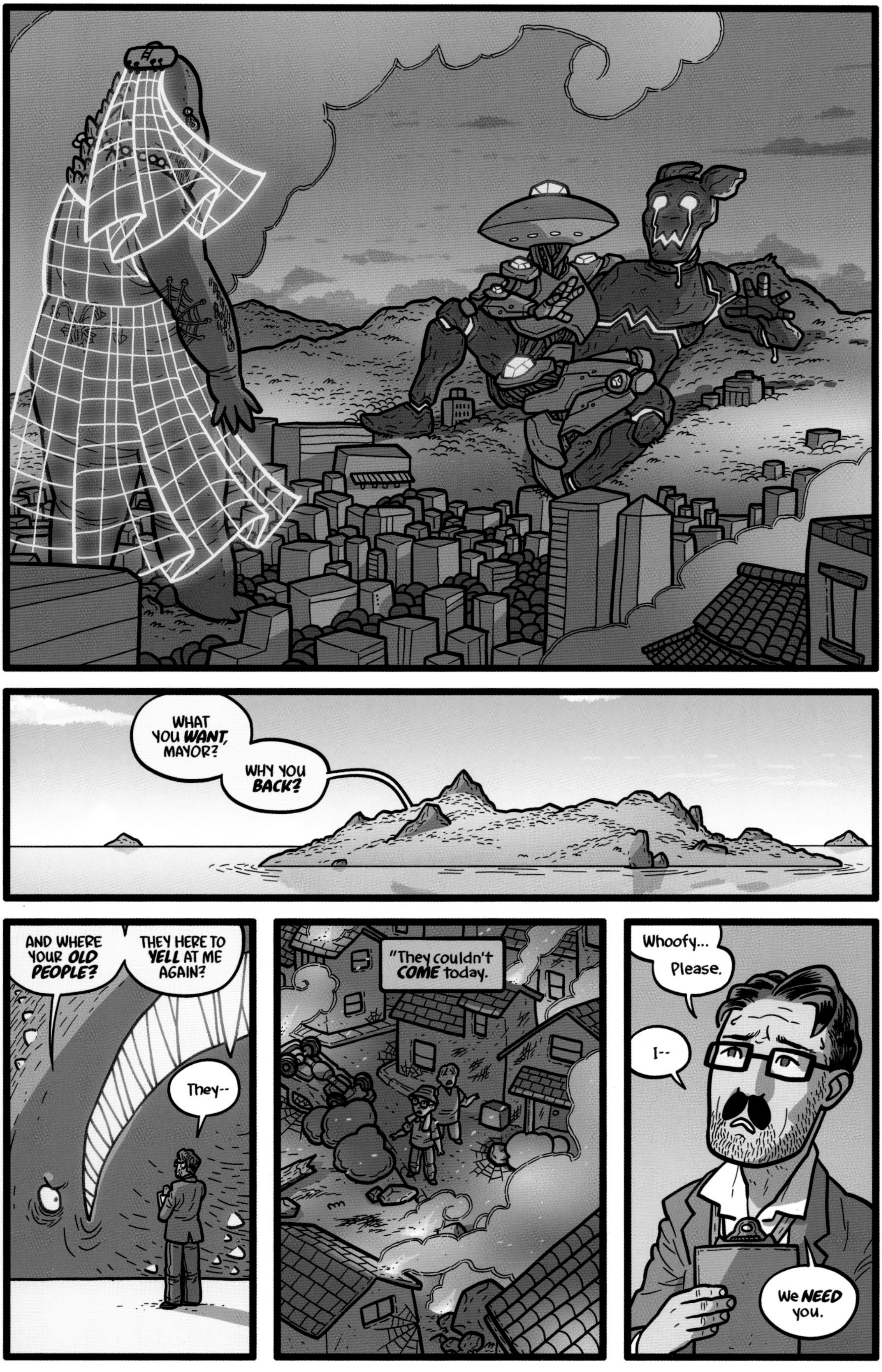
WHAT YOU WANT, MAYOR?
WHY YOU BACK?
AND WHERE YOUR OLD PEOPLE?
THEY HERE TO YELL AT ME AGAIN?
They--
"They couldn't COME today.
Whoofy...
Please.
I--
We NEED you.

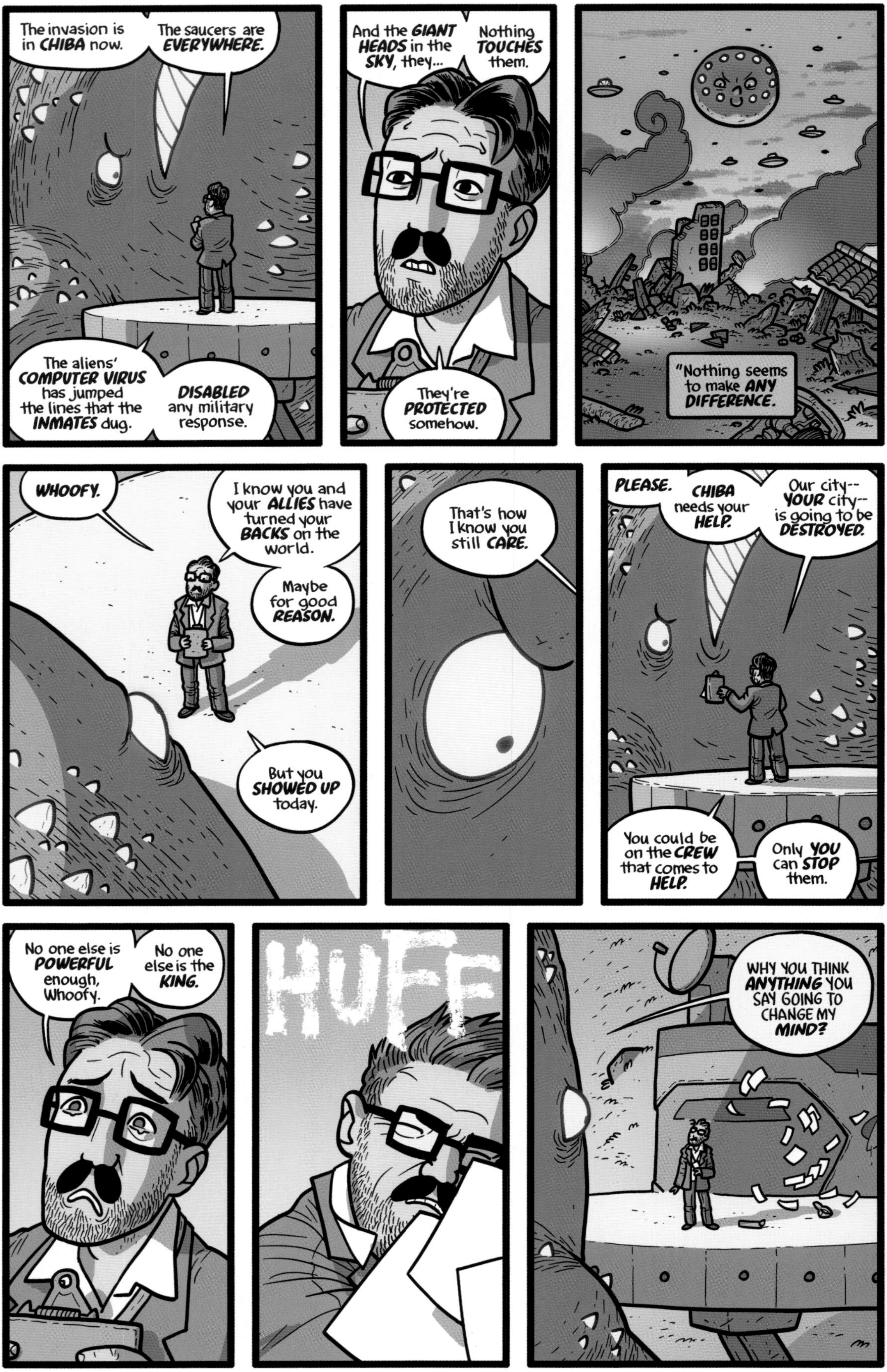
The invasion is in CHIBA now.
The saucers are EVERYWHERE.
The aliens' COMPUTER VIRUS has jumped the lines that the INMATES dug.
DISABLED any military response.
And the GIANT HEADS in the SKY, they...
Nothing TOUCHES them.
They're PROTECTED somehow.
"Nothing seems to make ANY DIFFERENCE.
WHOOFY.
I know you and your ALLIES have turned your BACKS on the world.
Maybe for good REASON.
But you SHOWED UP today.
That's how I know you still CARE.
PLEASE.
CHIBA needs your HELP.
Our city-- YOUR city-- is going to be DESTROYED.
You could be on the CREW that comes to HELP.
Only YOU can STOP them.
No one else is POWERFUL enough, Whoofy.
No one else is the KING.
HUFF
WHY YOU THINK ANYTHING YOU SAY GOING TO CHANGE MY MIND?

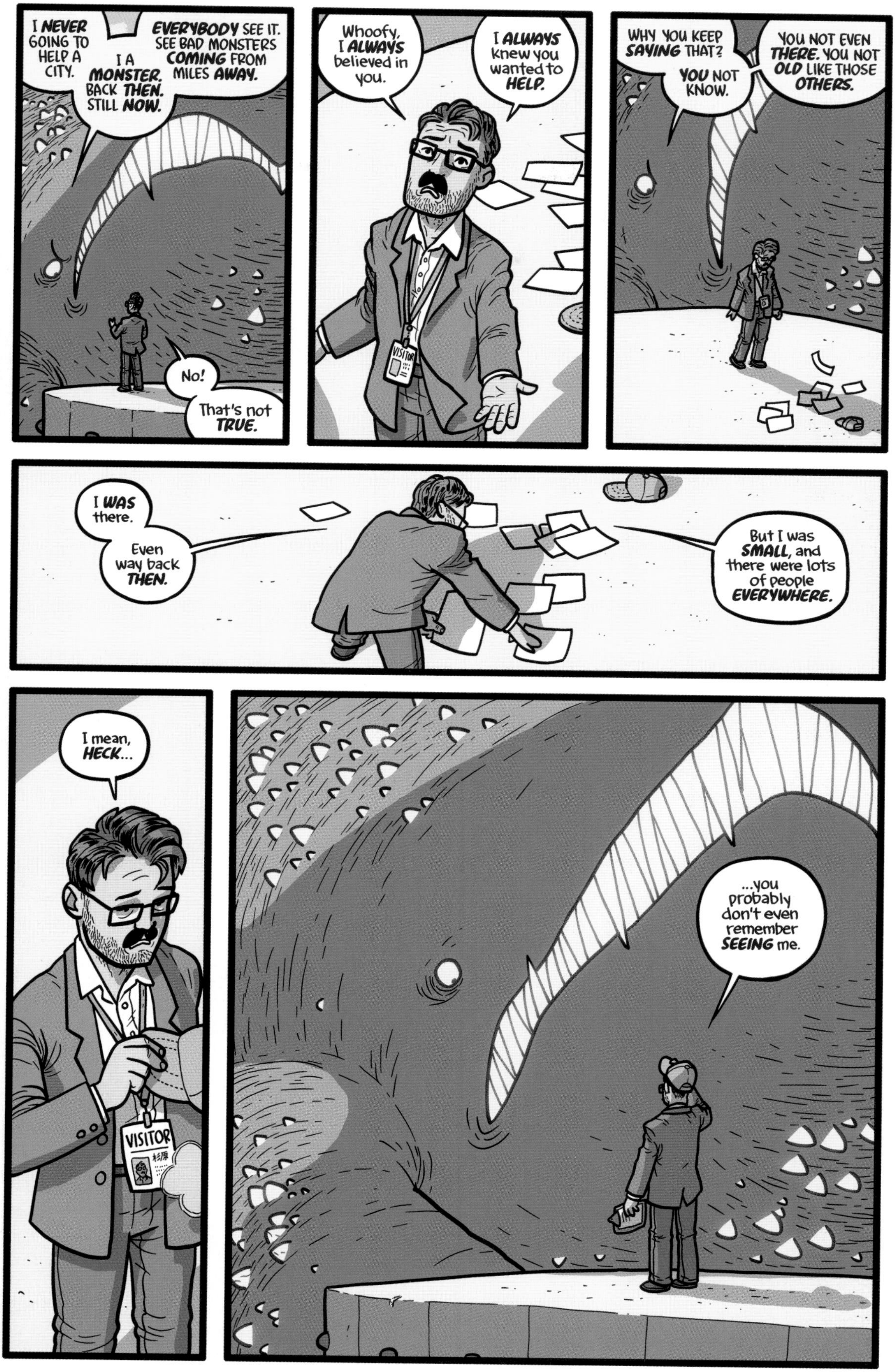

I NEVER GOING TO HELP A CITY.
I A MONSTER. BACK THEN. STILL NOW.
EVERYBODY SEE IT. SEE BAD MONSTERS COMING FROM MILES AWAY.
No!
That's not TRUE.
Whoofy, I ALWAYS believed in you.
I ALWAYS knew you wanted to HELP.
VISITOR
WHY YOU KEEP SAYING THAT?
YOU NOT KNOW.
YOU NOT EVEN THERE. YOU NOT OLD LIKE THOSE OTHERS.
I WAS there.
Even way back THEN.
But I was SMALL, and there were lots of people EVERYWHERE.
I mean, HECK...
VISITOR
...you probably don't even remember SEEING me.

L-LI'L BOY?
GRIDBOT
THE SEPTAGON, TOKYO
KCHAK
VEEEENN

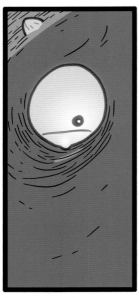

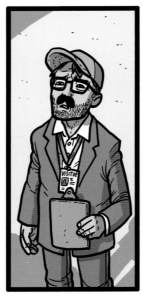

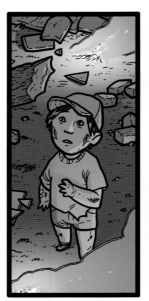

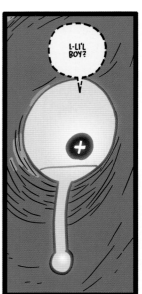

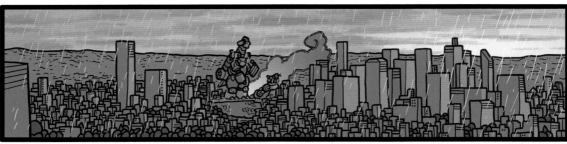

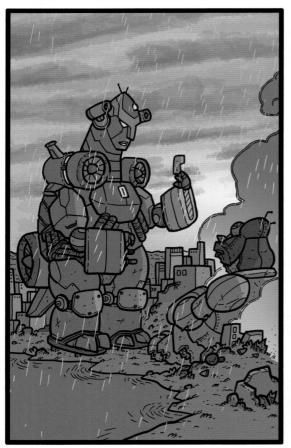

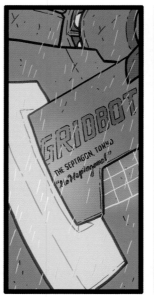

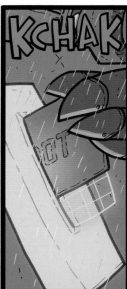

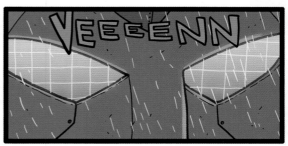

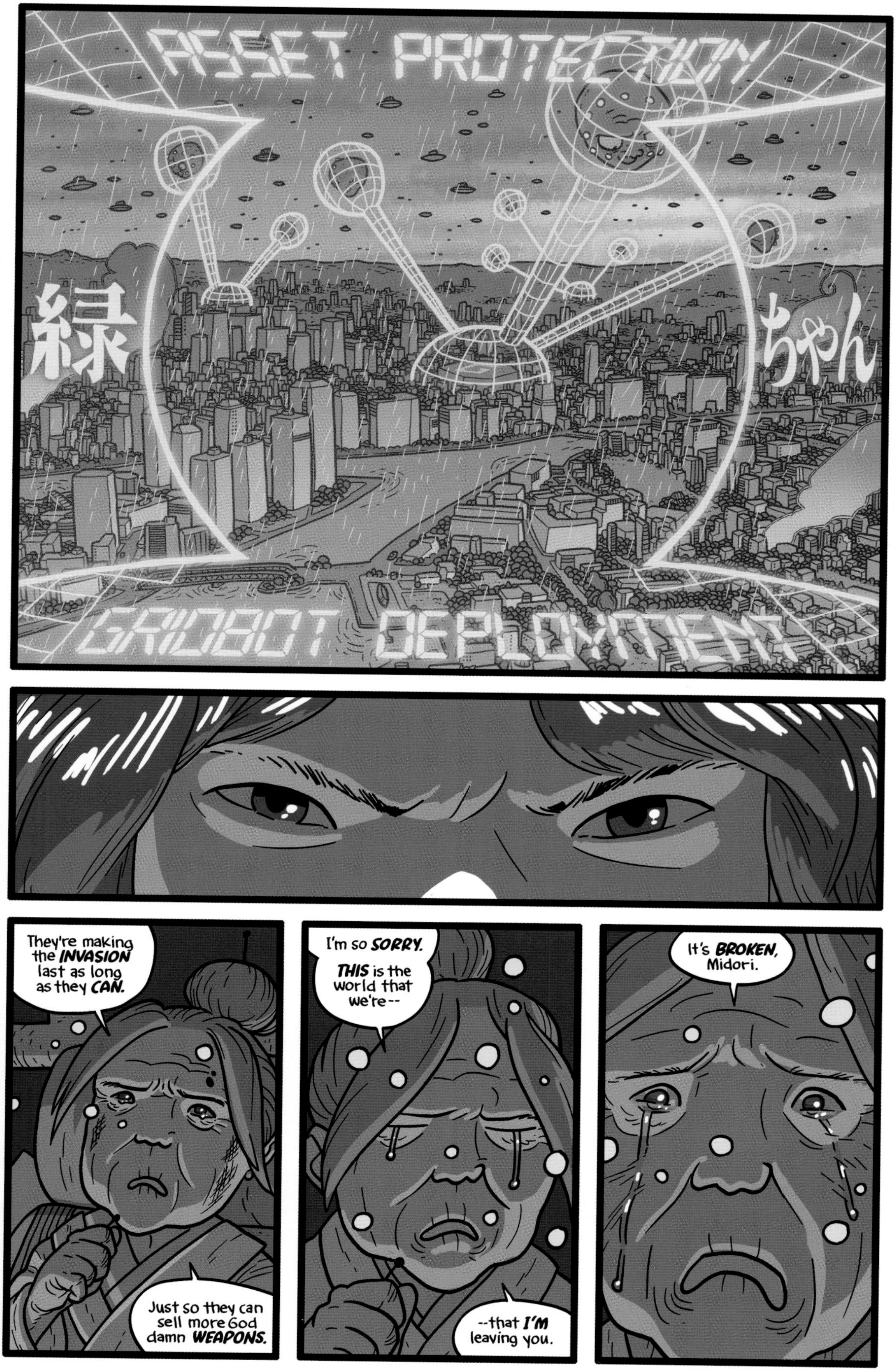
ASSET PROTECTION
緑
ちゃん
GRIDBOT DEPLOYMENT
They're making the INVASION last as long as they CAN.
Just so they can sell more God damn WEAPONS.
I'm so SORRY.
THIS is the world that we're--
--that I'M leaving you.
It's BROKEN, Midori.

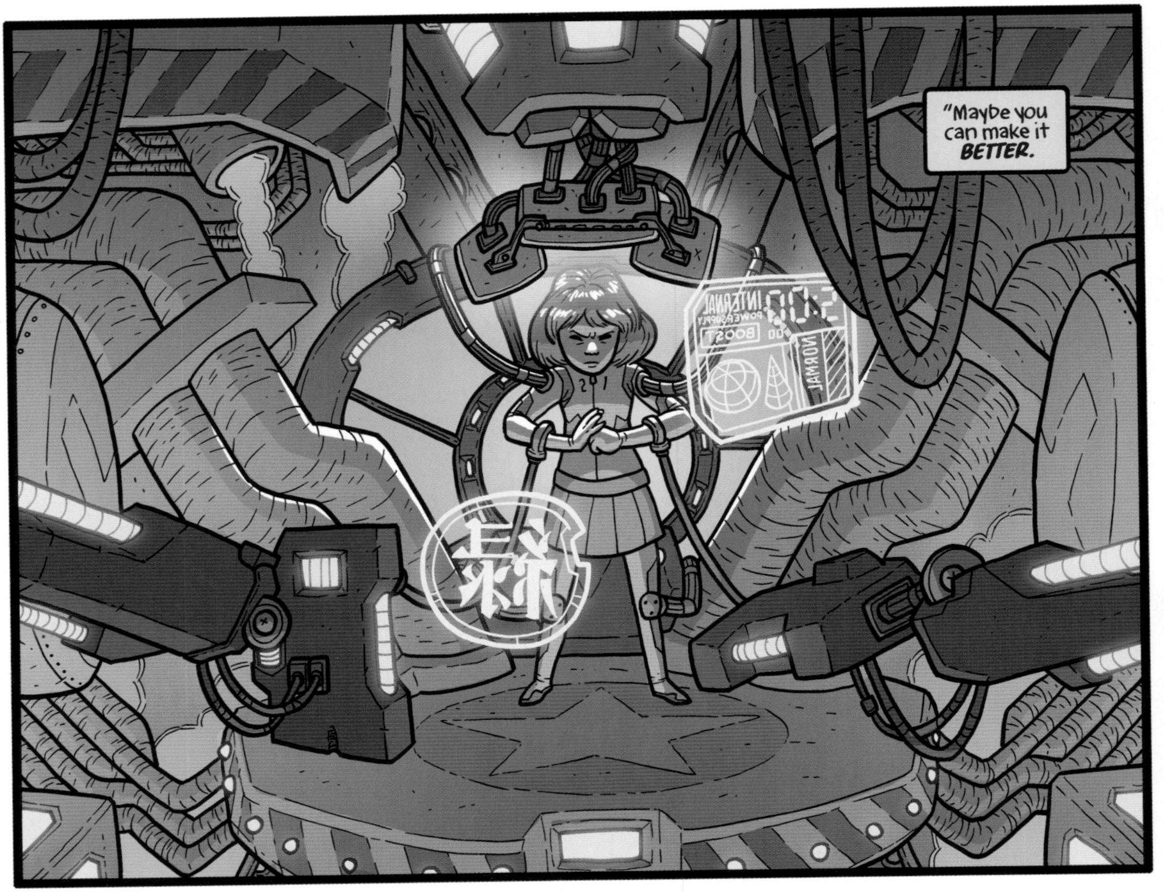
"Maybe you can make it BETTER.

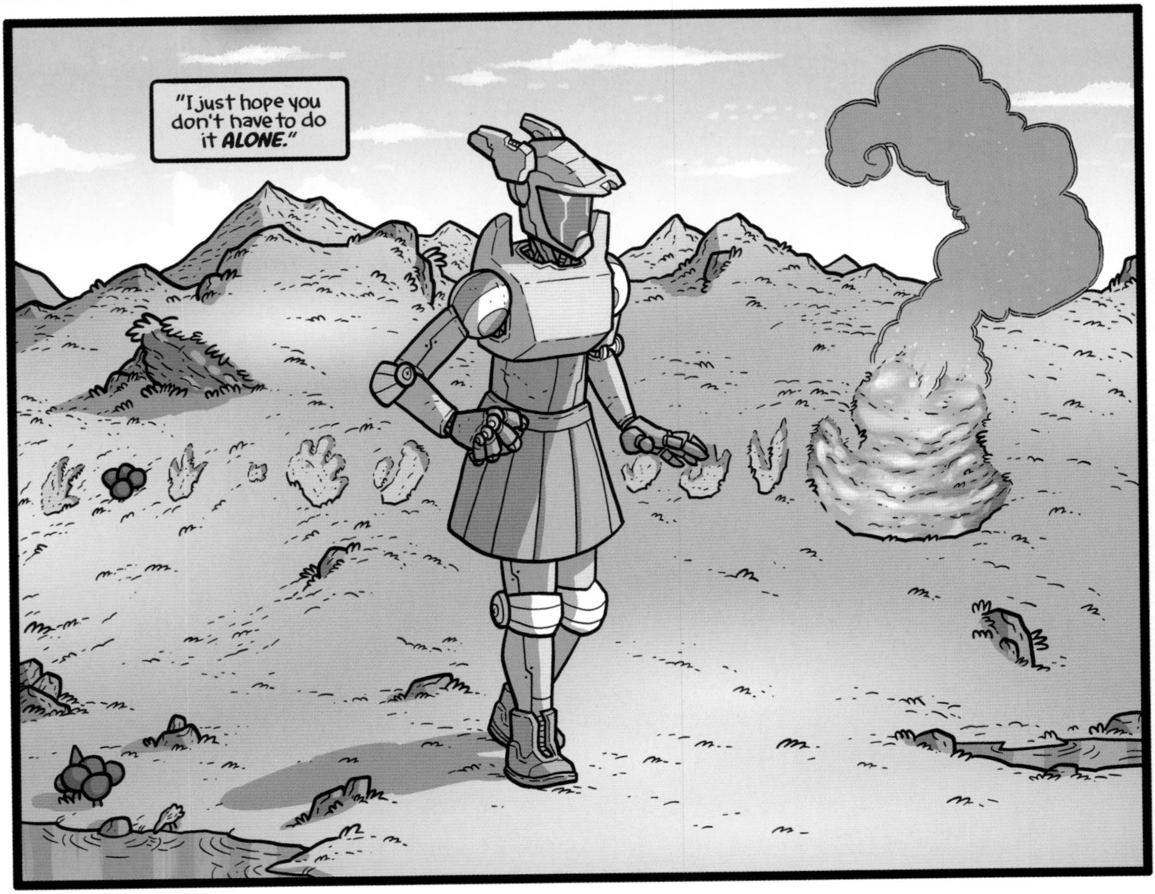
"I just hope you don't have to do it ALONE."

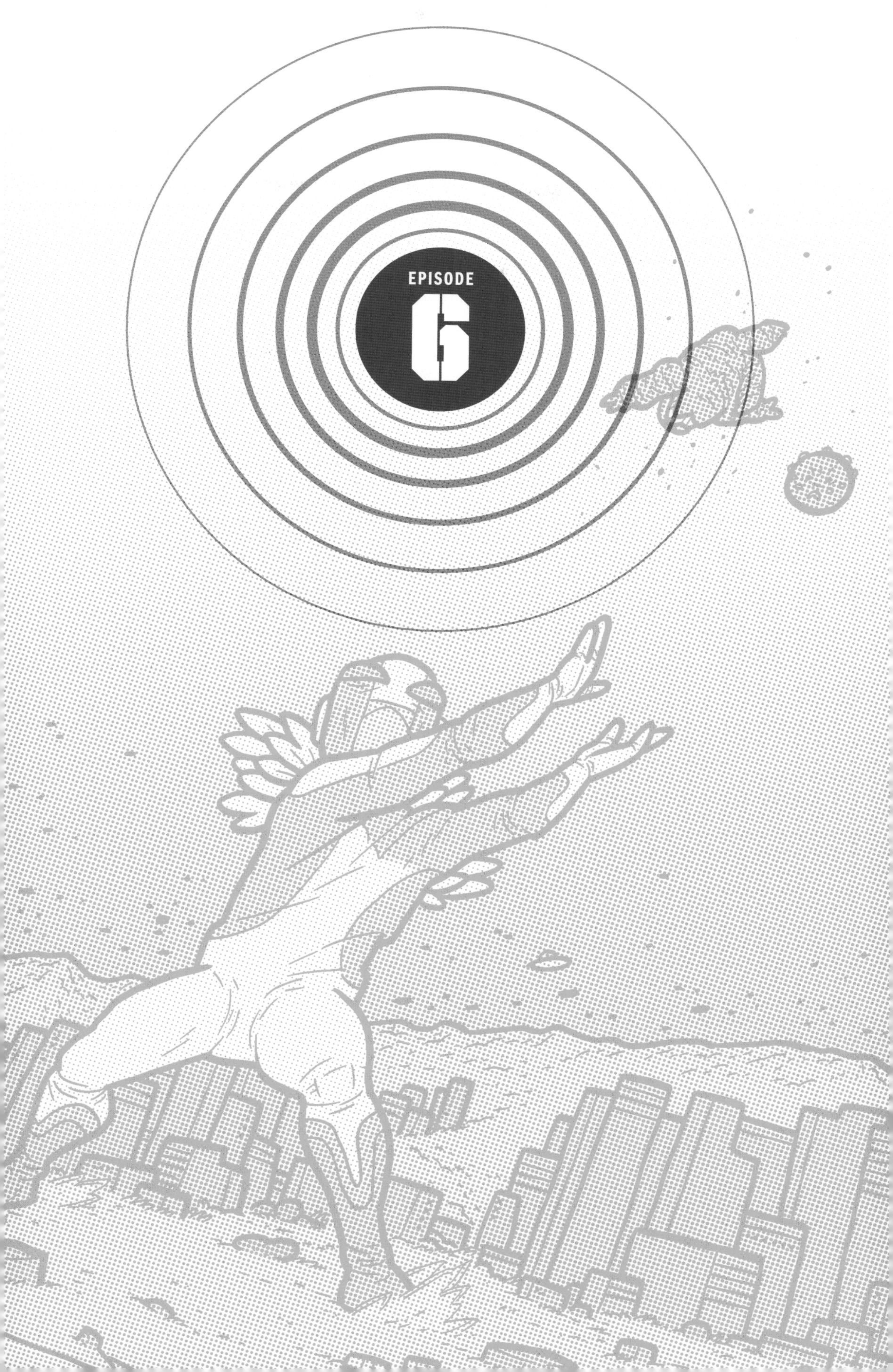
EPISODE
6

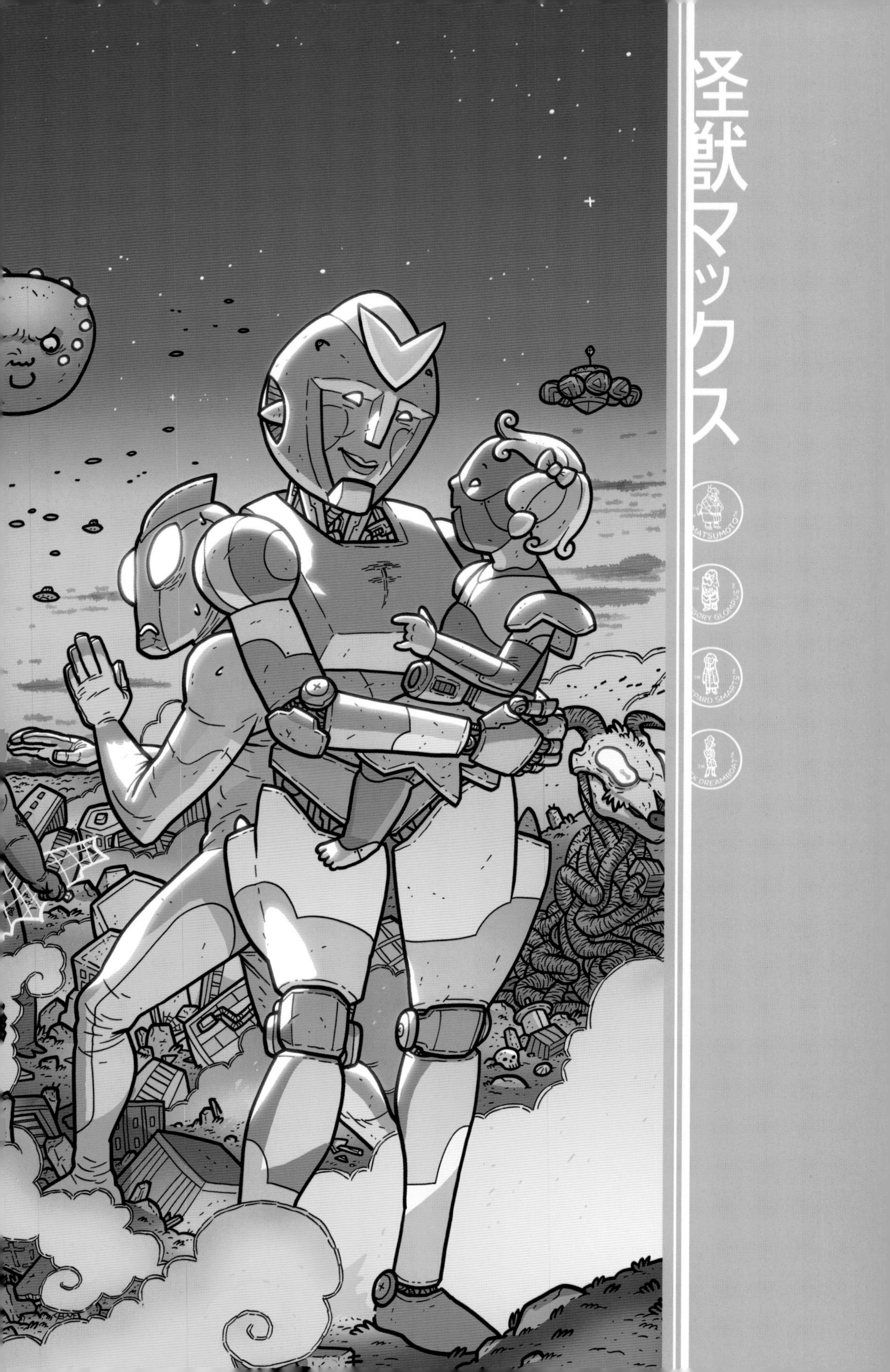
怪獣マックス

MONDAY ☆0700☆

YOU WANT *MY* TAKE?

I'D SAY IT WORKED OUT PRETTY MUCH THE WAY YOU'D *EXPECT*.

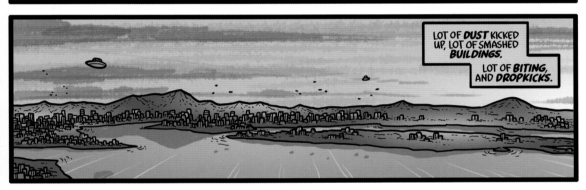

LOT OF *DUST* KICKED UP, LOT OF SMASHED *BUILDINGS*.

LOT OF *BITING*, AND *DROPKICKS*.

COUPLE OF US DEAD IN THE *WRECKAGE*, JUST TO SHOW WHAT THE *STAKES* ARE.

WHY *NOT*, RIGHT? WE'RE *DISPOSABLE*, AREN'T WE?

INMATES.

CONVICTS.

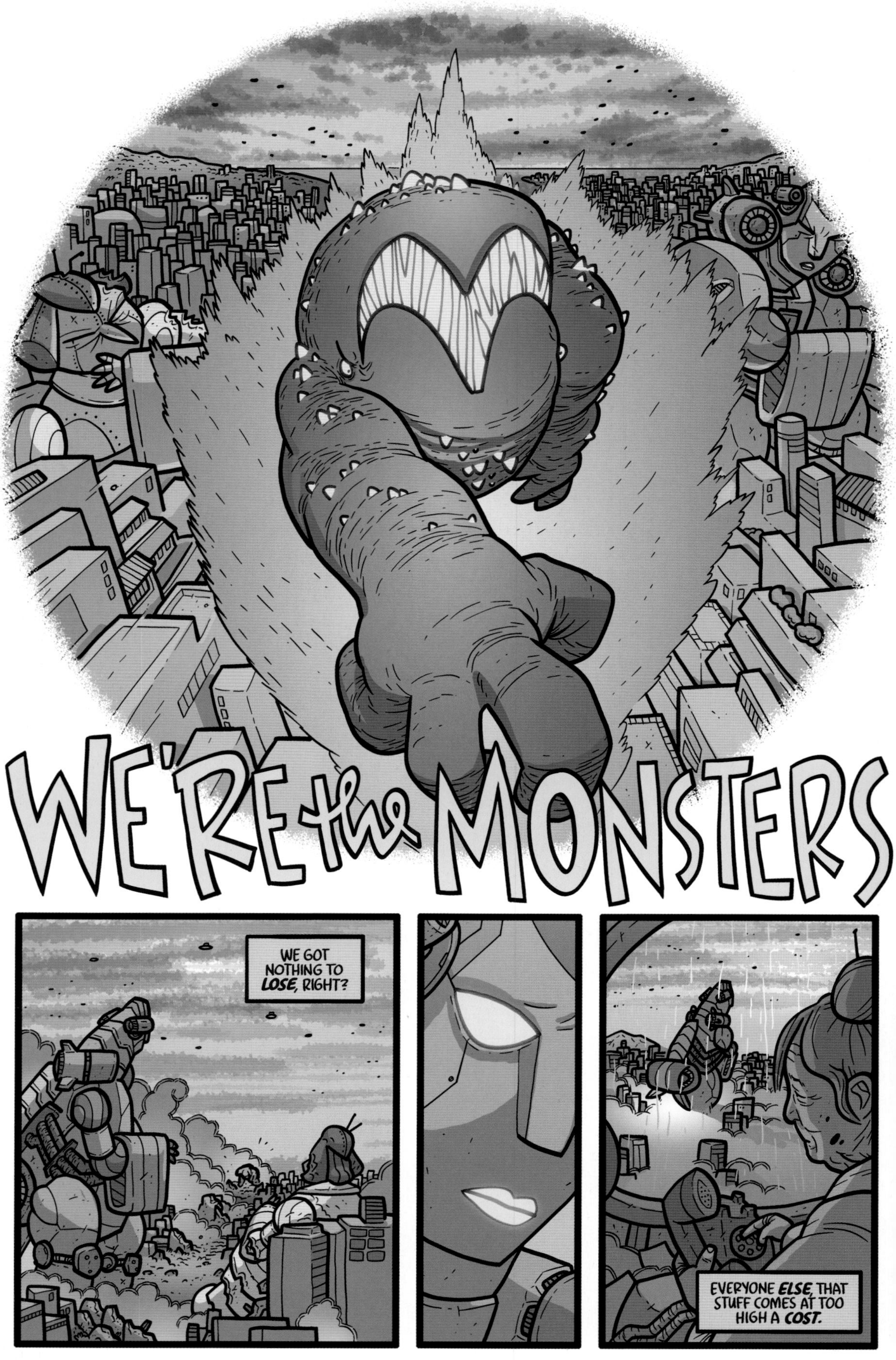
WE'RE the MONSTERS
WE GOT NOTHING TO LOSE, RIGHT?
EVERYONE ELSE, THAT STUFF COMES AT TOO HIGH A COST.

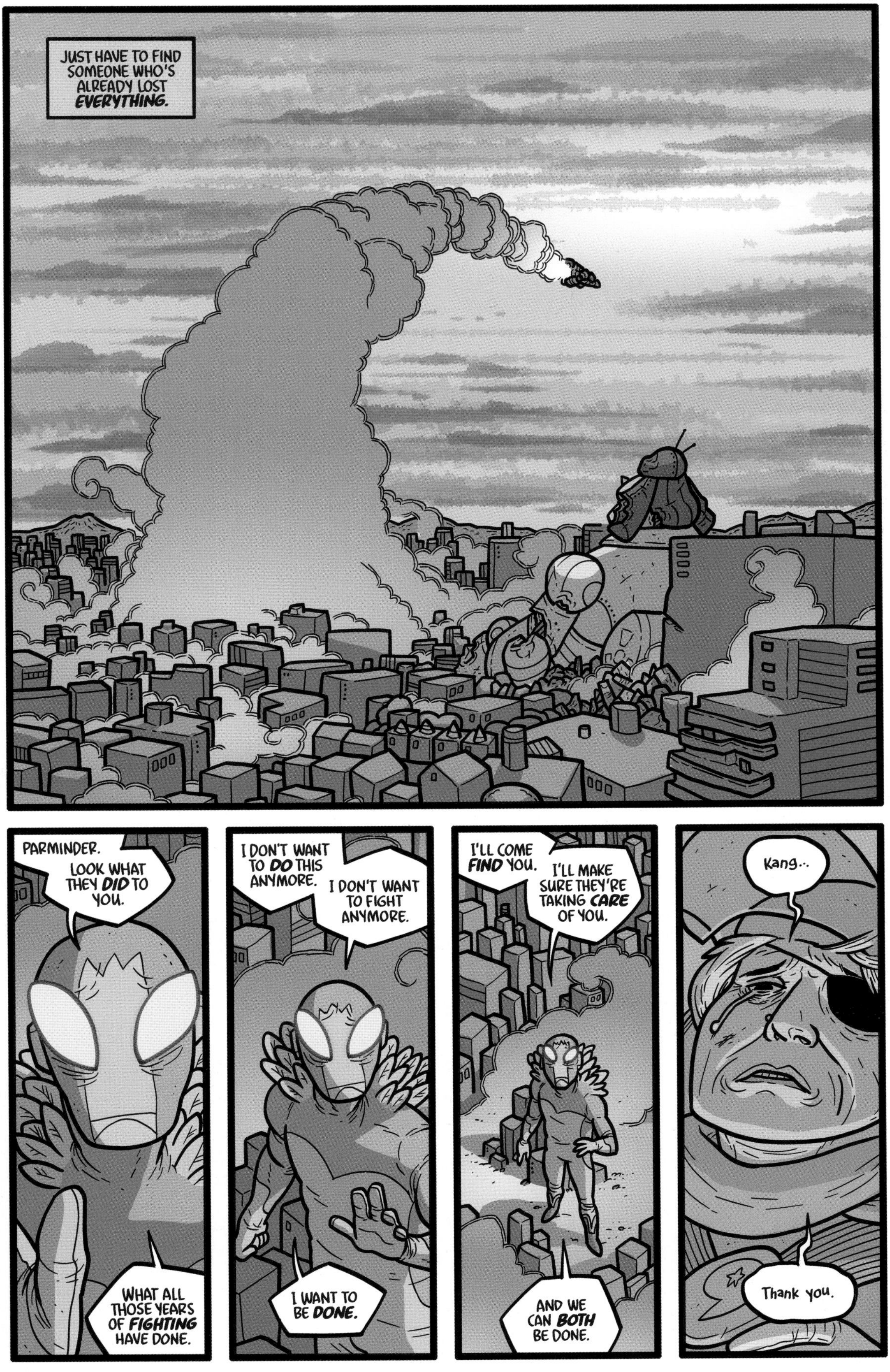
JUST HAVE TO FIND SOMEONE WHO'S ALREADY LOST **EVERYTHING.**
PARMINDER.
LOOK WHAT THEY **DID** TO YOU.
WHAT ALL THOSE YEARS OF **FIGHTING** HAVE DONE.
I DON'T WANT TO **DO** THIS ANYMORE.
I DON'T WANT TO FIGHT ANYMORE.
I WANT TO BE **DONE.**
I'LL COME **FIND** YOU.
I'LL MAKE SURE THEY'RE TAKING **CARE** OF YOU.
AND WE CAN **BOTH** BE DONE.
Kang...
Thank you.

YOU'RE A GOOD FRIEND.

GOD DAMN IT.

≈sniff≈

GOD DAMN IT

≈ahem≈

KANG HERE.

KANG!!

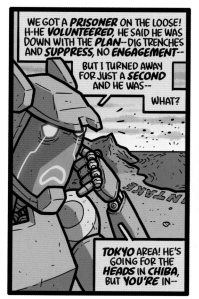

WE GOT A PRISONER ON THE LOOSE! H-HE VOLUNTEERED, HE SAID HE WAS DOWN WITH THE PLAN-- DIG TRENCHES AND SUPPRESS, NO ENGAGEMENT--

BUT I TURNED AWAY FOR JUST A SECOND AND HE WAS--

WHAT?

TOKYO AREA! HE'S GOING FOR THE HEADS IN CHIBA, BUT YOU'RE IN--

YEAH. I KNOW HOW FAR IT IS.

I'LL MAKE IT.

Y'KNOW, EVERYONE ALWAYS SAYS THE SAME THING.

THAT YOU'D THINK WITH A WAR THIS FINAL, WE'D ALL BE ON THE SAME SIDE.

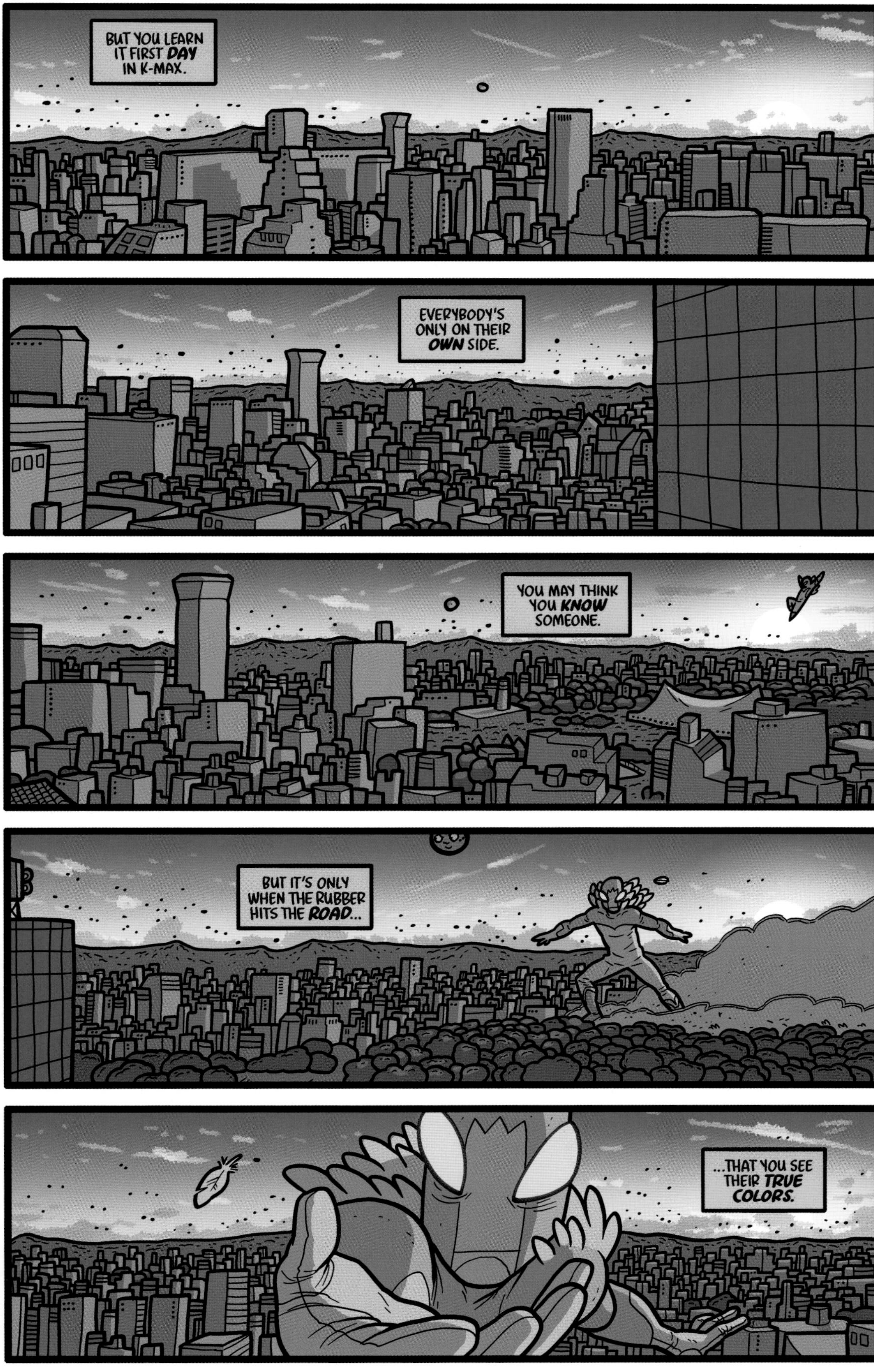
BUT YOU LEARN IT FIRST DAY IN K-MAX.
EVERYBODY'S ONLY ON THEIR OWN SIDE.
YOU MAY THINK YOU KNOW SOMEONE.
BUT IT'S ONLY WHEN THE RUBBER HITS THE ROAD...
...THAT YOU SEE THEIR TRUE COLORS.

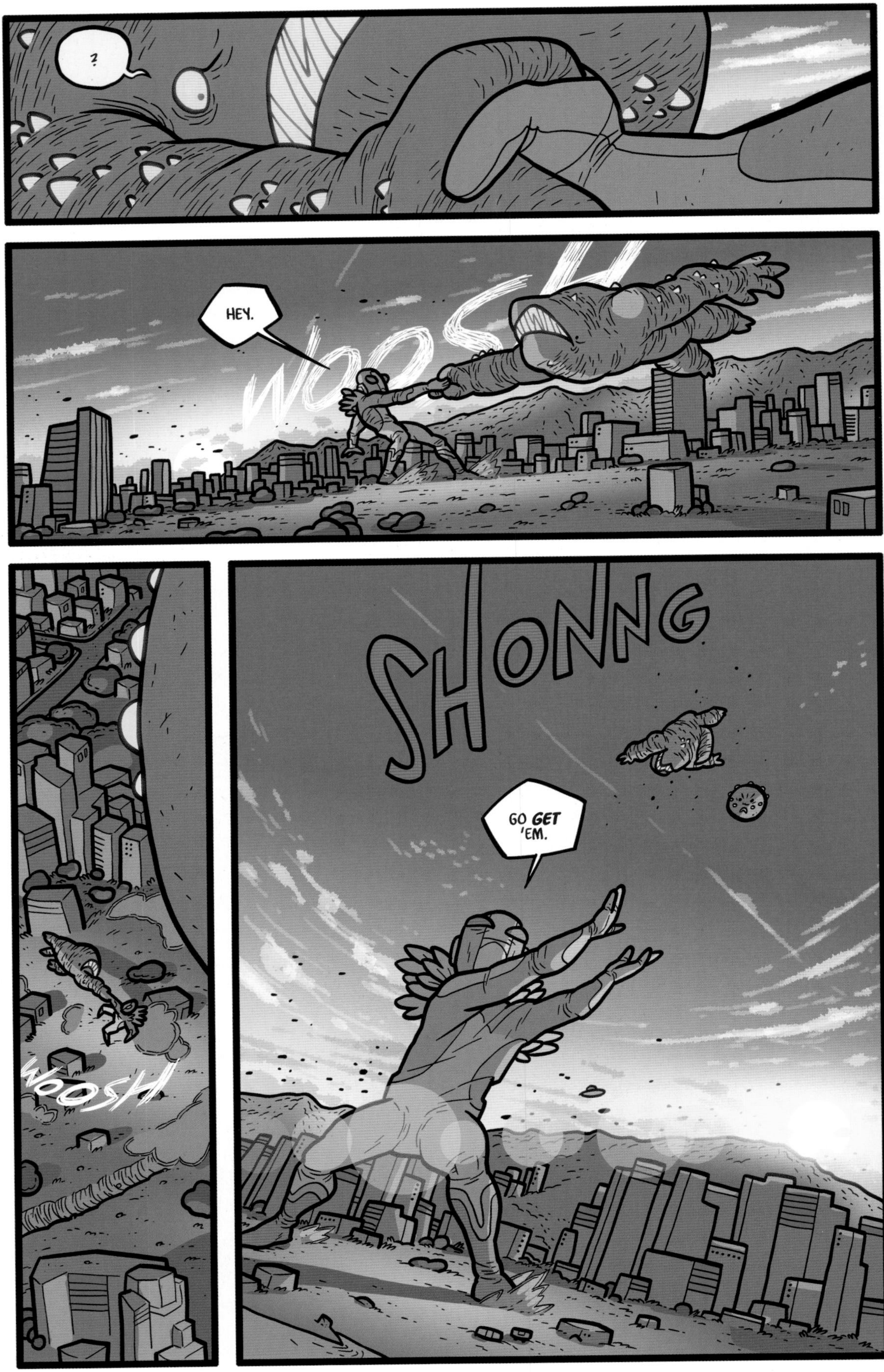
?
HEY.
WOOSH
WOOSH
SHONNG
GO **GET** 'EM.

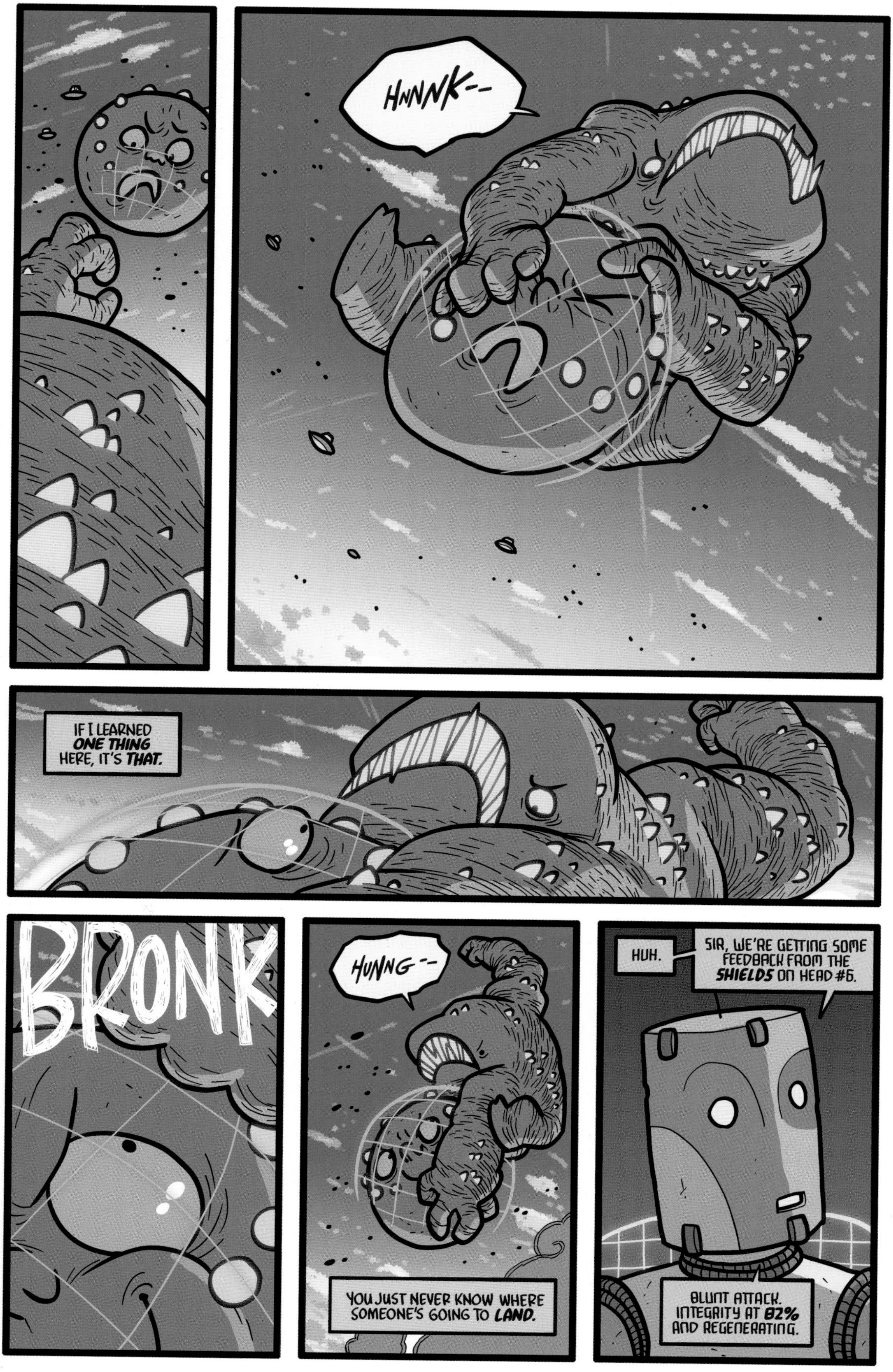
HNNNK--
IF I LEARNED ONE THING HERE, IT'S THAT.
BRONK
HUNNG--
YOU JUST NEVER KNOW WHERE SOMEONE'S GOING TO LAND.
HUH.
SIR, WE'RE GETTING SOME FEEDBACK FROM THE SHIELDS ON HEAD #6.
BLUNT ATTACK. INTEGRITY AT 82% AND REGENERATING.

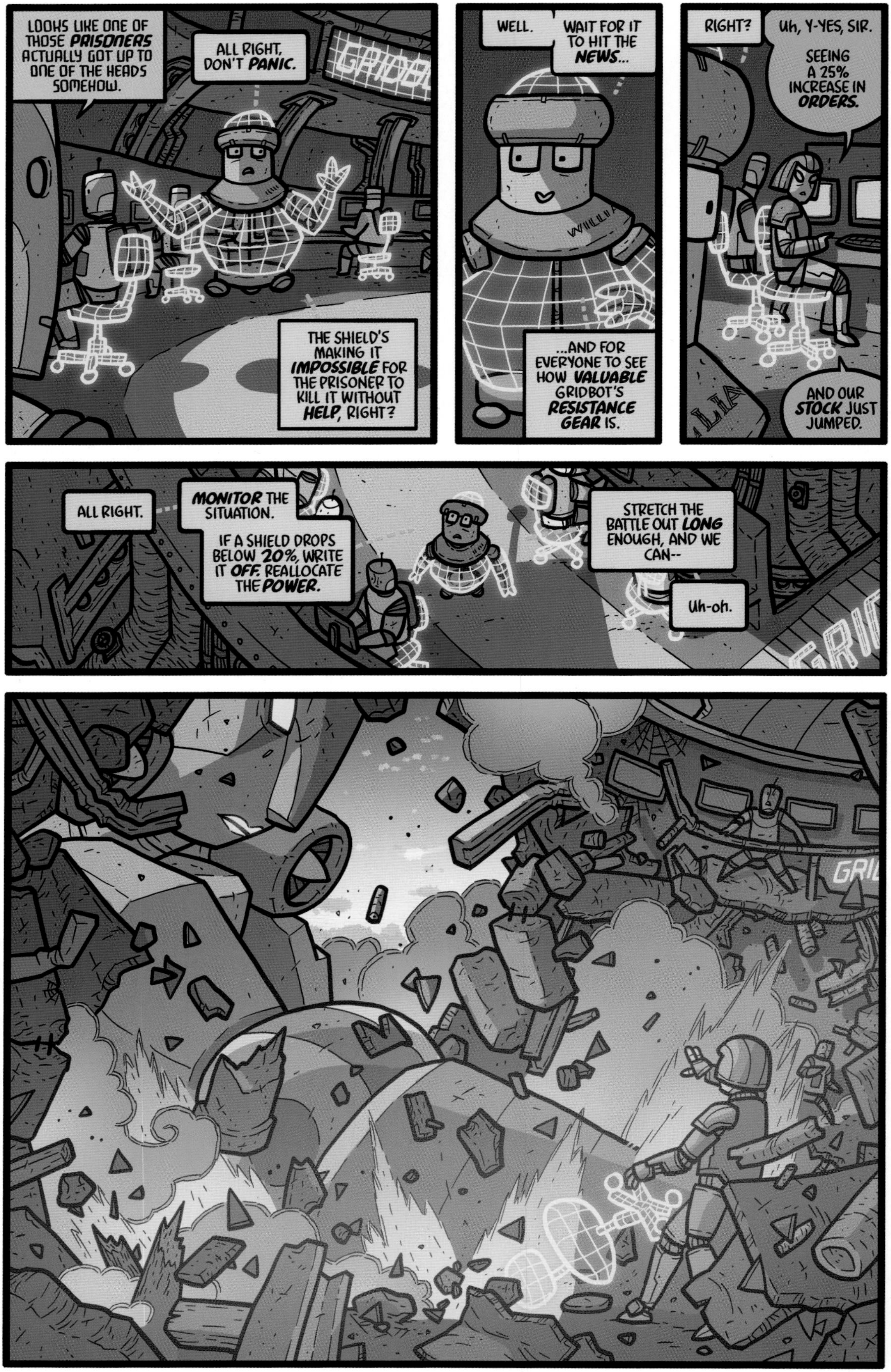
LOOKS LIKE ONE OF THOSE PRISONERS ACTUALLY GOT UP TO ONE OF THE HEADS SOMEHOW.
ALL RIGHT, DON'T PANIC.
GRIDBO
THE SHIELD'S MAKING IT IMPOSSIBLE FOR THE PRISONER TO KILL IT WITHOUT HELP, RIGHT?
WELL.
WAIT FOR IT TO HIT THE NEWS...
...AND FOR EVERYONE TO SEE HOW VALUABLE GRIDBOT'S RESISTANCE GEAR IS.
RIGHT?
Uh, Y-YES, SIR.
SEEING A 25% INCREASE IN ORDERS.
AND OUR STOCK JUST JUMPED.
ALL RIGHT.
MONITOR THE SITUATION.
IF A SHIELD DROPS BELOW 20%, WRITE IT OFF. REALLOCATE THE POWER.
STRETCH THE BATTLE OUT LONG ENOUGH, AND WE CAN--
Uh-oh.
GRID
GRI

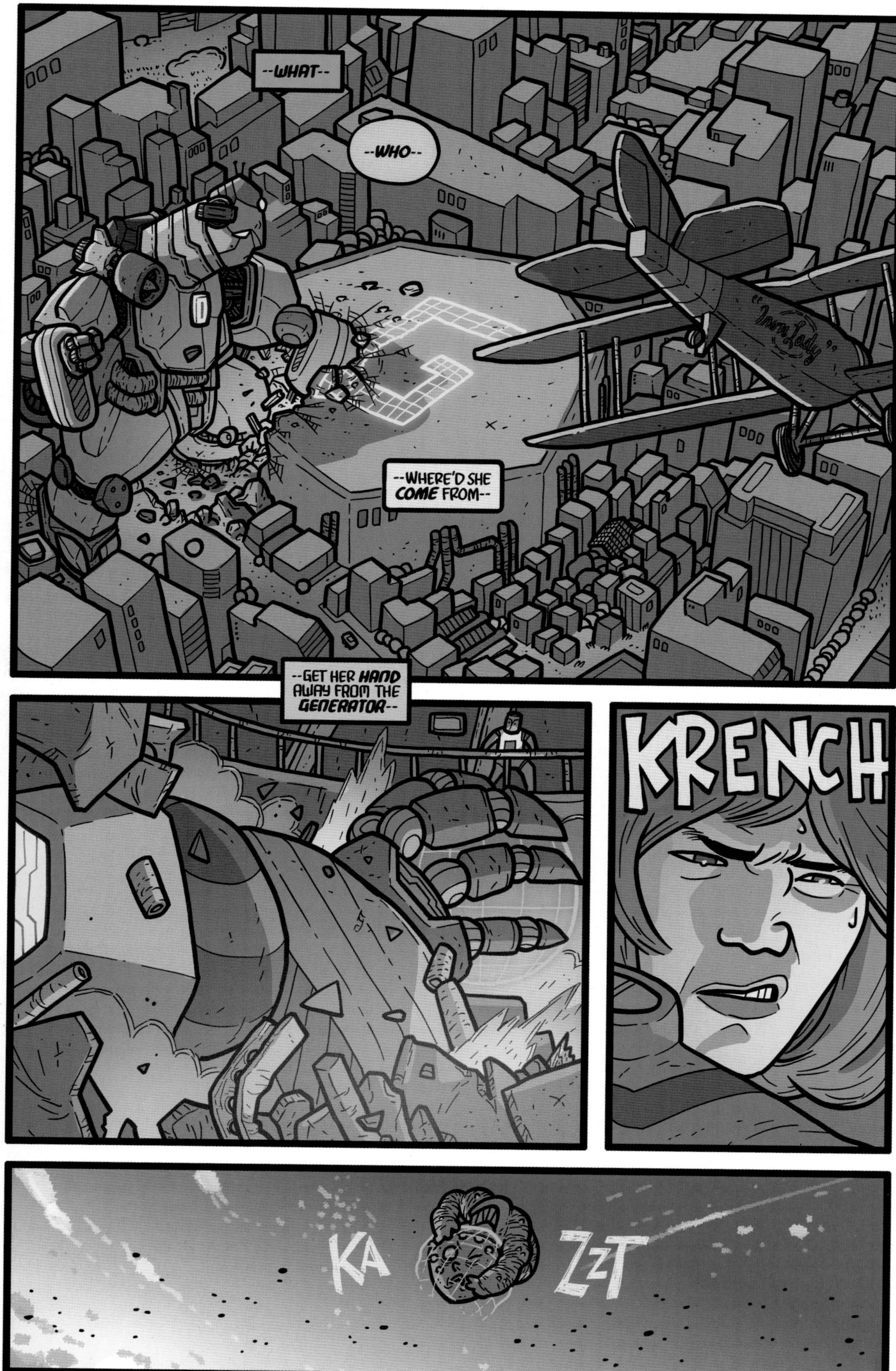
--WHAT--
--WHO--
--WHERE'D SHE COME FROM--
Iron Lady
--GET HER HAND AWAY FROM THE GENERATOR--
KRENCH
KA
ZzT

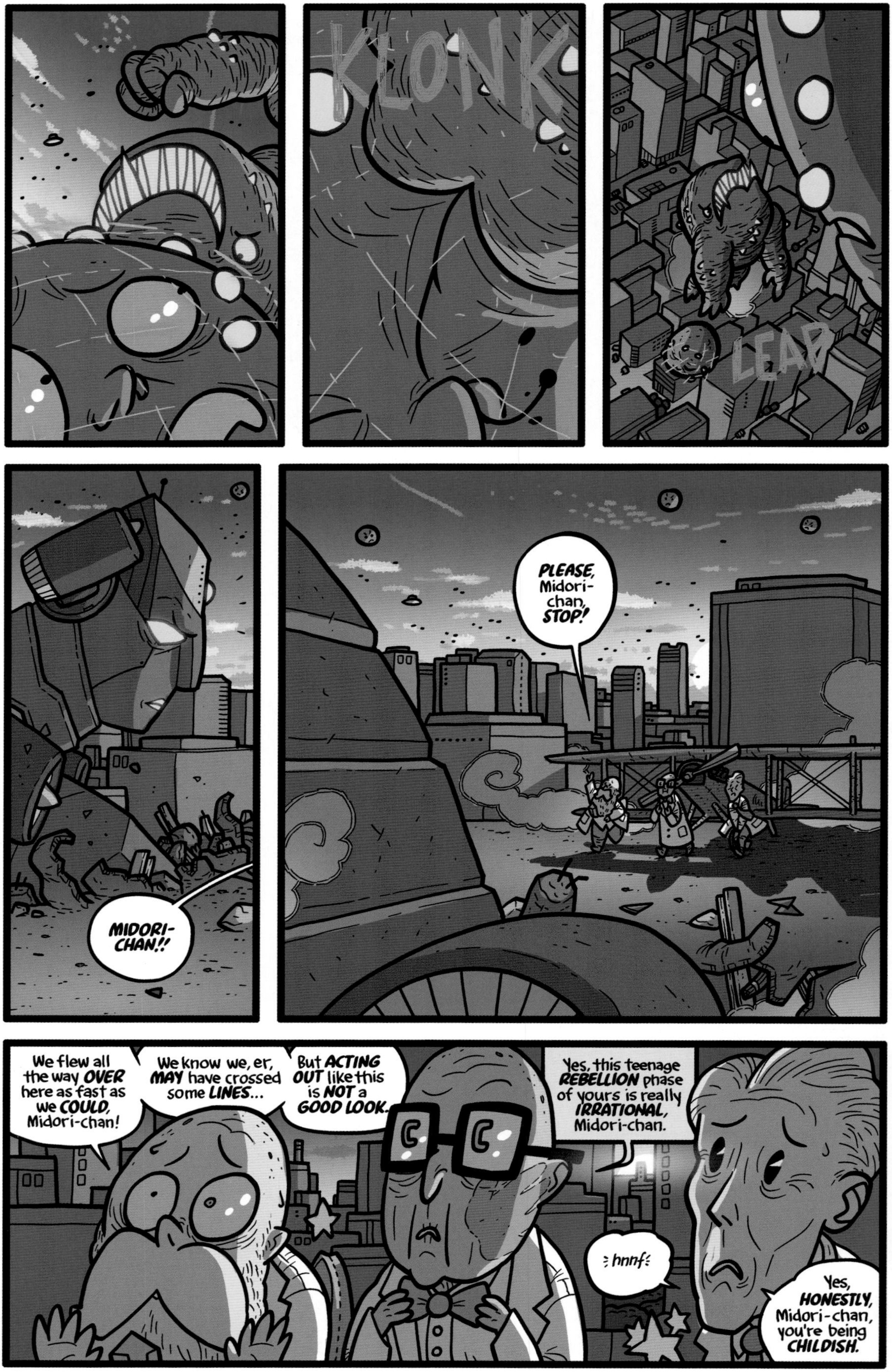
KLONK
LEAP
MIDORI-CHAN!!
PLEASE, Midori-chan, STOP!
We flew all the way OVER here as fast as we COULD, Midori-chan!
We know we, er, MAY have crossed some LINES...
But ACTING OUT like this is NOT a GOOD LOOK.
Yes, this teenage REBELLION phase of yours is really IRRATIONAL, Midori-chan.
hnnf
Yes, HONESTLY, Midori-chan, you're being CHILDISH.

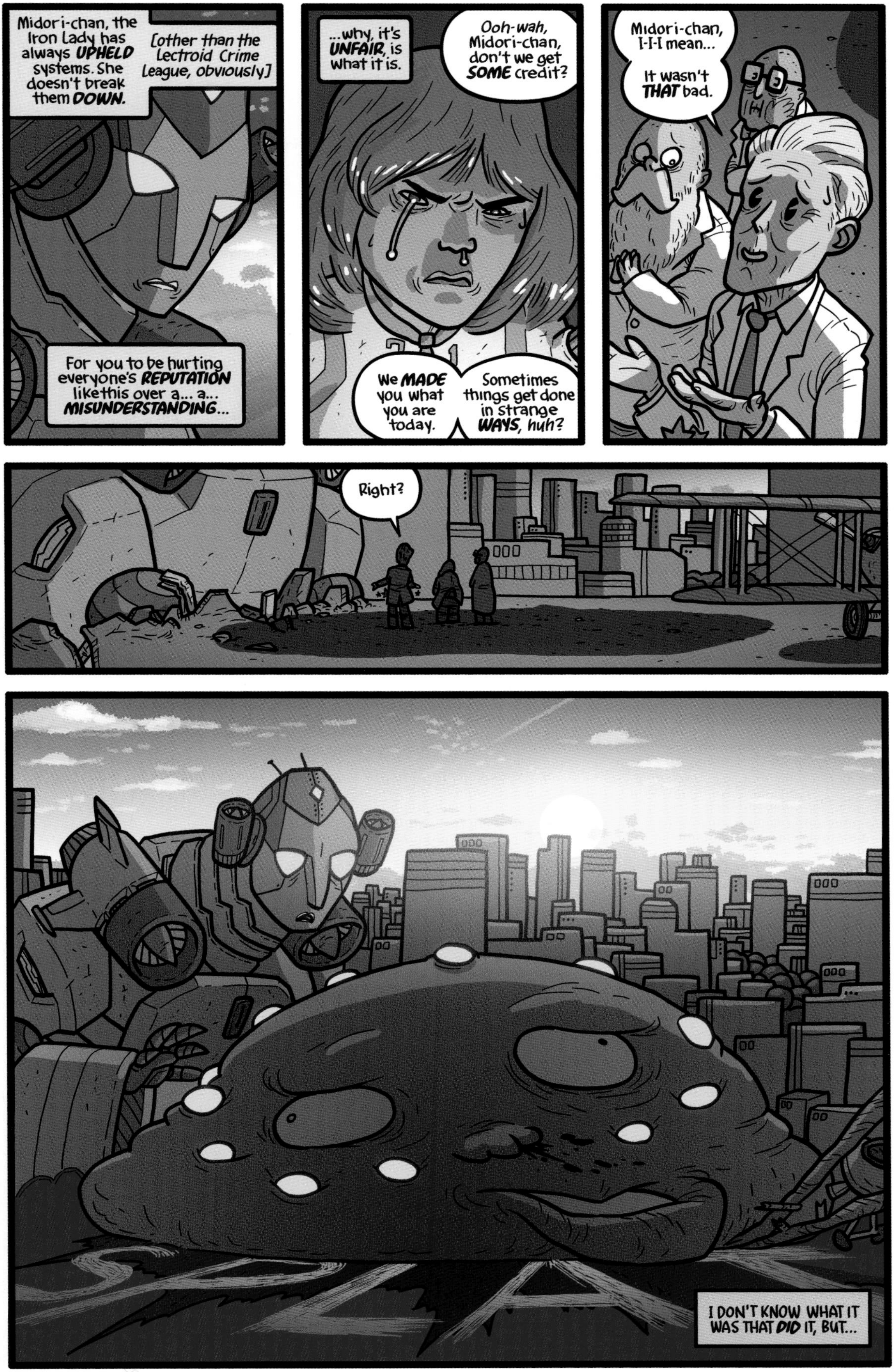

Midori-chan, the Iron Lady has always **UPHELD** systems. She doesn't break them **DOWN.**
[other than the Lectroid Crime League, obviously]
For you to be hurting everyone's **REPUTATION** like this over a... a... **MISUNDERSTANDING**...
...why, it's **UNFAIR**, is what it is.
Ooh-wah, Midori-chan, don't we get **SOME** credit?
We **MADE** you what you are today.
Sometimes things get done in strange **WAYS**, huh?
Midori-chan, I-I-I mean...
It wasn't **THAT** bad.
Right?
I DON'T KNOW WHAT IT WAS THAT **DID** IT, BUT...

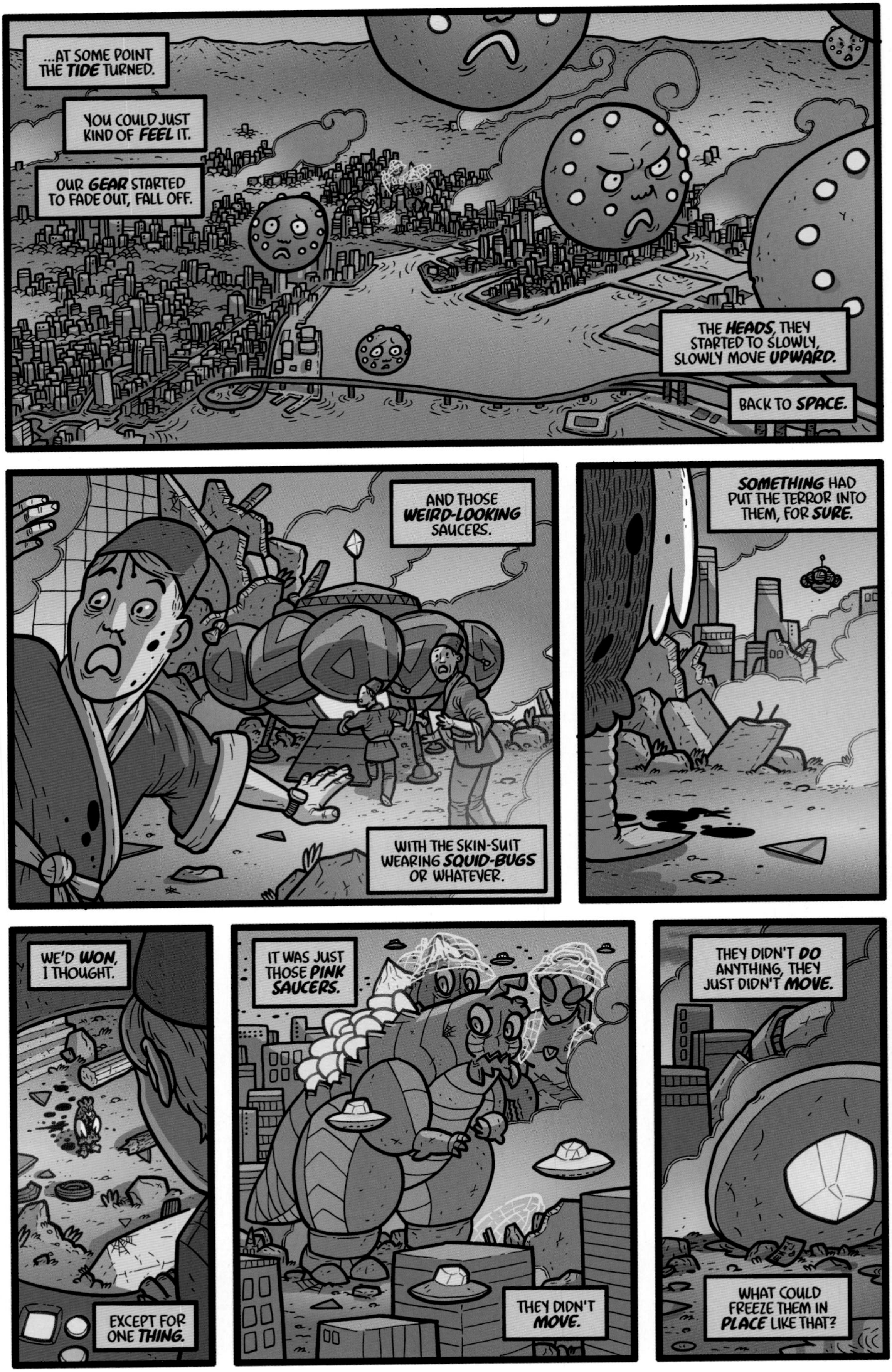
...AT SOME POINT THE TIDE TURNED.
YOU COULD JUST KIND OF FEEL IT.
OUR GEAR STARTED TO FADE OUT, FALL OFF.
THE HEADS, THEY STARTED TO SLOWLY, SLOWLY MOVE UPWARD.
BACK TO SPACE.
AND THOSE WEIRD-LOOKING SAUCERS.
WITH THE SKIN-SUIT WEARING SQUID-BUGS OR WHATEVER.
SOMETHING HAD PUT THE TERROR INTO THEM, FOR SURE.
WE'D WON, I THOUGHT.
EXCEPT FOR ONE THING.
IT WAS JUST THOSE PINK SAUCERS.
THEY DIDN'T MOVE.
THEY DIDN'T DO ANYTHING, THEY JUST DIDN'T MOVE.
WHAT COULD FREEZE THEM IN PLACE LIKE THAT?

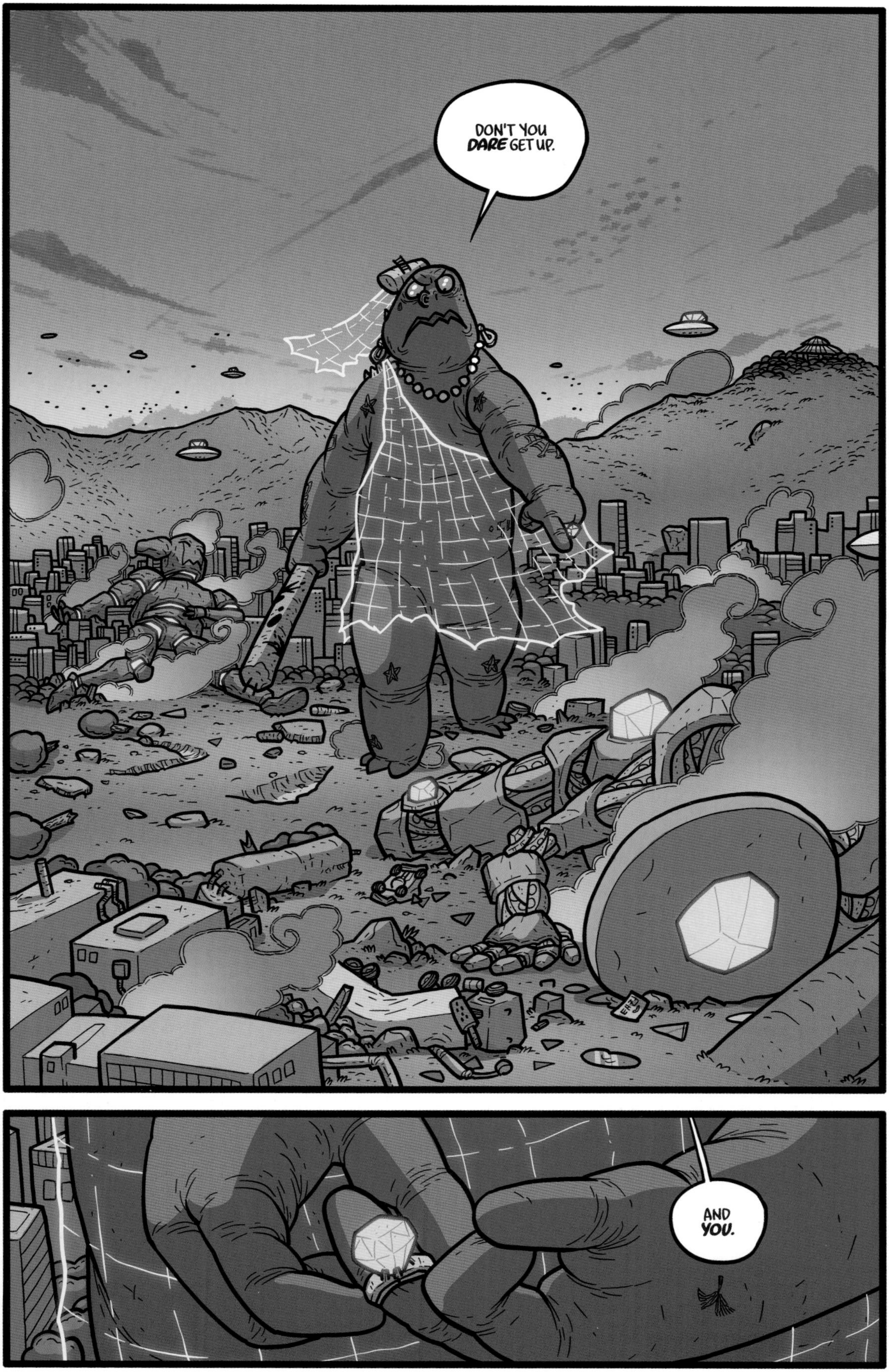
DON'T YOU DARE GET UP.
AND YOU.

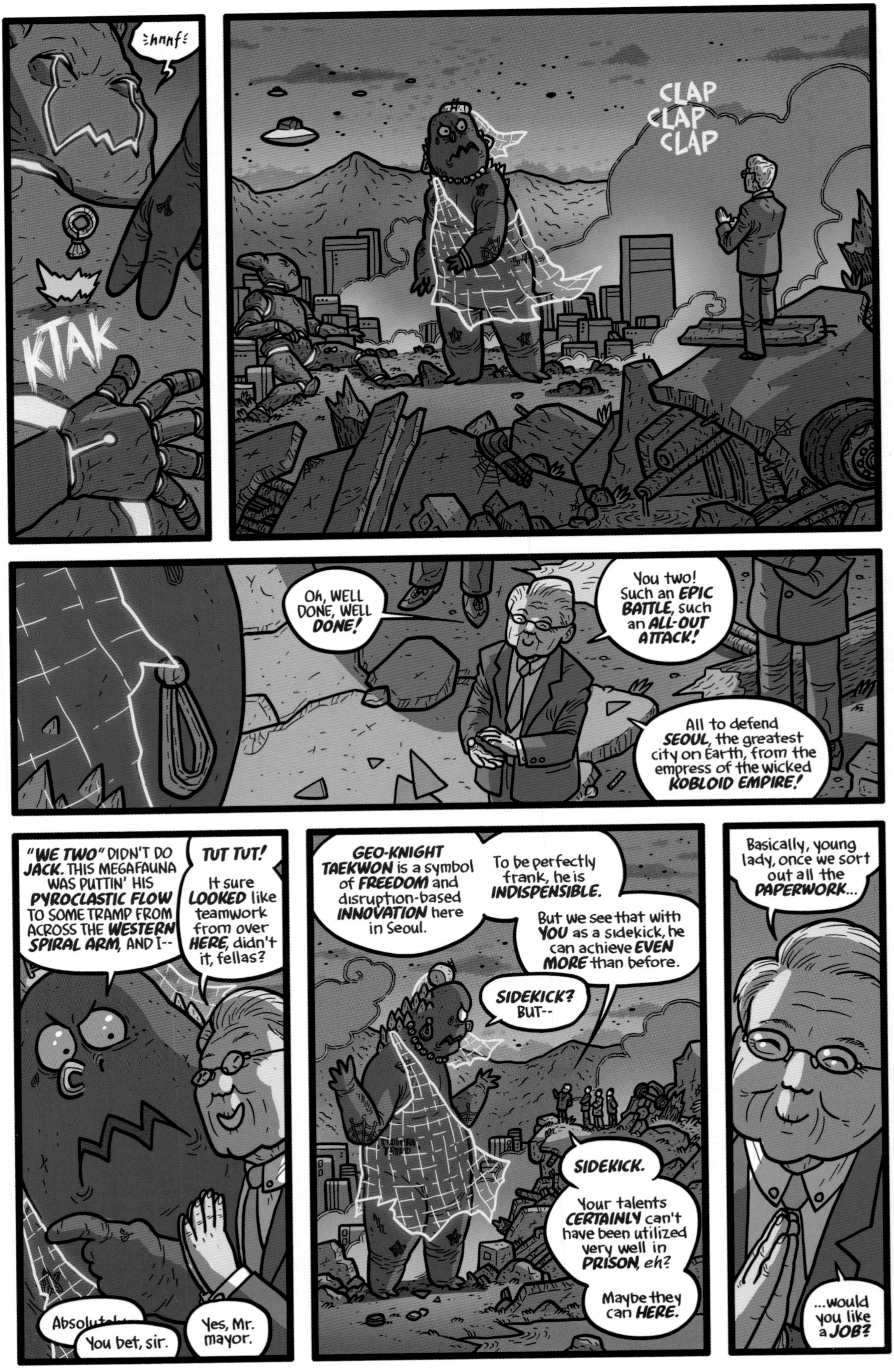
hnnf
KTAK
CLAP
CLAP
CLAP
Oh, WELL DONE, WELL DONE!
You two! Such an EPIC BATTLE, such an ALL-OUT ATTACK!
All to defend SEOUL, the greatest city on Earth, from the empress of the wicked KOBLOID EMPIRE!
"WE TWO" DIDN'T DO JACK. THIS MEGAFAUNA WAS PUTTIN' HIS PYROCLASTIC FLOW TO SOME TRAMP FROM ACROSS THE WESTERN SPIRAL ARM, AND I--
TUT TUT!
It sure LOOKED like teamwork from over HERE, didn't it, fellas?
Absolut
You bet, sir.
Yes, Mr. mayor.
GEO-KNIGHT TAEKWON is a symbol of FREEDOM and disruption-based INNOVATION here in Seoul.
To be perfectly frank, he is INDISPENSIBLE.
But we see that with YOU as a sidekick, he can achieve EVEN MORE than before.
SIDEKICK? BUT--
SIDEKICK.
Your talents CERTAINLY can't have been utilized very well in PRISON, eh?
Maybe they can HERE.
Basically, young lady, once we sort out all the PAPERWORK...
...would you like a JOB?

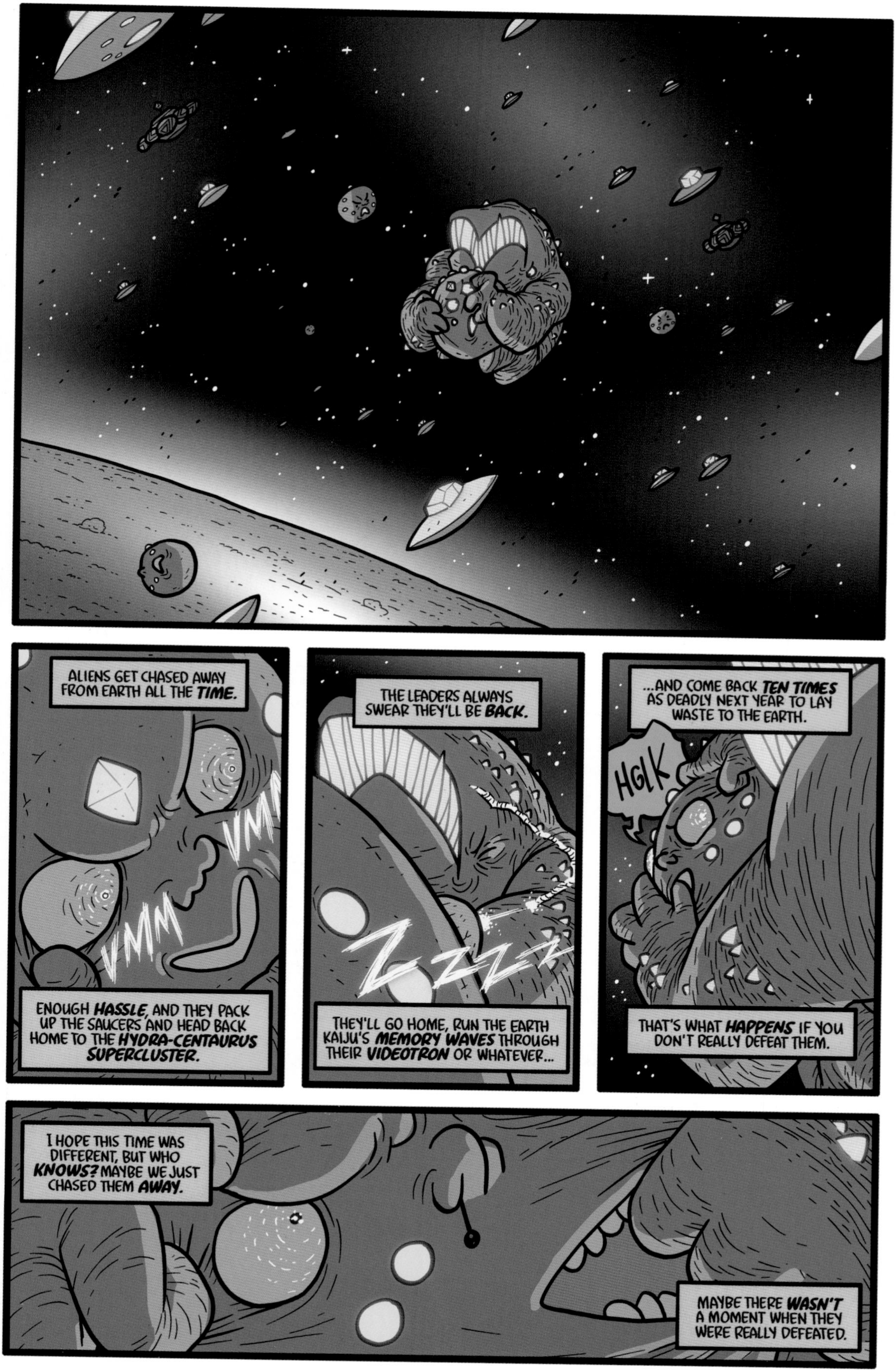
ALIENS GET CHASED AWAY FROM EARTH ALL THE **TIME.**
VMM
VMM
ENOUGH **HASSLE**, AND THEY PACK UP THE SAUCERS AND HEAD BACK HOME TO THE **HYDRA-CENTAURUS SUPERCLUSTER.**
THE LEADERS ALWAYS SWEAR THEY'LL BE **BACK.**
ZZZZZ
THEY'LL GO HOME, RUN THE EARTH KAIJU'S **MEMORY WAVES** THROUGH THEIR **VIDEOTRON** OR WHATEVER...
...AND COME BACK **TEN TIMES** AS DEADLY NEXT YEAR TO LAY WASTE TO THE EARTH.
HGLK
THAT'S WHAT **HAPPENS** IF YOU DON'T REALLY DEFEAT THEM.
I HOPE THIS TIME WAS DIFFERENT, BUT WHO **KNOWS?** MAYBE WE JUST CHASED THEM **AWAY.**
MAYBE THERE **WASN'T** A MOMENT WHEN THEY WERE REALLY DEFEATED.

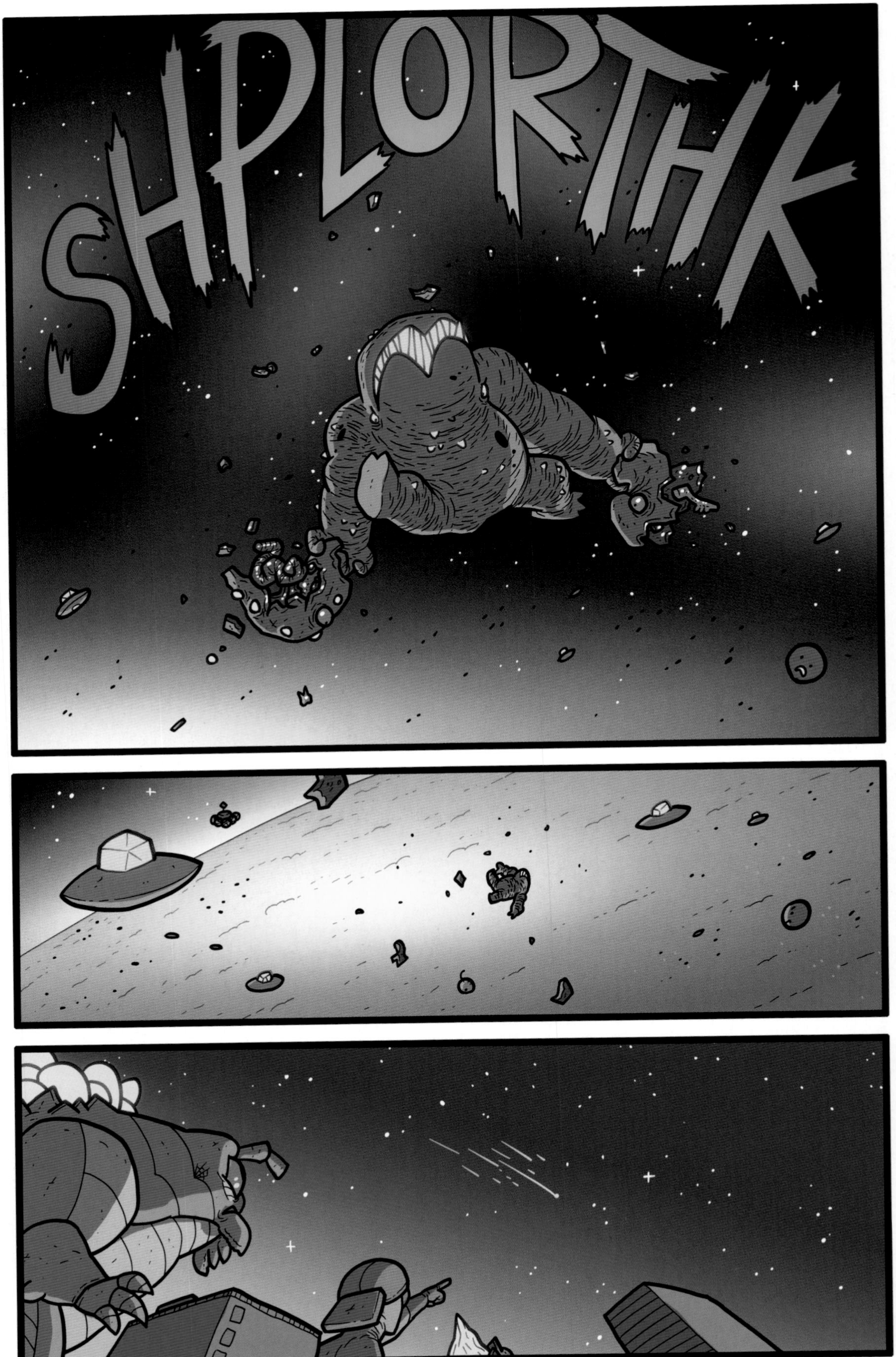
SHPLORTHK

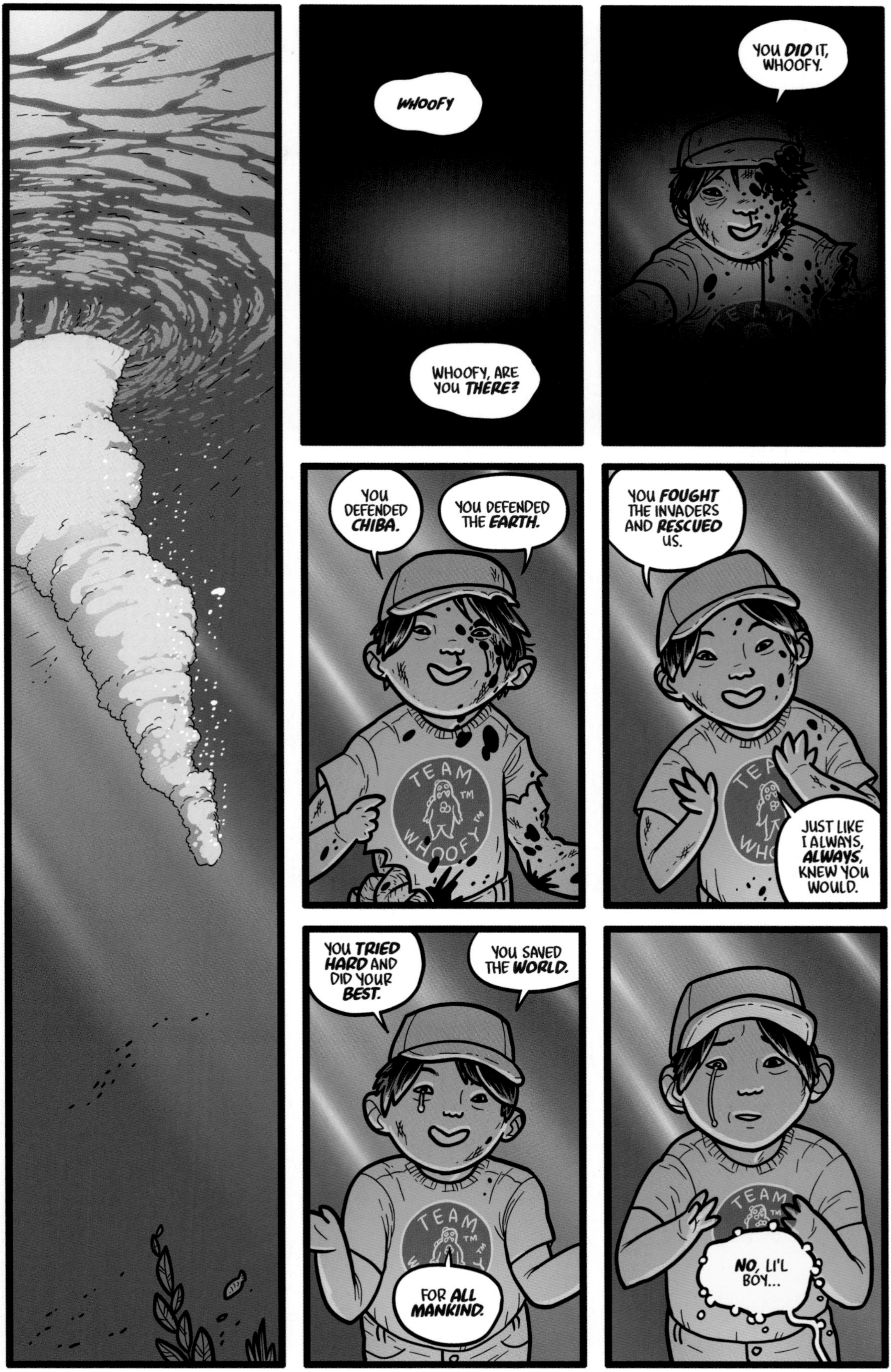
WHOOFY
WHOOFY, ARE YOU THERE?
YOU DID IT, WHOOFY.
YOU DEFENDED CHIBA.
YOU DEFENDED THE EARTH.
YOU FOUGHT THE INVADERS AND RESCUED US.
TEAM WHOOFY
JUST LIKE I ALWAYS, ALWAYS, KNEW YOU WOULD.
YOU TRIED HARD AND DID YOUR BEST.
YOU SAVED THE WORLD.
FOR ALL MANKIND.
NO, LI'L BOY...

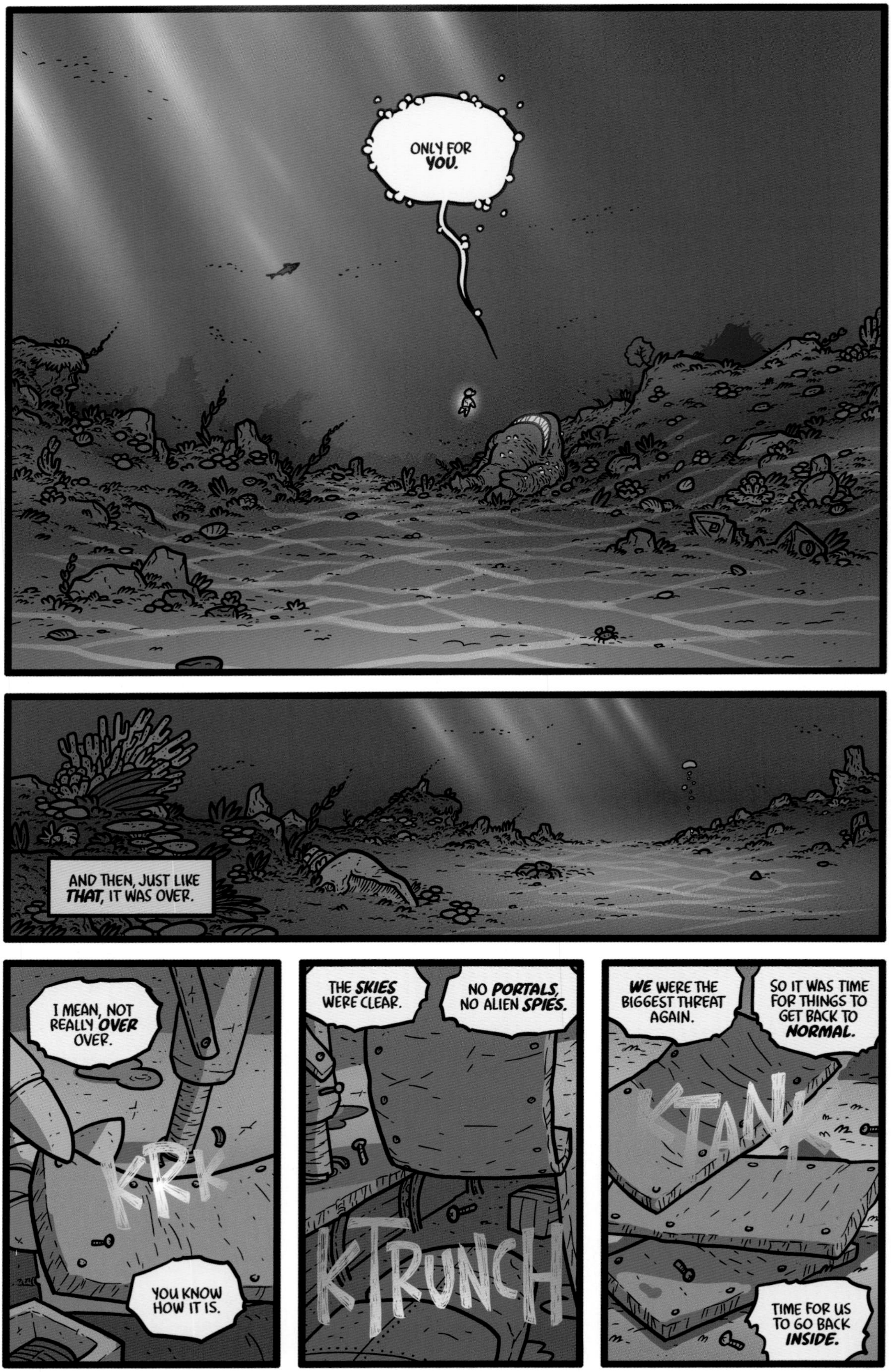

ONLY FOR **YOU.**
AND THEN, JUST LIKE ***THAT***, IT WAS OVER.
I MEAN, NOT REALLY ***OVER*** OVER.
KRK
YOU KNOW HOW IT IS.
THE ***SKIES*** WERE CLEAR.
NO ***PORTALS***, NO ALIEN ***SPIES.***
KTRUNCH
WE WERE THE BIGGEST THREAT AGAIN.
SO IT WAS TIME FOR THINGS TO GET BACK TO ***NORMAL.***
KTANK
TIME FOR US TO GO BACK ***INSIDE.***

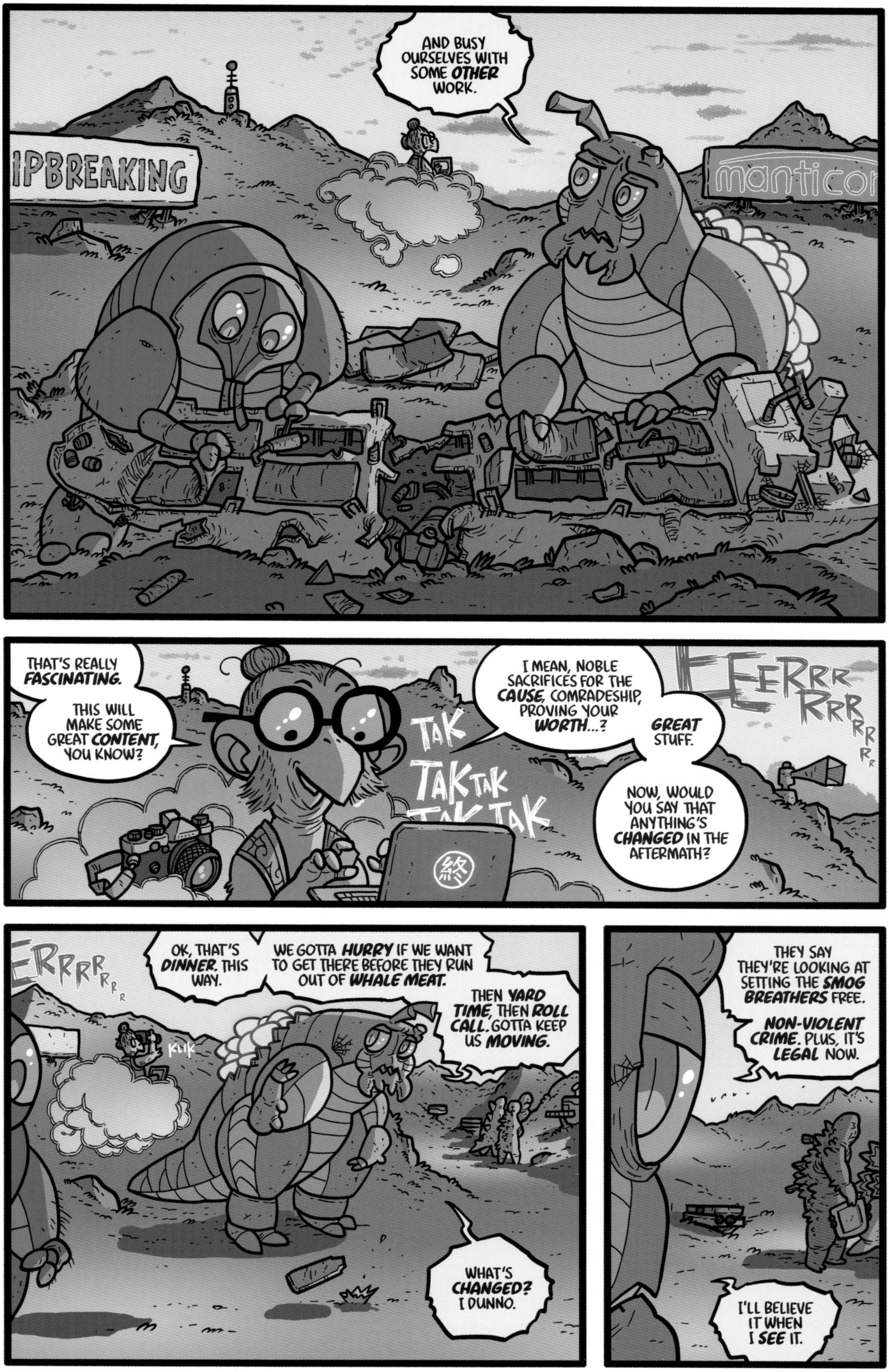
AND BUSY OURSELVES WITH SOME OTHER WORK.
IPBREAKING
manticor
THAT'S REALLY FASCINATING.
THIS WILL MAKE SOME GREAT CONTENT, YOU KNOW?
TAK TAK TAK TAK TAK
I MEAN, NOBLE SACRIFICES FOR THE CAUSE, COMRADESHIP, PROVING YOUR WORTH...?
GREAT STUFF.
EEERRRRRRRRRR
NOW, WOULD YOU SAY THAT ANYTHING'S CHANGED IN THE AFTERMATH?
EERRRRRR
OK, THAT'S DINNER. THIS WAY.
WE GOTTA HURRY IF WE WANT TO GET THERE BEFORE THEY RUN OUT OF WHALE MEAT.
THEN YARD TIME, THEN ROLL CALL. GOTTA KEEP US MOVING.
KLIK
WHAT'S CHANGED? I DUNNO.
THEY SAY THEY'RE LOOKING AT SETTING THE SMOG BREATHERS FREE.
NON-VIOLENT CRIME. PLUS, IT'S LEGAL NOW.
I'LL BELIEVE IT WHEN I SEE IT.

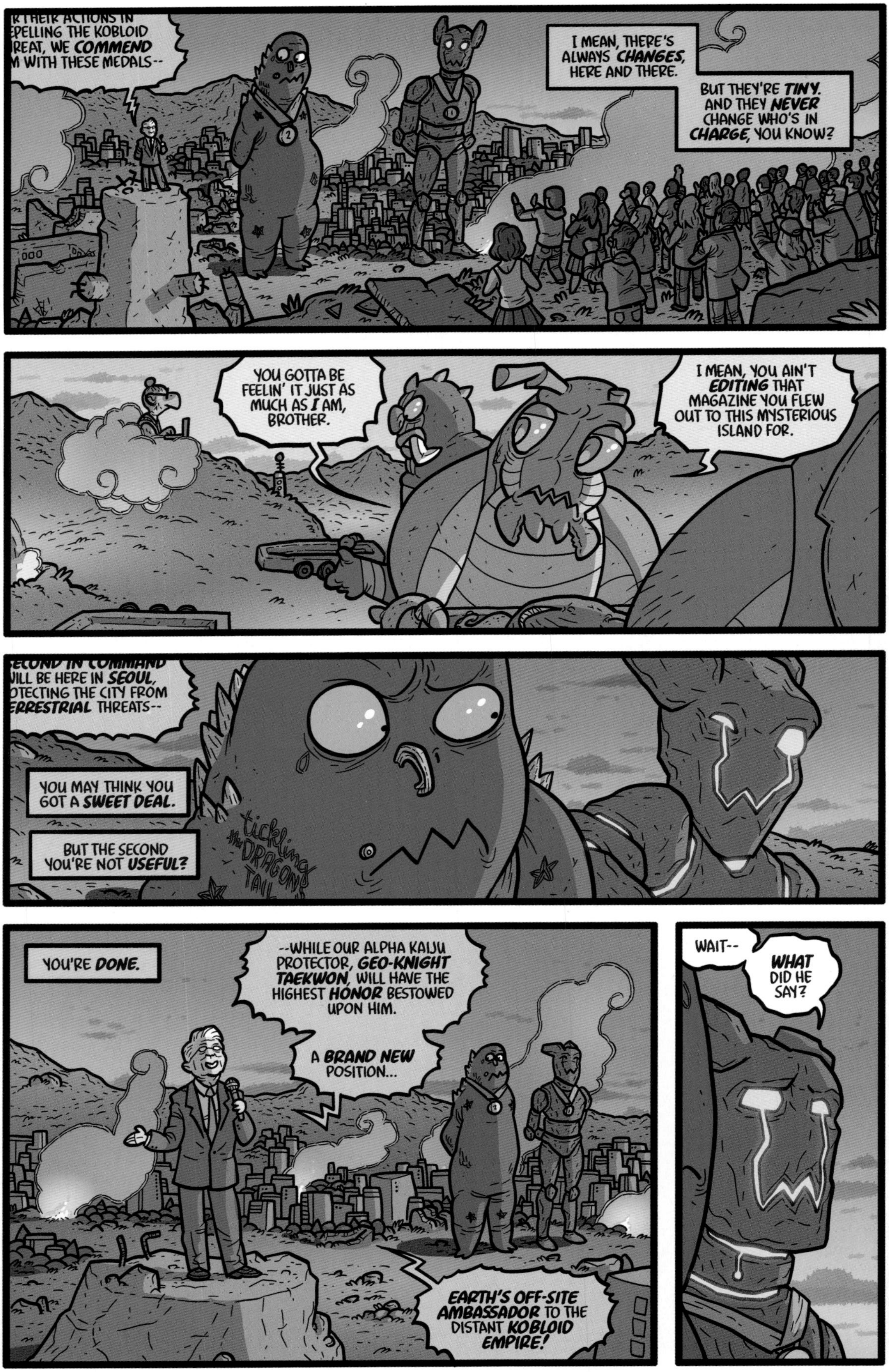
R THEIR ACTIONS IN
EPELLING THE KOBLOID
REAT, WE **COMMEND**
M WITH THESE MEDALS--
I MEAN, THERE'S ALWAYS **CHANGES**, HERE AND THERE.
BUT THEY'RE **TINY**. AND THEY **NEVER** CHANGE WHO'S IN **CHARGE**, YOU KNOW?
YOU GOTTA BE FEELIN' IT JUST AS MUCH AS **I** AM, BROTHER.
I MEAN, YOU AIN'T **EDITING** THAT MAGAZINE YOU FLEW OUT TO THIS MYSTERIOUS ISLAND FOR.
ECOND IN COMMAND
WILL BE HERE IN **SEOUL**,
OTECTING THE CITY FROM
ERRESTRIAL THREATS--
YOU MAY THINK YOU GOT A **SWEET DEAL**.
BUT THE SECOND YOU'RE NOT **USEFUL**?
YOU'RE **DONE**.
--WHILE OUR ALPHA KAIJU PROTECTOR, **GEO-KNIGHT TAEKWON**, WILL HAVE THE HIGHEST **HONOR** BESTOWED UPON HIM.
A **BRAND NEW** POSITION...
EARTH'S OFF-SITE AMBASSADOR TO THE DISTANT **KOBLOID EMPIRE!**
WAIT--
WHAT DID HE SAY?

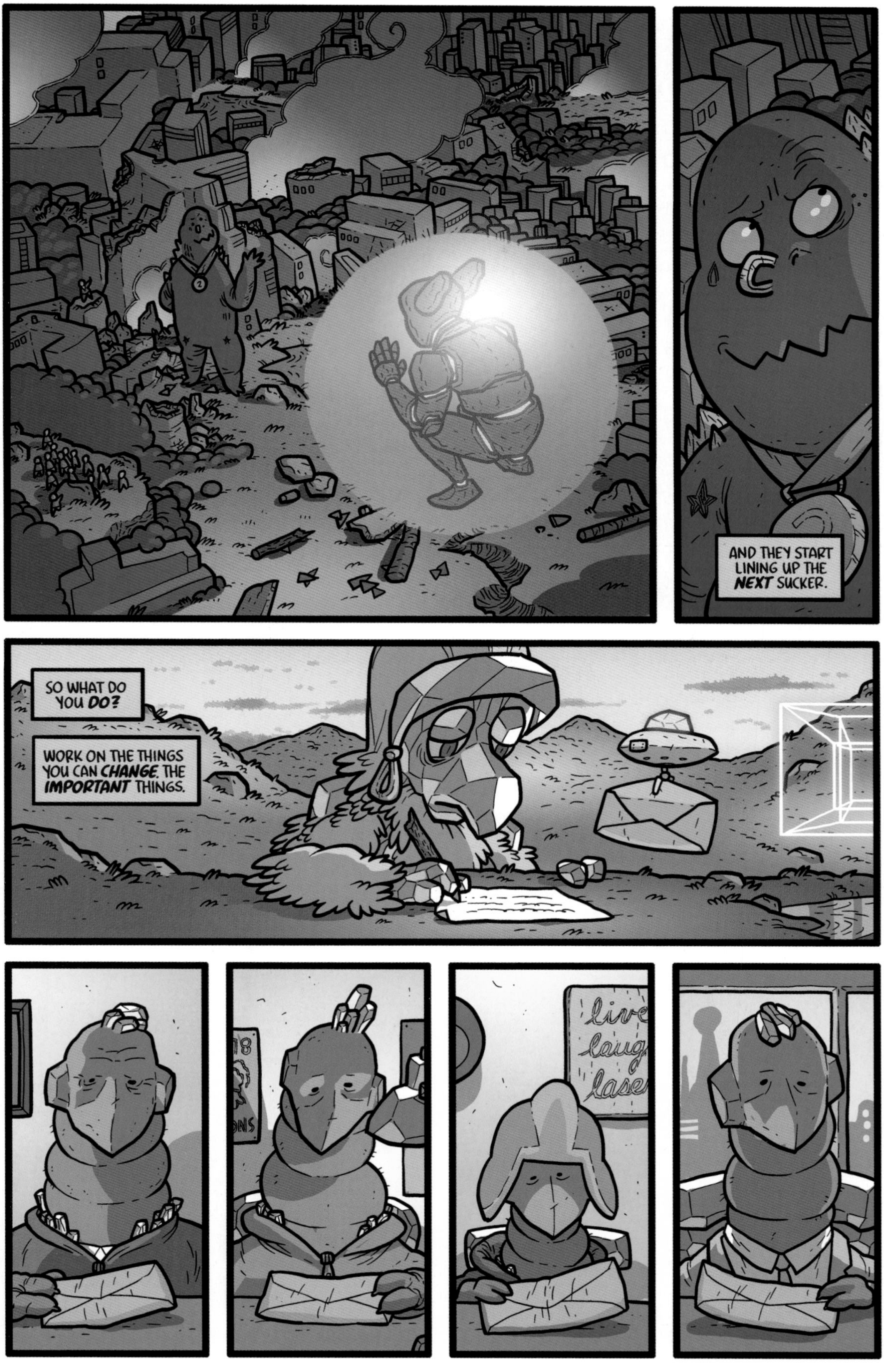
AND THEY START LINING UP THE **NEXT** SUCKER.
SO WHAT DO YOU **DO?**
WORK ON THE THINGS YOU CAN **CHANGE**, THE **IMPORTANT** THINGS.

YOU GO WHERE YOU'RE MOST *NEEDED*.

JETT

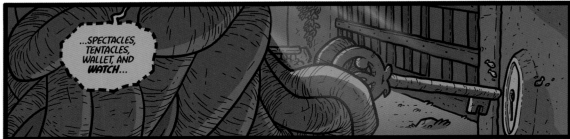

...SPECTACLES, TENTACLES, WALLET, AND *WATCH*...

ALL RIGHT, NEXT IN *LINE!*

CLINIC

ONE DOSE OF KADATHODONE *PER* PATIENT

MAYBE IT'S THANKLESS *WORK*.

MAYBE YOU GET NO *RECOGNITION*.

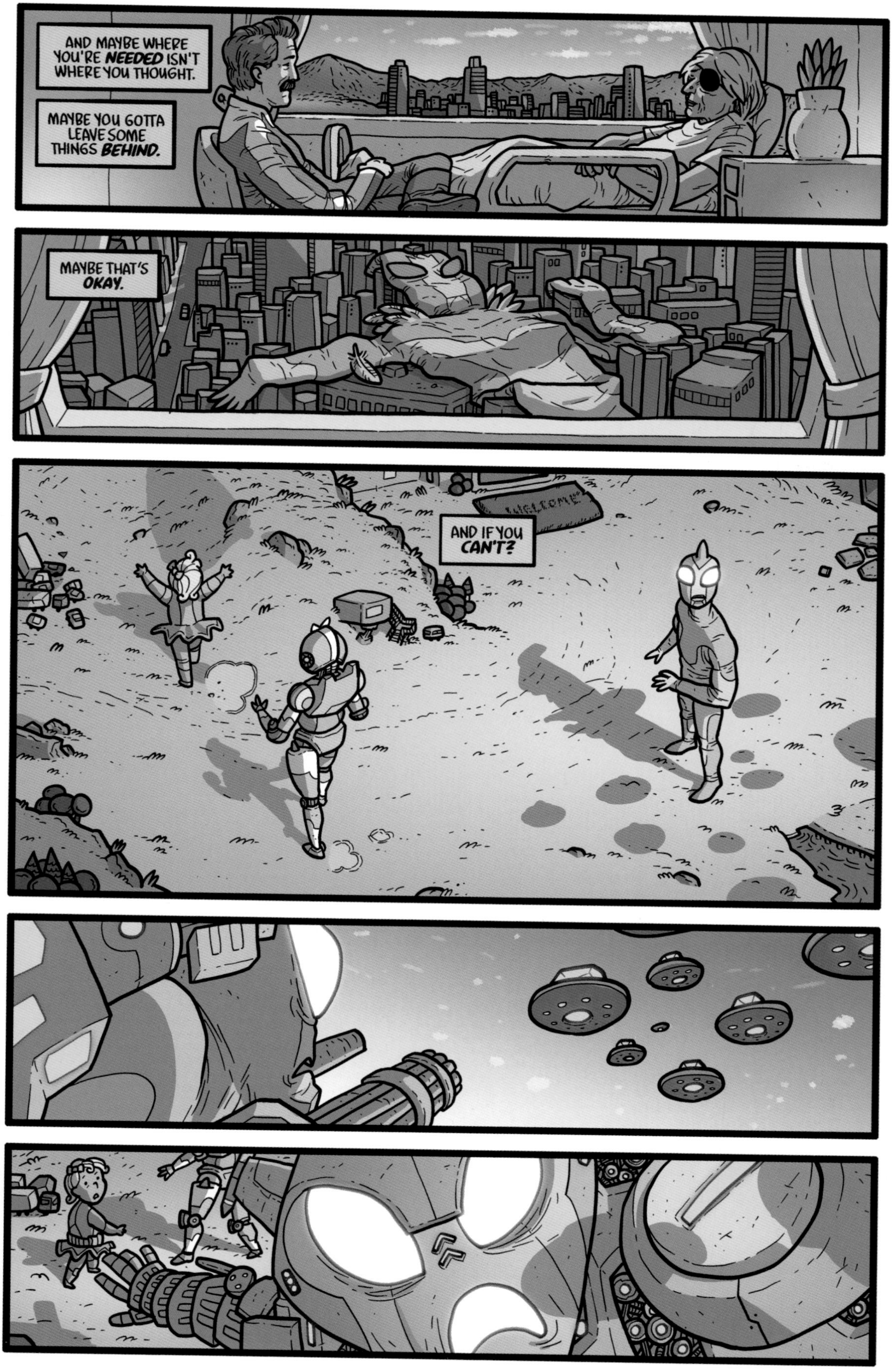
AND MAYBE WHERE YOU'RE ***NEEDED*** ISN'T WHERE YOU THOUGHT.
MAYBE YOU GOTTA LEAVE SOME THINGS ***BEHIND.***
MAYBE THAT'S ***OKAY.***
AND IF YOU ***CAN'T?***

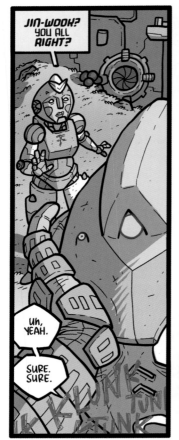

JIN-WOOK? YOU ALL *RIGHT*?

UH, YEAH.

SURE. SURE.

YOU BET.

MAYBE THAT'S OKAY *TOO*.

IT'S JUST A MATTER OF HOW WE *DEAL* WITH IT.

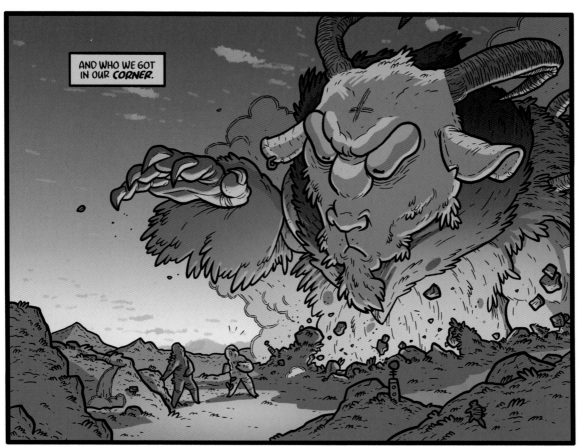

AND WHO WE GOT IN OUR **CORNER.**

Atlas
Death's Head
Luna
Exc...

Atlas
Death's Head
Luna

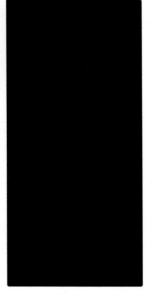

THAT'S **IT**, AIN'T IT? MORE THAN ANYTHING.

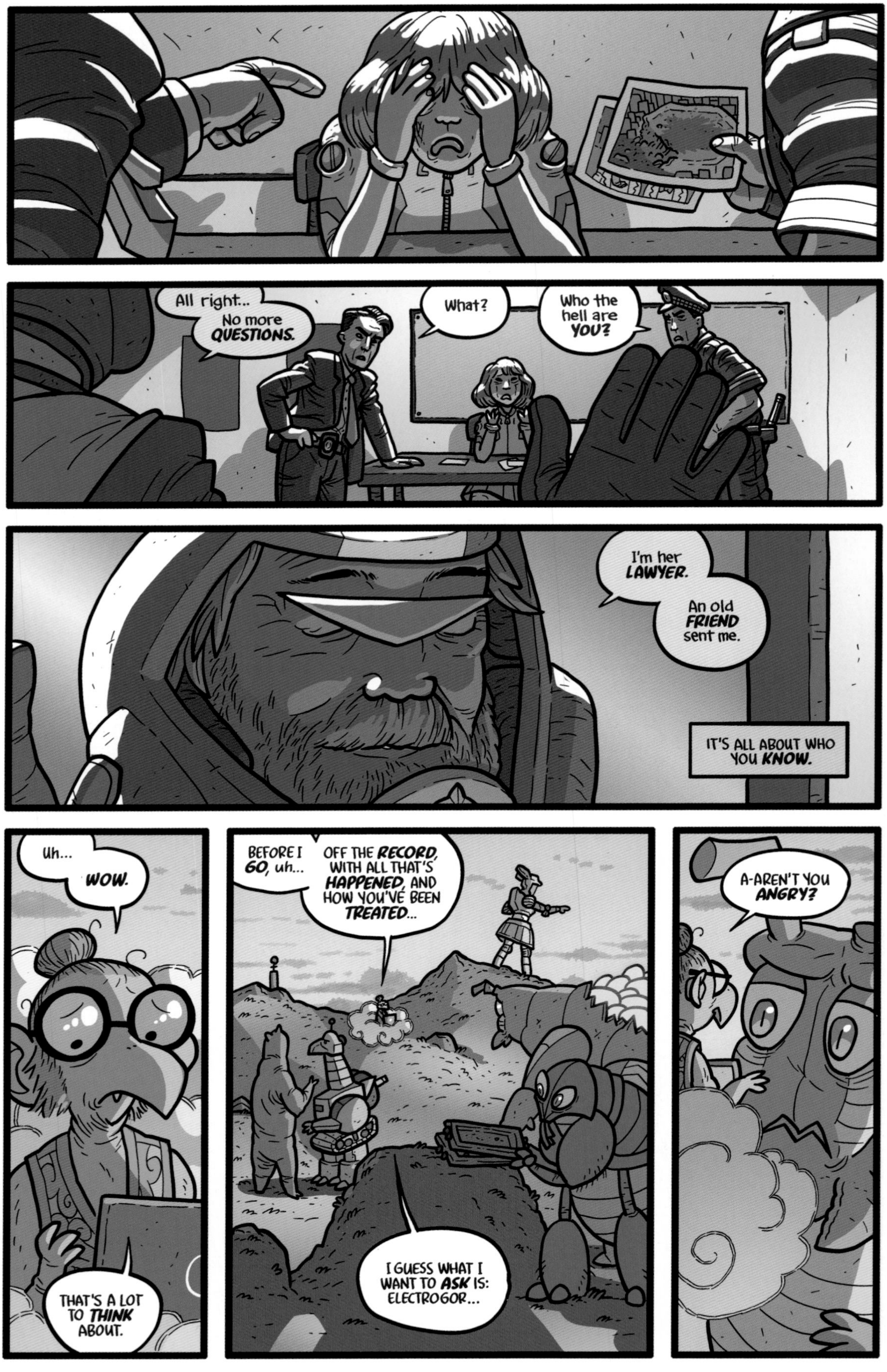
All right... No more QUESTIONS.
What?
Who the hell are YOU?
I'm her LAWYER.
An old FRIEND sent me.
IT'S ALL ABOUT WHO YOU KNOW.
Uh...
WOW.
THAT'S A LOT TO THINK ABOUT.
BEFORE I GO, uh...
OFF THE RECORD, WITH ALL THAT'S HAPPENED, AND HOW YOU'VE BEEN TREATED...
I GUESS WHAT I WANT TO ASK IS: ELECTROGOR...
A-AREN'T YOU ANGRY?

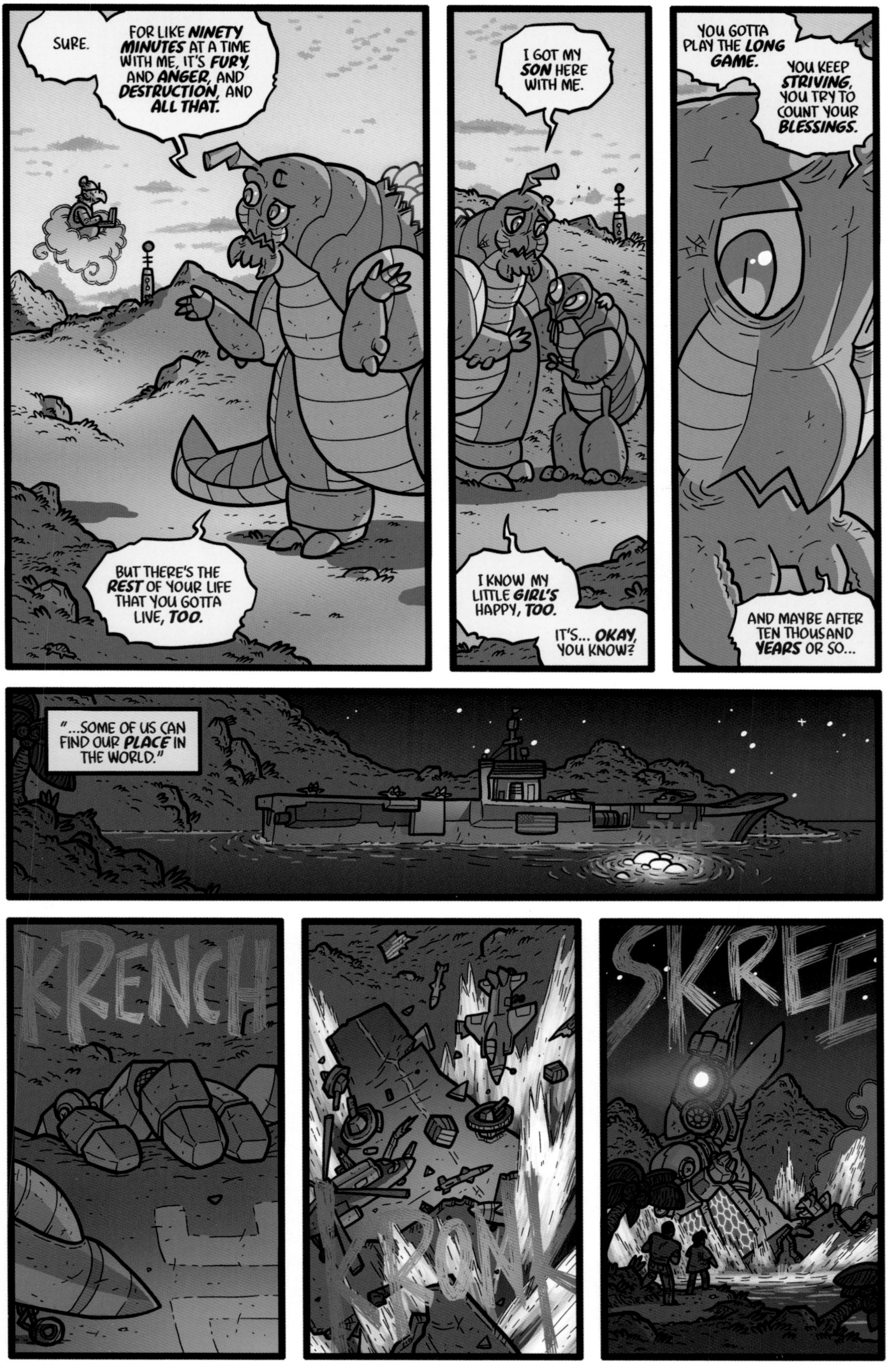
SURE.
FOR LIKE NINETY MINUTES AT A TIME WITH ME, IT'S FURY, AND ANGER, AND DESTRUCTION, AND ALL THAT.
BUT THERE'S THE REST OF YOUR LIFE THAT YOU GOTTA LIVE, TOO.
I GOT MY SON HERE WITH ME.
I KNOW MY LITTLE GIRL'S HAPPY, TOO.
IT'S... OKAY, YOU KNOW?
YOU GOTTA PLAY THE LONG GAME.
YOU KEEP STRIVING, YOU TRY TO COUNT YOUR BLESSINGS.
AND MAYBE AFTER TEN THOUSAND YEARS OR SO...
"...SOME OF US CAN FIND OUR PLACE IN THE WORLD."
KRENCH
KRONK
SKREE

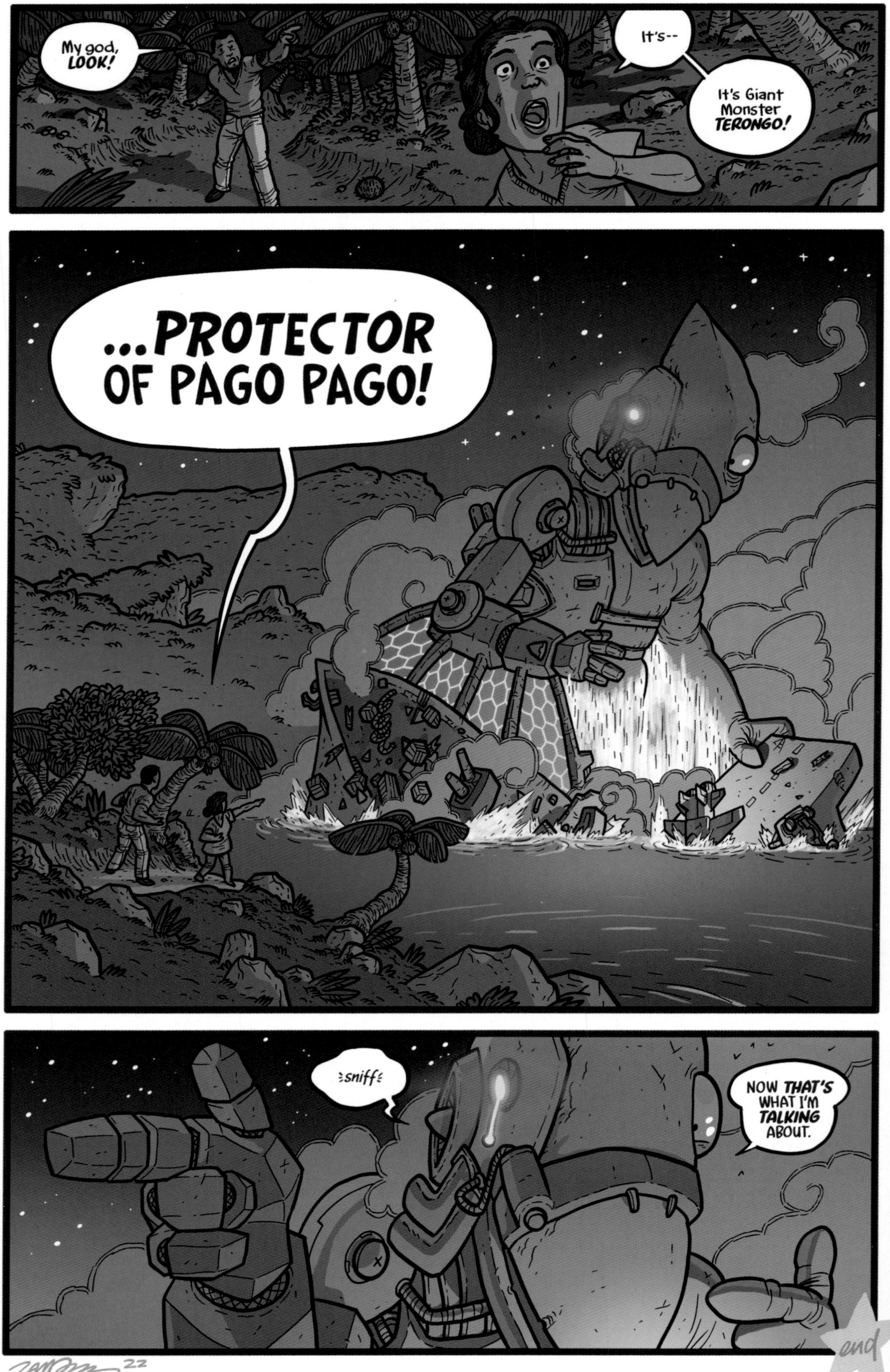
My god, LOOK!
It's--
It's Giant Monster TERONGO!
...PROTECTOR OF PAGO PAGO!
sniff
NOW THAT'S WHAT I'M TALKING ABOUT.
end

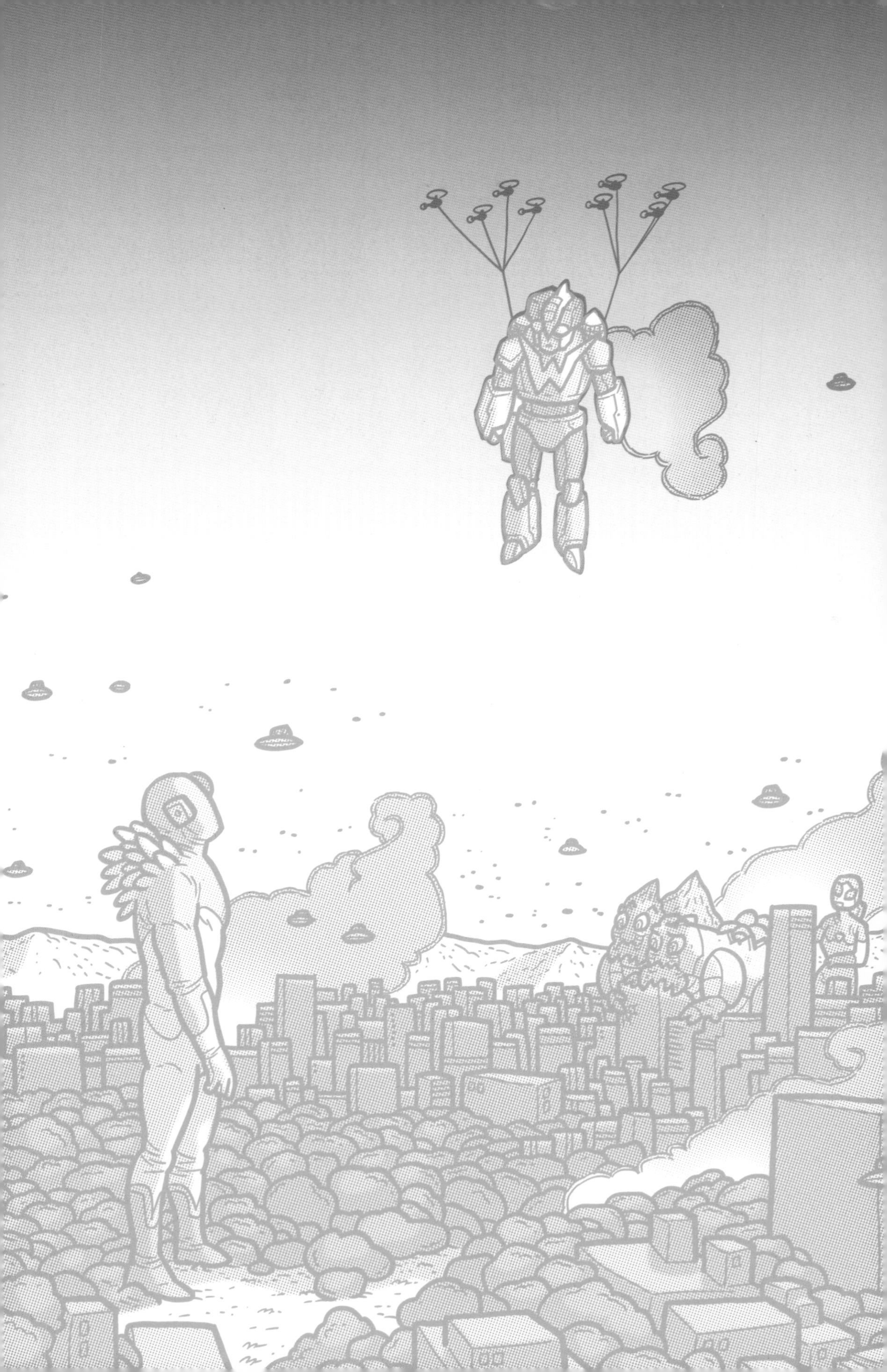

FAREWELL FROM MONSTER ISLAND

Well, friends, we made it. Thirty-six issues, seven years, and some eight hundred-plus pages after I idly thought to myself, *I wonder what city-destroying monsters would be like if they just, ya know, hung out?*, we are here, at the end of all things. First, some FAQs:

Q: Did the series end up the way you expected? The way you wanted?

A: Pretty much. It had the right tone, it had the right amount of character stuff, and it paid off on plots the way I wanted it to. It was both sillier and more heartbreaking than I thought it would be. I think it became less cruel and trope-y as it went on, which I saw as an improvement. It became way less sci-fi and way more satire than I originally planned. Basically, all matters of logistics were streamlined out of it with some space superhero magic, and I feel like the series was better for it. It definitely ended up the way I wanted: an immense soup of likable (and hateable) characters that lived observable lives.

Q: Was there anything weird that you planned that didn't make it in?

A: Sure. Daniel was going to have some kind of "bad luck" power, the prison was originally going to use guards that had been kidnapped, drugged, and brainwashed for some reason, and all of Season 1 and 2's content was originally going to be crammed into Season 1. There was going to be some kind of katakana and hangul writing system for the cell/crater numbers that I wisely de-emphasized. There was going to be more of a language barrier between the human and monster languages, as well as a tiny roaring interpreter. That would have still been a good gag, but an exhausting thing to keep straight as the stories got longer and more complex.

Q: What was the best skill you learned after all that comics-making?

A: Couple of 'em. *Writing:* I learned how to pretty quickly cobble together a decent story from some unrelated threads. *Lettering:* I got a pretty consistent, conventional hand-lettering style out of all that practice. *Coloring:* I learned how to light and render a scene with minimal "pen mileage" and as few layers as possible. *Workflow:* I learned what to listen to when writing (soundtracks), penciling (podcasts, audiobooks), lettering and inking (talky TV), and coloring (soundtracks again). Broadly, I also learned that doing everything on a project from writing to coloring—which always seemed like an impossibly large task—is doable if you have good support, a thought-out workflow and tools, and a priority of speed over perfection (still working on that last one).

Q: Who else worked on this series?

A: *Kaijumax* is frequently described as a one-man show, so I want to dispel that rumor real quick and give some shout-outs to the people who helped this series chug along as I dragged my occasionally lazy, occasionally perfectionist, always sluggish feet.

Editors Zack Soto, Desiree Wilson, and Sarah Gaydos kept me moving along when I wasn't always feeling it, and helped me with navigating which cultural avenues, shall we say, are better than others to venture down. EIC/publisher James Lucas Jones has been there to rah rah a pretty weird book even when it didn't exactly fit in.

Dylan Todd and Fred Chao did crisp, unbelievable design work for the trades and back matter throughout the series, saving me untold hours of drawing new stuff.

Jason Fischer has been there since the beginning with color assists, nailing it page after page, providing great feedback and comradery, and—to be perfectly frank—being the only one around here who remembers what color any character is.

Ryan Browne helped me create the original version of this series and kicked the whole thing off with a request to collaborate.

My studiomates at Minneapolis' own World Monster HQ have been amazing collaborators, supporters, and friends for the life of the series.

Most of all, original series editor Charlie Chu has been the absolute mastermind behind *Kaijumax*, finding the charm in this series when even I wasn't seeing it, shamelessly hyping it to anyone who would listen, and being a great sounding board and friend from the very start.

And, as always, this is dedicated to my cool wife, Julie, and my awesome son, Jin, without whom I would never have thought to watch *Ultraman*, and none of this would ever have happened.

Thank you, everyone, for sticking with us all this time! I'll be diving into other projects soon (after I've had a long refreshing nap at the bottom of the ocean), but you can find me on my Patreon page at patreon.com/zandercannon and on Twitter at @zander_cannon.

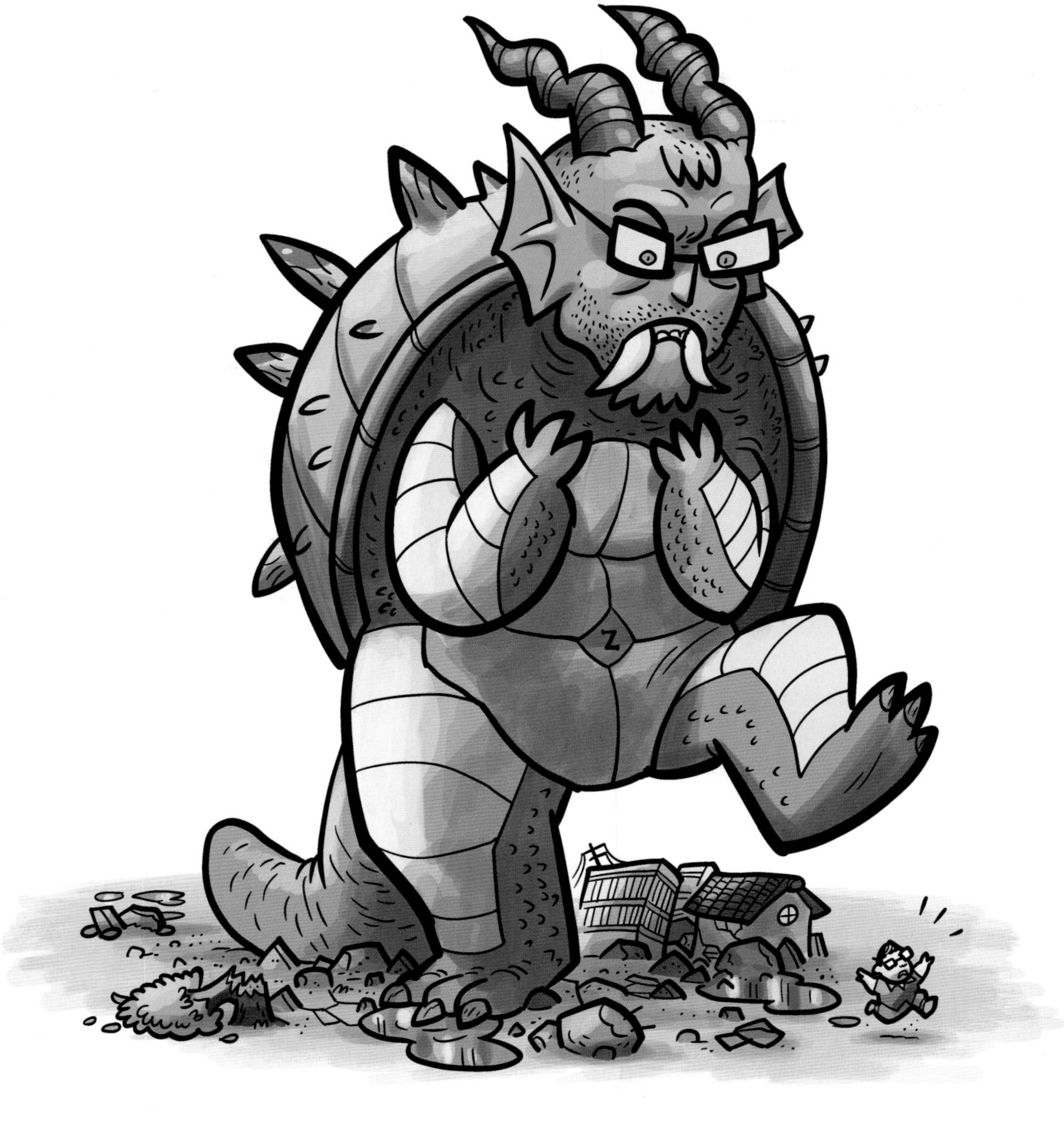

SINCE 1993, ***ZANDER CANNON*** HAS WRITTEN AND DRAWN COMICS ABOUT GODS, ROBOTS, ASTRONAUTS, POLICE OFFICERS, PALEONTOLOGISTS, ALIENS, FENG SHUI MASTERS, SUPERHEROES, AND MONSTERS.

HE LIVES IN MINNESOTA WITH HIS STRONG WIFE JULIE AND ABOVE-AVERAGE SON JIN.

KAIJUMAX.COM
@ZANDER_CANNON